THIS IS WHERE I CAME IN

OTHER BOOKS BY JACK SAUTER

SAILORS IN THE SKY

TAILFINS ACROSS EUROPE

HISTORY OF THE USS LAKE CHAMPLAIN

THIS IS WHERE I CAME IN

Growing Up in New York City during the 1930s and 40s

JACK SAUTER

With a Foreword by John Robben

ISBN 10: 0-9787854-0-1
ISBN 13: 978-0-9787854-0-6

Printed in the United States of America

For Marianne, Karen, Laurette and Keith.

And to my guiding light growing up,
my sisters Rita Palmer and Dorothy McDonald

"Young man, rejoice in your youth"
—Ecclesiastes: Chapter 11; 9

FOREWORD

Jack Sauter came late to writing, but when he finally arrived he brought an entire world with him, one that many of will recognize as our own. It isn't as if Sauter woke up one day after turning 60 and started writing out of the blue, such things are unlikely to happen, but he'd been practicing, without even realizing it. When I first met him in the Navy he was already writing letters back home to his family and fiancé. When he wasn't flying off the deck of our aircraft carrier as a radar/navigator aircrewman in his three-man Douglas Skyraider, he was tucked away in a hidden corner of the ship scribbling letters, some as many as 20 and 30 pages long, to his girl back in the States. In these letters Sauter would pour out his heart to the girl he'd left behind, describing to her not only his feelings about her and his hopes for their future together, but also his experiences of that day, whether of the plane's dangerous launch off the ship toward the Korean coastline, or the equally hazardous return landing onto a pitching flight deck. It was through these letters that he maintained his distant love affair temporarily shut down by their separation, but kept alive in words until his return could not only reunite them, but also reignite their passion for one another.

In those days Jack Sauter thought of himself as a letter-writer, not as a writer. He read voraciously, authors like Thomas Wolfe, Scott Fitzgerald, Graham Greene and others. They were real writers, he believed, belonging to another world, one beyond his, and though his words flowed freely into his letters never did he think of himself as someone capable of writing a book. His fiancé saved his letters, as did his parents, and when the war ended and Jack returned from it those hundreds of letters he'd written in Korean waters were there, all safely set aside, someday perhaps to be read again in his twilight years.

From time to time he might read one or more of them, and be surprised at how vividly they captured his experiences. But he was busy then, trying to make a living for himself and his new wife, and then for their expanding family, and there was little time or inclination, to take up the pen again. The letters had served their purpose, they'd kept him bound in the same way that letters can to his wife-to-be, but that part of his life was behind him. His letters were good for memories, but little else.

Years went by, good years and many of them, and then one cold and rainy January night in Florida, shortly after turning 60, Jack Sauter, inspired by a military memoir he'd just finished reading, began thinking about his own wartime service, and astonished himself at how much he was able to recall. He picked up a legal pad, and began writing in long-hand. Before he knew it, he'd filled twenty pages.

It took him two years to write his "book," if that even what it was, and then wondered, "Ok, what now?" Some of his friends, of whom I was one, to whom he'd sent copies of his manuscript, urged him to try to get it published. He sent query letters to 40 publishers, none of whom expressed much interest. "I just about gave up," Jack remembers. "Then, purely by accident, I came across the name of a small publisher, McFarland. They were publishing a few military memoirs a year and I thought,' what the heck! What have I got to lose?" Instead of following his usual procedure, he sent them the entire manuscript, all 496 pages of it! A week later he had a contract! When his book was finally published he was 65 years old.

This is not quite a Cinderella story. SAILORS IN THE SKY didn't make the best-seller list. Neither was it made into a movie. But Sauter's book got plenty of attention and found many readers. Today his book can be found in the libraries of 50 or more universities, including Oxford, Princeton, Harvard, Yale, Notre Dame and at the military, naval and air force academies. It's still on sale in the bookstores of the Smithsonian and the Naval Air Museum at Pensacola. And the first printing sold out. Not bad for a sailor who thought of himself as only a "letter –writer."

Following SAILORS IN THE SKY, Sauter then wrote TAILFINS ACROSS EUROPE, an account of a nine-week trip to Europe that he took with his wife, Marianne, in 1959. One reader called his second book, "Every-one's first trip to Europe." A writer compared it to OUR HEARTS WERE YOUNG AND GAY.

A year later he was commissioned by Turner Publishing to write the history of his aircraft carrier in Korea, USS LAKE CHAMPLAIN, for that ship's association. And now there's his fourth book, THIS IS WHERE I

CAME IN, Jack Sauter's memoir of growing up in New York City in the 1930's and 1940's. I've read this book twice, both prior to publication. The first time chapter-by-chapter, which Jack sent to me as his finished each one. Then I reread it from start to finish after it was completed. I wrote a review of it for the "Greenwich Time," even when it was only half done. How many authors have had that experience? But that was two years ago, and now I'm looking forward to reading it again, this time "between covers" as authors like to boast.

Titles for books, especially catchy titles that are easy to remember, are difficult to come by, but when one is found it can make a difference in the book's appeal. Sauter has a knack for good titles, and this one's no exception. THIS IS WHERE I CAME IN is a popular catchphrase from the 1940sand 50s, when people attending movies would often walk in on a film after it had started and then stay until the movie brought them back to where they'd come in.

We choose books to read for a variety of reasons, some because they're popular, others for being entertaining or informative, but another reason—and perhaps a more important one—is because the author has the ability to remind us of something that happened to us. I used to watch my aging grandmother sitting in her rocking chair; her eyes closed a flicker of a smile crossing her lips. "Nana," I'd ask, "What are you smiling about?" "Oh," she'd coo softly, "I'm just remembering the old days."

In THIS IS WHERE I CAME IN, Jack Sauter reminds us not only of his "old days," but ours as well. People are going to read his story and be surprised that he's also describing theirs. His book is not one that primarily instructs, persuades, or enlightens, though it does that too. But what it excels in is recalling his past, as well as the reader's. And what a gift this is his because he is able to give it and ours because he's presenting it to us. The byproduct of a work of art, besides its beauty, is that it captures the truth not just of the artist but also of the recipient. There's a kind of miracle when this happens, and just as certain music or a painting stirs the fire in our souls by blowing life into the embers of memory, so does the written word when it reminds us that there is no end, the writer and the reader, forever linked.

Jack Sauter's sentences dance and twirl, his scenes ignite, memories explode into life. His truth mirrors the truth of ours and because of this his book will last as long as we do, and we as long as his book does.
John Robben

PREFACE

Writing this book has been the means of reliving a wonderfully happy childhood. When I began to think it over in sentences and paragraphs, I was astonished at the vividness of certain memories.

Some of the dates may not be accurate, but in this type of story, that's not too critical. I'm sure the facts are correct.

Back in the days when movies were four-a-week and less structured, patrons often paid little attention to the starting times, buying tickets whenever the urge came over them. Reaching the point in the plot where they'd sat down, one would turn to the other and say, "Let's go. This is where we came in." This memoir will carry my life from "where I came in" –the year 1929, to when I left the Bronx to join the Navy at the start of the Korean War; a period of twenty years. I couldn't imagine a more turbulent and rewarding time to be growing up.

While I'm naturally the focus of the narrative, I've tried to give equal time to the world that surrounded me. This is in response to a question that I'm often asked, "What was it like growing up in New York during the Great Depression?" Essentially, this is a story of that world. The cloistered neighborhoods, the stores we shopped in, the dominant effects of radio and movies, the rigid social structure where most workers wore a uniform, the importance of religion, and finally the everyday heroes and heroines of the Great Depression, who faced economic disaster with fortitude and good cheer.

All the timeless aspects of growing pains are here: the loneliness, the importance of friends and being accepted, the agonies of puberty, the fear of rejection, our initial encounters with girls, and trying to make sense of a world where our parents were struggling just to make rent money.

THIS IS WHERE I CAME IN is a story of adversity and humor, the unfolding mystery of sex, of family bonds and family tensions. It's a story everyone can relate to.

CHAPTER ONE

REMEMBERING

My mother was dying and all we could do was watch and wait and pray. There was nothing that her doctors or I could do. She wasn't old—only 70, but a series of strokes had taken their toll. Since my father's death three years earlier in 1968, she'd gone steadily downhill, and she was spending the last pennies of her life in a nursing home in Peekskill, New York.

Most of our visits had been filled with frustration. From our home on Long Island, it was a tortuous drive that always seemed much longer than it looked on a map. Extended delays at the bridges were just a prelude to the twisting, endless curves of the Bronx River Parkway, always made worse in the rain or snow. Marianne usually brought flowers, but my mother barely acknowledged them—when she did she always told her nurses: "Look at the beautiful flowers my SON brought me!" Like most mothers, no daughter-in-law was ever good enough for her only son. There was no love lost between them—their relationship might best be described as an "armed truce," or an irresistible force meeting an immovable object.

Intent on staring blankly at the flickering television monitor above the foot of her bed, it was as if we weren't in the room. After ten minutes of a monologue: "How are you feeling? How's the food? Have you been walking?," we'd just give up and sit in silence. When she finally turned away from the screen, her usual query was, "When are you leaving? There's a good program I want to watch." At that point Marianne and I were ready to take the suggestion (secretly we felt like throttling her!), but we usually persevered and remained at least for an hour. Her nurse was far more talkative, but we hadn't driven all this way to chat with her.

Then a few months before she died everything changed. Unknown to us, her doctor had been giving her a mind-altering drug: L-Dopa. It had an extraordinary effect on her demeanor. In one week she was transformed from a chronic complainer into a sterling new persona.

We arrived one Friday to find her sitting up in bed, with color in her cheeks and fully alert. Her famous thousand-watt smile, a long time gone, was back in full force. The TV was off and she began to relate in great detail much of what had occurred around the time of her marriage. Recalling everything from her courtship to dancing the two-step, she was happily back in the early twenties, a new bride and mother. "What a wonderful time we had, your father and me, living in the twenties. We went dancing every Friday and Saturday, staying out till all hours. He was a marvelous dancer. We never got tired."

Jumping from subject to subject, knowing somehow that this might be her last chance to get it all out, she remembered with uncanny exactitude each and every house and apartment that she and my father had occupied in the decade before I was born. The names spilled out as water from a broken dam: Staten Island, Central Islip, Edenwald, East Moriches, Unionport...Rattling off the names, she put Rand McNally to shame. I was astonished at the number of moves they made in a relatively short period of time, particularly since my father didn't drive. It appeared that my parents rarely stayed in one place for more than a year. I don't know if it was my arrival or the Great Depression that brought this wandering to a halt. (Strangely, my life has been just the opposite—chalking up only two addresses since I married more than a half-century ago.) Her memory, something that she was always proud of, had returned with startling clarity.

Listening to her speak, it was as if all these address changes had occurred last month and not fifty years before. She maintained that bright, upbeat attitude throughout our stay, and for once we were sorry to see the visiting hour come to an end.

Her doctor wasn't available that night, and we assumed that this was a permanent breakthrough and that soon she would be her old self. Sadly, the change was short-lived, and by the next visit she had returned to her previous condition. I was very angry. How could I be so easily disillusioned? There were so many questions I wanted to ask and now it was too late. Her journey into her past had been all too brief. That gate of memory had opened but a crack, offering me only a tantalizing glimpse into her early life. I wanted to know so much more. What had attracted her to my father? What was her childhood like, her school days on the eastside of Manhattan just after the turn of the century? Why hadn't she gotten along with her mother-in-law? Was she content with her marriage and her children?

Our greatest pleasure is remembering. It's a time-tunnel to the past—a way of restoring part of a lost life. People speak of love at first sight, but true love evolves and ripens with repeated sights and sighs. The delight in renewing an old friendship or re-reading a favorite book is often far more enriching than the initial encounter. Just like music, the joy is in the rehearing.

Sons and daughters rarely take the time to dig into their parent's early life. They're too busy living in the present and planning the future. All too often by the time advancing age stirs their curiosity, there's no parent left. Like the aging sailor, he rarely thinks about his ship and his service memories until he reaches his sixties, and by then it's often too late to find a shipmate to share them.

Retracing our steps, it's clear that there's more to a life than one individual. Are we not the historical result of many ancestors stretching back unbroken into the distant past— everything that enriched the lives of our parents, grandparents, aunts, uncles and cousins? Each one adding a little DNA or a dollop of some ingredient, much like the spices and condiments that go into a gourmet dish How I would have relished filling in all those blank spaces in my own years from the time I was born until I was old enough to be aware of what was going on around me. I read every scrap of history from that "dark age," but that's no substitute for a mother's recollection. I've quizzed my two older sisters, but they suffered from the same blackout that I did.

Like the tribal elders of old, I have to continue this story and pass along my experience in the hope that it enhances the knowledge of these two decades—one of the most pivotal periods in American history. I also hope it will afford my children something I was denied, the inner processes and events that shaped their father's character. What I would give to have a written account of my parent's early life, but that opportunity is long past. I hope that this effort will help to make amends.

CHAPTER TWO

THE BIG APPLE

Manhattan

This reminiscence is a love letter to New York, the city where I was born and raised. I spent my entire working life in the boroughs and never lived more than a mile from the city-line. The metropolis never fails to entrance me. Driving into Manhattan at dusk on the Long Island Expressway, one is afforded one of the most luminous and breathtaking views imaginable. Descending behind a mass of soaring towers, the sun's afterglow silhouettes the skyline, and here and there, the first evening lights—our own urban fireflies—are making their appearance. I've witnessed this sight hundreds of times, but it never fails to send a shiver up my spine. I have to remind myself to concentrate on my driving for no image could be more distracting.

Gotham has much to complain about, and its residents will be quick to tell you: scorching summers, frigid winters, overcrowding, noise, dirt, expensive living, and at times, even dangerous. All those descriptions are true, and yet, along with millions of tourists from every nook and cranny of the globe that yearn to visit the "Capital of the World," thousands of young people come here every year to live and work and find fulfillment. Many older residents find the city an ideal retirement spot. For those who desire far more than just a warm, sunny locale, the vibrancy of New York helps to keep them young. The city is essentially a universal "pot au feu," one that's constantly being replenished year after year. Within its borders is an array of delights and attractions found nowhere else. The best in art, theatre, movies, dance, jazz, rock, concert music, opera, ballet, foreign films, restaurants, newspapers, publishing, fashion and shopping—all in infinite variety and unmatched depth.

New York City is certainly crowded, but where else can one live happily without the need of a car? Public transportation is reliable, accessible and operates 24 hours a day. The climate can remind one of Siberia one season and the jungles of Southeast Asia in another, but close by are some of the world's most attractive beaches, boasting white sand that stretches as far as the eye can see and ocean water you can swim in. When the snow flies, pristine ski slopes are but a few hours drive from mid-town. A lot closer to home, one can find the unexpected gem of an open-air ice-skating rink smack in the middle of the soaring towers of Rockefeller Center—the kind of delightful surprise for which the city is famous.

With four out of five boroughs perched on islands, the river, the sound and the ocean are never far away, offering unmatched vistas and opportunities for swimming, boating and sunning. Driving down the Westside, one may chance on a stately ocean liner heading toward the open sea. Every street in Manhattan ends in a river, and lingering sunsets behind the Palisades are a given. When the weather keeps you indoors, its museums run the gamut from huge world-class art and library structures, to more intimate enclaves like the Frick Collection and the Trolley and Fire Department archives. Not to forget the extraordinary American Museum of Natural History. This attracts visitors from every continent. Monuments reflect the same eclectic tone, with a Broadway composer

(George M. Cohan) and an Army Chaplain (Father Duffy), sharing the same slender atoll in the middle of Times Square.

If you're a sports fan, its heaven on earth, with the Yankees, Mets, Knicks, Rangers, and Jets. Even tennis has its own stadium where the world's best compete. And the streets of the five boroughs are the site of the annual New York City Marathon, drawing more than a million spectators.

When it comes to money, Wall Street is synonymous with the Big Apple, and we boast all three major stock exchanges and the home of some of the largest banks in the nation. For those who want a quicker way to put a dent in their assets, one can usually find a Three-Card-Monte Game on a city sidewalk.

But money always takes a second place to the exhilaration I always feel walking up 57th Street on an early autumn evening, with gusts of wind chasing fallen leaves along the sidewalk. After a superb French dinner at Le Perigord, one of my favorite restaurants, I'm headed for a performance by a world-class symphony orchestra in Carnegie Hall. And all the while I'm less than an hour from home. Walking, to be sure, is one of the city's delights. Just like London, Paris or Rome, the Big Apple is best seen on foot. If I'm making my way cross-town, I can nearly always beat the automobile traffic.

While there's never a lack of company, one of New York's biggest assets is the anonymity it bestows on its residents. For the most part, unless you try to blow up their apartment, your neighbors couldn't care less what you're doing. "The city that never sleeps," is more than just a popular lyric. Paris and London for the most part, close up shop, not to mention their public transport by midnight. Here I can mail a letter at a 24-hour post office, sit down to a hot pastrami sandwich and beer at 3 A.M., or listen to live jazz while the rest of the country is in dreamland. And where else can I buy literally ANYTHING, whether it's a love potion from Trinidad, or a mink coat for my dog?

With a veritable United Nations of dialects, customs, and gastronomy, one can experience a fair chunk of the world without leaving the five boroughs. Queens County alone boasts more than thirty ethnic groups and the city's natives speak more than one-hundred twenty languages. (I sometimes wonder if English was counted in that total!). Walking along the Lower Eastside, the aroma of sizzling spare ribs easily blends into the unique Mediterranean scent of Parmesan or oregano, all within the confines of one short street. Seemingly infinite varieties of Indian,

Thai, Chinese, Japanese, French and Italian restaurants all thrive cheek by jowl, block after block in the narrow canyons of Manhattan.

Perhaps I'm prejudiced, but most of us who live here still think, "It's a wonderful town. (And the Bronx is up and the Battery is down!") Scanning the diverse notables who called Gotham their home, we find, among others—George Washington (New York was the first capital of the United States), Mark Twain, F. Scott Fitzgerald, Irving Berlin, George Gershwin, Douglas MacArthur, George Ballanchine, Arturo Toscanini, Fiorello LaGuardia, Leonard Bernstein, Babe Ruth, Richard Rodgers, Woody Allen, Thomas Wolfe, Edgar Allen Poe, Cole Porter, Theodore and Franklin Roosevelt, John Lennon, Marilyn Monroe, and Walt Whitman. They can't all be wrong.

CHAPTER THREE

BEGINNINGS

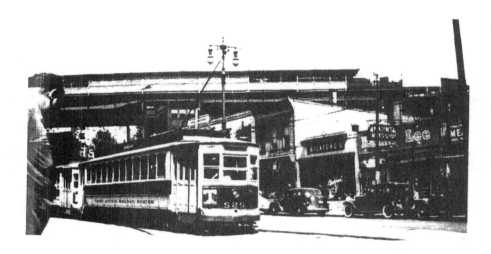

Trolley car

Sometimes in the quiet of the night I can almost hear it: that one-of-a-kind, rasping sound of the "Z" trolley descending the hill. Starting her westbound run at Castle Hill Avenue, it accelerated on its downward path, and the distinctive melody of steel wheels on rails rose and fell as it completed its three-block journey. Lying in my bed, in that fifth floor apartment on Gleason Avenue, it was a "tune" that never changed: "the 177th Street blues."

We lived within walking distance of the Long Island Sound, and the "Z"s journey would carry her clear across the sleeping Bronx to the Hudson. I'd always think of that trolley when I sang "America the Beautiful" in school and recited the line, "from sea to shining sea." But the real adventure lay in riding the trolley from beginning to end. Sometimes, I'd venture the last few blocks on foot to the George Washington

Bridge and walk half way across— just far enough to be able to see the wide river opening a path to the Atlantic. Linked to the majestic sweep of the parkway, it wound its way south into the great city. This was the world I grew up in: The New York of the 30's and 40's.

The trolleys disappeared in the late forties, replaced by supposedly more efficient buses. For a while the tracks remained, but gradually even they were lost as the roads were rebuilt and repaved. Like some ancient fossil from another age, it's still possible from time to time to come across a few feet of old track half buried in blacktop. I wonder if the current generation ever wonders where these rails went and what rode on them. Like the steam trains that once dominated America, these trolleys and the way of life they represented, are gone forever.

When I first read H.G. Wells, "Time Machine," I thought it was a wonderful piece of pure fantasy. As I grew older, I gradually came to realize that we all possess our own "time machine," one that we can enter anytime the mood strikes us.

How often have I hitched myself to this device and traveled across the decades as easily as if I'd crossed the street? And what infinite riches lay hidden in the soft folds of this human storehouse we call memory? Are we not made of memories? Every moment of our lives is the mirror of all the moments preceding it. The media has spent literally tons of ink writing about the "glories" awaiting us when cable TV has 500 channels, but this is but a speck compared to the dramas we can conjure up on our own personal "screens." I'm constantly astonished at how much I can remember of events I'd thought were long forgotten. In time I learned that nothing is ever truly lost: it's just waiting there to be stirred into action. One just has to find the right key.

My Aunt Irene, who died in 1988 at the age of 95, was a master at this trick. One day we were talking about ice-skating and she was reminded of an incident that occurred over seventy years before. Once she started, all the details fell into place. In reality, Irene was no longer in 1985, but had been transported back to Wilson's Woods (she always called them Woodsy Woods) in the year 1916. It was an unbelievable feat. She could recall with startling clarity and immediacy what she and her friends were wearing, what they had for lunch, and to a large extent, what they talked about.

Plumbing the depths of my own memory was just as easy. Down the spiraling path I'd spin on my excursion through the years, never knowing till I reached my goal just how clear the images might be. If I didn't like the decade I was living in, it took but an instant to redial a simpler time. If the "good old days" weren't as radiant as we imagined, there was little doubt that in many respects a change of date could only mean improvement over today. What passes for music on our current radio is a perfect example. One would have to harken back perhaps beyond written history to find a period so bereft of melody and tunes that make you smile. Some critics maintain that music is merely a reflection of the times we live in, but I find that theory too simplistic. One only has to listen to the joyous songs of the Depression Thirties' to punch holes in that theory.

The Thirties' are as good a decade as any to begin this story because that's the starting point of my earliest memories. I could open at the turn of the century when my parents were born, but they'll have their day in the sun a little later on. Their era was infinitely more exciting than mine, at least up until 1940, but I knew nothing of this when I entered the scene in December, 1929. My fading baby pictures in the family album show a sleeping infant doted on by several figures young and old. They surround me as they would some prized trophy won in competition. As the first and only son in my family, the first grandson on my mother's side, and carrying the full name of my great-grandfather (John Charles Martin) who still lived, it appeared I'd won the Triple Crown. I was called John after my father, my paternal grandfather and my mother's younger brother. (My godmother, Flo said, "There are too many "Johns." Let's call him Jack." It stuck. More often it was "Jackie." If, in those early photos my carriage, my clothes, and my accompanying sisters appear elegant, there was good reason. I was born at the peak of my father's financial success.

Baby picture with Rita and Dorothy -1930

At thirty, he was something of a boy-wonder. Putting aside a career in art after his marriage in 1919, he'd found his niche on Wall Street. A natural flair for figures, coupled with hard work, imagination and an ingratiating manner, had vaulted him into the chief cashier's position at some of the most prestigious brokerage houses. Born two months after the Stock Market crash, it was not as many think, an instantaneous blow to all levels of society. What happened in October 1929 could be likened to a stone dropped in a pond, and the latter events to the ever-widening ripples. My father, the second John Sauter, was on top of the world. Like nearly everyone else, he viewed the recent happenings as merely a temporary dip in an economic graph that would only continue to rise.

I know all this because I come from a family of story-tellers. Whether it was my Aunt Irene or Flo; my Grandpa Ludwig, or my mother, none of them ever seem to tire of telling all the tales of their youth. If my parents could have chosen a period to grow up in, they couldn't have picked a better era. New York was bursting at the seams. Their childhood memories mirrored this phenomenal city as it took center stage in every-thing from the longest bridges to the best baseball teams. In the first two decades of this century it rode this crest to bigger and better things. On a more personal level, every year brought more spectacular new wonders with the automobile, motion picture, the phonograph, and radio.

As you read on, you'll notice that nearly all the storytellers are women. This is true for a number of reasons. As in most families, I saw more of my mother's side, and although she had three sisters and four brothers, two of the boys had died in their twenties, and another, John, had made a career of the Navy, shortly before I entered the picture. My aunts regaled me with accounts of what it was like to live on 96th Street on the east side of Manhattan. They left nothing out: the World War (it didn't have a number in those days), sleigh-riding down Lexington Avenue, walking across the frozen East River to Long Island on frigid nights (that grew colder with each telling), and the granite hard times of their youth. My grandfather was a custom furniture craftsman and a decorative plasterer, professions that were disappearing with the demise of extravagant mansions, the ones that used to dot 5th Avenue. But regardless, even when he was fully employed, he had his work cut out for him, trying to raise eight children on one salary.

Already leaning toward the navy

How all these people (two parents, eight children, and on occasion, my grandmother's father), managed to squeeze into a railroad flat containing only two bedrooms has remained to this day, a mystery. Incredibly, their relating of the Ludwig epic was never tinged with bitterness, envy, or despair. Everything was generously coated with the bright patina of optimism and a healthy sense of humor. An incident where all the children are sent out scouting for loose chunks of coal in a railroad yard was transformed into an adventure to wondrously recapture. How the evening meal would have been cooked had their mission been unsuccessful was never mentioned. Regardless of their grim circumstances, they studied hard, worked together, and had an unstinting belief in what would later be referred to as the "American Dream."

CHAPTER FOUR

MEMORY

I t was so long ago, and yet it seems like only yesterday.

For those of us who grew up before and during World War II, this period calls up a time as distant and remote as another planet. The Great Depression tested this country far more rigorously than any war. In a very real sense it was a war, one that would determine whether our system of capitalistic democracy could survive. We won that war, and the safeguards we put in place in the early 1930s to prevent it happening again, shaped not only my life, but that of every American. My recollection of this period is as a child and an adolescent, a time of lasting impressions. As you read on, you'll see that compared to today, it was also an era of true innocence. Words like "honor," "discipline," "sacrifice," and "patriotism" held real meaning. These virtues held us in good stead for the rest of our lives.

For the most part, the Bronx I knew no longer exists. But in my mind's eye it's just as real as it was when I was growing up on the streets of Unionport. The empty lots, the little girls jumping rope, the old people sitting on their folding chairs in front of our apartment; ticking off the minutes of their lives. Giant elm trees spreading their huge branches across the street, reaching out to their brothers; and always in the background, the silver-toned chimes of St. Peter's Church on Westchester Avenue, tolling the quarter-hours.

Coming on the scene in December1929, just after the Great Crash, New York and the world were so totally different then that not even as prolific a futurist as H.G. Wells could have imagined what has been described as a roller coaster ride through history. The double whammy of the Great Depression and World War II had a profound and dampening effect on just about every American, but my young memories are mostly positive. In most cases my friends and I remember these years as the great adventure of our lives. We were witnesses to an unparalleled world stage.

1934 in front of apartment

My Bronx of the 1930s could have been anywhere in "small town" America. I say "Small Town" because except for the close proximity of the "city," as we always referred to Manhattan, we could have just as easily been living in Peoria or Poughkeepsie. Each neighborhood encompassed a few square blocks—an intimate enclave unto itself. I never kept a diary or journal, but a few old, musty family photo albums survive, along with those faded black and white images secured by arrow-shaped black gummed corners. Incredibly, these pictures are still held firmly in place just as they were during Roosevelt's First Term. It seemed everyone owned a Brownie camera. And everyone religiously placed those pictures in an album that was passed around until the pages became dog-eared.

Those little, yellowing 2 ¼ x 3 ¼ prints were my sole link to those hidden years before I became aware of the world around me. Pictures of my parents before the Depression left its mark; images of my sisters as budding young girls, my aunts and uncles in the rounded collars and long dresses and hats of the twenties; my grandparents before they looked like grandparents. The whole family saved forever on film. A mosaic of recaptured time out of time.

So what you are about to read is the product of my memory. Recollecting the events from sixty-odd years ago is an easier task for a seventy-something than trying to recall what I ate for dinner last night. I can't explain it. It just happens.

Each of these stories had a trigger—sometimes it would be meeting a long-forgotten relative at a wake or wedding. Other times a fragment of a Jerome Kern melody or an Ira Gershwin lyric would do the trick. I'm convinced that every sight, sound, smell, taste and touch we've experienced from birth is locked away in the folds of our memory—one of the miracles of the human brain. Finding that key is easier than one thinks.

As a writer, one learns to record the "How, What, Why, Where and When" of every arresting experience, so the same formula can be applied to resurrecting those days and nights when our biggest concern was finishing our homework. A three by four photo of my godmother will be the overture to a myriad of adventures simply because Irene was a living "Auntie Mame."

But no one had greater tales to tell than my grandparents. Their formative years placed them, in our eyes, in the covered wagon era. Born in the 1880s, they were well into raising a family before they laid eyes on an automobile or an airplane. Subways had yet to make their appearance in New York, and horses still held center stage. My father, the oldest of twelve children, recalled having to help his dad hitch up a team of horses at the crack of dawn for his daily bread delivery route. Of course, with each telling, the temperature got colder and the snow deeper. But the important thing was that those stories were told.

The Unionport of my youth was a contentedly insular neighborhood. Much like the villages of France or Italy, our homes and apartments nestled close to the church or synagogue. A subway station or trolley car line was always nearby, and a nickel could carry you practically everywhere in the city. Mothers walked to a dozen stores and knew every butcher, baker and grocer by name. Shopping was communication. Jobs lost, babies born, couples joined, customers who died. All this gossip was exchanged before the first transaction. If you needed credit, it was offered —with no interest. After buying some cold cuts and bread at Max's deli across the street from our apartment, Max would look at me and say, "Yakeeboy, you want I put in the book?" The answer was always yes. Out from under the counter would came the dog-eared school writing tablet and the amount was duly noted. On payday, everyone anteed up.

All this activity was accomplished on foot. Because of the Great Depression and World War II, few of our parents owned cars. Even a bicycle was a luxury for many—myself included.

My world was defined by a score of streets in every direction, easily viewed from my fifth-story window. Inside that quadrangle lived grandparents, four aunts and uncles, and cousins galore. Within walking distance were all the important way stations of my life: the church and school, the public library, the stores, the post office, the movies and the subway station. There was little crime. Drugs were unknown, and personal assaults in my neighborhood were as rare as Brooklyn Dodger World Series victories. There was the occasional break-in or liquor store hold-up, but rarely was anyone hurt. Most families in our apartment building left their doors open during the hot summer months. In any event, locked in the grip of the Great Depression, we had little to steal.

Those of us who were Catholic identified ourselves by parish. The rest would call their neighborhoods Unionport, or Fordham or Throggs Neck. The second street I grew up on — Olmstead Avenue, boasted that it was the only block in New York City that had a synagogue, a Protestant house of worship and a Catholic church on succeeding corners. The Irish bar, the Hebrew National delicatessen, the German bakeries, and the Italian barbershops were sprinkled throughout the locale, and were as ubiquitous as the golden leaves of autumn.

With no video games or television we entertained ourselves on the sidewalks and streets. Ring-a-Liveo, Take a Giant Step, or just plain Tag, kept us running on summer nights. The Good Humor Man and Bungalow Bar ice cream trucks were a familiar sight; those jingling bells a Pavlovian call to the young—a Pied Piper on wheels, perhaps. When it was too hot to run we told ghost stories, pitched pennies or sat in one of the scores of abandoned cars left in the empty lots. Some of the older boys used these cars for other games, but it held no interest for us. We might sneak a kiss, but it was all pretty tame by today's standards. At our age, most of us thought that girls were "soft boys."

Our grammar school classrooms harkened back to another era. In St. Raymond's, where my most of my aunts and uncles had once been taught, the heavy oak desks were fitted with inkwells. Utilizing wooden straight pens with a removable stylus, our writing instruments were not that far removed from the quill that Jefferson had used to write the Declaration. I heard stories about mischievous boys who had dunked the pigtails of the girl sitting in front of them in these receptacles. Perhaps that's why my classmates and I were separated by sex. School was serious stuff with the slower learners being left back to repeat a year. No one seemed to question that practice. Discipline was freely meted out by the teachers, some of it fairly harsh, especially by the Christian Brothers. But times were hard and there was no appeal to parents who were often worrying about where the rent money was coming from. Everyone in the family was expected to do his or her part, whether it was washing and drying dishes, folding laundry, running errands or scrubbing the kitchen and bathroom. In most families everyone over twelve worked, full or part time.

Right up until the end of World War II, horses were a common sight on our streets. A familiar image was the fruit and vegetable wagon, invariably led by an Italian, who more often than not had raised the very produce he was hawking. Every turnip, carrot, pear, peach and potato was grown within a few miles of the city. Their natural flavor is still nostalgically recalled, the peach and apple juice running down our chins with the first bite. Just about every pie was homemade, as was the chocolate pudding. To lick the bowl clean would be the highlight of my day.

Money being very tight, often exotic (or what we thought was exotic) fare would reach our table. Fried spaghetti, hash mixed with an egg or onions, and potato pancakes with apple sauce, were regular "menu surprises." For most of us, toasters were an unfamiliar item. Toast as we knew it was made by holding a piece of bread on a fork over an open gas flame on the stove. It had a unique flavor, never forgotten. Even when the iceman could "cometh," during the winter perishables were placed on the fire escape. I'm sure it saved some precious money, but more important, it left vivid images of the frozen cream rising out of the milk bottle, reminding me of a submarine conning tower, surfacing from the depths.

Before microwave ovens and frozen food (the kind you found in a store, not on the fire escape) everything was cooked or baked at home. Heavenly smells lured us to the kitchen without any urging. Observing our mothers, we had the unparalleled opportunity to watch how a cake or pie was created from scratch; other days it was viewing the formidable preparation required to deliver a roast chicken or holiday turkey dinner to the table. Cholesterol was a word yet to be minted, so butter, eggs and cream were liberally found in every dish. Times were hard, but food was relatively cheap.

Climbing the five flights of stairs to my apartment, especially during the hot summer months when all the doors were open, was a crash course in international cuisine. When the weather turned brutally cold those same staircases and landings became our indoor playgrounds. We punched Spaldeens off the walls, played hopscotch or engaged in serious card games like Go Fish, War and Fan-Tan.

In an era when few people owned cars, many items were delivered right to the door. The horse-drawn milk wagons of Borden's or Sheffield's were a familiar sight to every early riser. Besides milk and cream, one could order bread, muffins, cheese, butter or orange juice. (Strangely, the one item that nearly everyone has delivered today—the morning newspaper—wasn't available then, the sole exception being the Bronx Home News, an afternoon local journal hawked by schoolboys. That was the sole purpose of the stationary-candy store.) The milkman wore a uniform, and for the most part, so did every other worker. It was a time when everyone's place in the scheme of things was clearly delineated, whether that person was a police officer, a nurse, a sanitation man or a Western Union Messenger.

Regardless of social station, everyone wore a hat. Women and young girls were rarely seen outside the house without a head covering, along with gloves and stockings. Aside from fedoras or woolen caps, men and boys relied on gooey hair tonic that would keep their locks in place through the hurricane of the century. Brylcreem, Wildroot or Vitalis were found in every medicine cabinet. Both adult sexes wore garters to hold up their silk stockings or socks, and undershirts were de rigueur for boys and men. The long-suffering distaff side was additionally burdened by an array of undergarments that defied description. At the beach, both sexes wore one-piece woolen bathing suits, usually black. Men's suits covered their chests. These garments were ideal for just about everything except going in the water, and they did a marvelous job of disguising the gender of their wearer. As I recall, they also itched like hell.

Knickers were mandatory for every boy until the magical age of thirteen, when, as a rite of passage, we were all delivered on Easter Sunday into a suit with long pants. Before being sent out to face the world, we had to endure a long lecture on the necessity of always pulling up the trouser legs before sitting down. This marked change was equivalent to a young girl receiving her first brassiere, whether she needed one or not. (The word "bra" didn't enter the vocabulary until sometime later.) For us, this change was strictly hearsay, as this "unmentionable" item was buried under innumerable layers of clothing.

Teenage girls used enough "pancake" make-up to keep Pillsbury in clover, and the strong scent of Sen-Sen identified a young man on the prowl long before he came into view. If you were really "in," you sported a long key chain hanging from your belt loop into your pocket. Along with a house key, that ring usually held a pocketknife, a rabbit's foot and a St. Christopher's medal. I could never quite understand the need for the latter since none of us ever roamed more than a few miles from home.

Cleanliness may have been next to Godliness, but a bath more than once a week, except in the heat of summer, was a rarity. Showers, incidentally, were strictly reserved for public pools and gyms. Some older people had a theory that taking baths during the winter was downright unhealthy. They firmly believed that the body produced some protective oils that prevented one from acquiring cold germs or worse. There may have been some truth to this speculation, as it's commonly known that the best way to catch a cold is to be in close contact with large numbers of people. Those who didn't bathe much from November till April were never, but never, in close proximity to large numbers of people—that's for sure!

Walking in the fresh air, even in the dead of winter was considered to be healthy and invigorating. One was labeled "soft" if he complained about the heat or cold. That's just the way life was, and no one tried to alter it. Except for few theaters on the style of Radio City Music Hall, air-conditioning lay far in the future. No one imagined it would ever cool an apartment.

While few of us traveled, we were constantly exposed to foreign languages. Most of my schoolmates' parents were born in Ireland or Italy, with a sprinkling from Germany. Other neighbors spoke Yiddish. (My family was immune to this with both sides having roots going back more than a hundred years.) Newspapers such as the Jewish Daily Forward, IL Progresso, and Die Stats Zeitung were found cheek-by-jowl with the New York local sheets: the Daily News, the Mirror and the Herald Tribune. Most of the older foreign-born women never learned to speak or write English, content to remain wrapped in a protective family cocoon of local dialects originating from Catania to Vilna. My classmates translated for them. I learned to eat matzoth-ball soup from kosher plates in one friend's house, and lasagna and spaghetti Bolognese in another.

Both tables held wine, something I only saw on Sundays. My parents enjoyed an occasional highball—the Carstairs bottle with the plastic seal balancing a ball on his nose a familiar sight in the cupboard. Beer was seldom found on our table, but it was, by far, the most popular drink in the neighborhood. I never saw bottled or canned beer until I was much older. The most common source of supply was from the local gin mill in a metal container supplied by the drinker. This process was known colloquially as "Rushing the Growler." No one ever questioned your age, and many a six-year old could be seen waiting on a barstool for the growler to be filled. Everyone knew who you were.

Religion was far more intrinsic to our lives than it is today. Much of the neighborhood revolved around the church, whether it was an evening of Bingo or the various societies that enlisted most of the women and girls. The American Catholic church had a distinct "separate but equal" philosophy that encompassed nearly every aspect of our lives. Aside from the Holy Name Society and the Children of Mary, there were Catholic Mothers of the Year, Catholic War Veterans and Catholic Boy Scouts. Even the radio got into the act with the Catholic Hour, and three Catholic newspapers were sold outside the church every Sunday. That Bing Crosby's Academy Award portrayal of a parish priest in GOING MY WAY was the most popular film of 1944, was a fair indication of the power of religion in America. It took most of us more than a few years to join mainstream America. Some never did.

It was a period marked with little alteration. The world was changing, often violently in places like Spain, China and Germany, but here our existence seemed set in stone; held firmly in the yoke of the Great Depression. Among my friends it was the rare father who held a steady job. With my dad unemployed, my mother worked full time and later pulled my older sister, Dorothy, out of high school and enrolled her in a crash course in typing and steno. Every dollar counted.

Families doubled up, often with seven or eight people sharing the same bathroom and kitchen. Dispossessed households sitting disconsolate on the sidewalk surrounded by all their earthly possessions was an all-too-common sight on the streets of the Bronx. This happened to my schoolmate, Vinny Vitale, but he was parceled out to an aunt and uncle in the same parish, so he remained in our class. When another schoolmate, Tony Conforti, celebrated his ninth birthday I was invited to his party. Tony's father worked as a stevedore unloading ships. With the sharp decline in trade, his working days were few if any. With no unemployment insurance they were living on the edge. This party brought home far more intensely than any headlines or radio announcements just how bad the Depression was. Poor Tony received no gifts from his family. I brought two Hersey bars that were very welcome. A few pieces of fruit and homemade birthday cards adorned the kitchen table. No matter how tough things were, I'd always received some birthday and Christmas presents from my Aunt Irene and my sisters, along with my parents, humble as they might be. At least Tony's mother had baked a cake. There were no candles so his father stuck wooden matches in the top. Same effect. We only got through half of "Happy Birthday to you..." After Tony blew out the matches the desperateness of his situation finally sank in and he began to cry. Pretty soon he had a lot of company. It was a memorable birthday, but not for the usual reasons.

Avoiding bill collectors became a 1930s art form. My own family used a number of ploys, and I well recall everyone being commanded to remain absolutely silent as the old life insurance man came climbing up five flights of stairs to pick up his monthly premium. "Everybody keep still. Here comes Mr. Silver," my mother commanded. Hungry men constantly knocked on our door, looking for a sandwich or a piece of pie, offering to do any chore at my mother's bidding. On occasion, there would be a real shock when the shadowy figure in the hall turned out to be a former store manager or a bank officer we'd known in better times. There were also times when my mother was approached by some neighbors, who chided her on giving out food. "You'll only draw more beggars," they cautioned. My mother replied, "That's ok. I'll just keep offering them food until I run out." On Saturday mornings in warmer weather we were always awakened by singers or musicians in the court-yard, looking for a few nickels or pennies. When there was little money my mother would often give them a leftover or a piece of fruit. With no unemployment insurance or public assistance, it was for many a rock hard existence. Many families we knew broke up under the strain and the inability to meet the rent and food bill. Children were sent to their relatives.

All during the time I was growing up in Unionport, the only thing harder to find than a job was a Republican.

President Roosevelt was the only beacon of hope in this long dark tunnel.

Like most other American cities, New York had a grimy, weathered look. Essentially this was caused by a lack of any new construction since the early thirties,' and the effects of coal heating in every home and business. While there were no new private homes, apartments or commercial structures being built, it was oddly, a time of tremendous public works. Among the completed projects in the thirties' were the East River Drive (later the F.D.R.), the Long Island parkways, the Triboro and Whitestone bridges, and the Queens Mid-town tunnel, to name but a few. In a last gasp of commercial building before the Depression shut everything down, the two tallest buildings in the country were completed: the Empire State and Chrysler skyscrapers.

Another thing that didn't change was the political lineup. All throughout grammar and most of high school we had the same President, Franklin Roosevelt, and the same Governor and Mayor: Herbert Lehman and Fiorello H. LaGuardia respectively. Even our borough president, James J. Lyons, remained a fixture. If nothing else, it made our civics lessons easier. In sports the baseball Yankees dominated the thirties'—the Bronx Bombers continuing their reign for another generation. Another Bomber, a Brown one, in the guise of Joe Louis did the same thing for boxing. It was an exciting time to be growing up in the Big Apple.

With few automobiles on the streets, our playgrounds spilled out beyond the curb. Stickball and punchball were always in vogue. In the winter, hilly roads became toboggan runs for "Flexible Flyers." Less affluent youngsters slid down on large pieces of cardboard; not as maneuverable, but just as much fun. Often two or three of us would pile on a sled, rocketing down an icy roadway, screaming our lungs out. We built snowmen and bored large tunnels in the massive white mounds. Every day and every week was filled with the joy of life being lived to the fullest.

Summers were entirely different. Life's tempo slowed to a crawl and we dreamed of places like Orchard Beach and the Bronx Pool. But for a couple of years none of us went near the beach because of an epidemic of infantile paralysis—the scourge of our youth. If one needed any reminder of just how debilitating this disease could be, he only had to look at our President in the newspapers or newsreels, either on the arm of an aide and wearing heavy steel braces. Fortunately, many empty lots dotted the landscape, often containing the remnants of half-built apartments halted due to a lack of money. What ideal places to let our imaginations run wild. That uncompleted wall became the fort in BEAU GESTE, a favorite film; the empty window a perfect firing point from which to repel an attack from the other gang. We had a tailor-made Bronx Pompeii—the ruins of a city, in this case unfinished, rather than destroyed. Few of us ever used the formal playgrounds that sprang up around the city. They could never match an empty lot when you wanted to erect a hut, build a fire, roast "mickeys," or just enjoy the unsupervised freedom that we needed. We all longed for adventure and here's where we found it— along with the movies.

CHAPTER FIVE

SATURDAYS AT THE MOVIES

Movies dominated our lives. Casting a mystical spell; we often thought they were the "real thing" and not the other way around. Transported into a rarefied fantasy trip, we lived separate lives. The memory lingers, even after seventy years. Who can forget the oppressive smell of heavy summer heat just after exiting an air-conditioned theater? I had some relatives who saw 200 films a year, and all from the same theater! The actors and actresses were as familiar as our own family, and they remained permanent icons for our entire childhood and puberty.

Castle Hill Movie theater.

"Jackie's mother! Jackie's mother!" the sing-song chant rang out; "Can Jackie go to the Castle Hill with us? It's a good pitcha' and all of us are goin'," This was the familiar Saturday recitation from my friends in the courtyard. My mother quickly doled out twelve cents and off we went, entering into a world of flickering images and utter darkness. It was 1941, and by now this Saturday afternoon (or sometimes morning) gathering had become as much a ritual as the weekend bath and confession. Every neighborhood had its theater and they were imbedded into the landscape like houses of worship, which in a way I guess they were. In the east Bronx we had two: the Square and the Castle Hill, each part of huge chains that dominated local movie-going throughout the city. These houses never showed the same films, so there was always a choice; in addition, there were a few independent theaters that thrived on reruns. Living in the wilds of the Bronx, we were, so to speak, at the very end of this Hollywood food chain. Our appetites were skillfully nurtured all along the way by clever advertising. A movie would initially open in a "first run" Broadway theatre to much hoopla. Radio City Music Hall would skim the cream right off the top; equally good "features" would open at the Roxy, the Paramount, the Capitol or the Astor. All of these opulent theaters would also feature name bands and well-known vocalists: the top entertainers in the country—Sinatra, Duchin, Cugat, and Connie Boswell. By contrast, patrons of the Square or the Castle Hill were lucky to be treated to a "Dish Night."

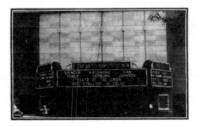

Marquee of Loew's American

Our Saturday movie scene never varied. For much of the day the auditorium bordered on bedlam, with kids screaming, fighting and creating sheer pandemonium until the lights were dimmed. The sole keeper of the peace (usually a losing battle) was a white-uniformed older woman who was always referred to as Matron. A flashlight her only weapon, she roamed the aisles breaking up scuffles and trying to keep her restive audience seated. Whatever her salary, it couldn't be enough for such a thankless job, but at the height of the Depression there never appeared to be any difficulty attracting these poor souls. Aside from keeping order, these matrons were more often than not pressed into service stopping nosebleeds, retrieving lost children and changing the underpants of many a small fry whose older brother was too busily engrossed with "Don Winslow of the Navy" to take him to the toilet. Besides the verbal abuse that came with the territory, they were the perennial target of countless spitballs and water bags. Astonishingly, in spite of all these tribulations, their particular occupation endured for as long as I can remember. For twelve cents our mothers got their money's worth: the cheapest baby-sitting ever devised. Sadly, by the time it was our generation's turn, the system had disappeared.

In addition to the double-feature, a first-run picture linked to a B-movie, we were treated to a cartoon, the Movietone News and the ubiquitous serial. Usually presented in twelve or fourteen segments, the "chapters," as they were always known, included such stalwart heroes as Dick Tracy, Captain Marvel or Captain Midnight. Each week at the serial's conclusion, our champion would be trapped in a burning building or bound and gagged in a car about to go over a cliff. Then the screen would erupt in a dazzling light and a message would flash, "Next week, Chapter 8, Trapped in the Mine!" In spite of our knowing that Dick Tracy, or whoever was featured, would survive whatever fiendish trap was laid, we still ate it up and came back nail-biting week after week.

Since most of us never read anything more involved than the comics or the sports page, the Pathe or Movietone News provided us with at least a modicum of what was going on outside the Bronx. One thing I distinctly recall was that whenever President Roosevelt's image appeared on the screen the audience would break into spontaneous applause. But this custom wasn't repeated with Truman or his successors. However, our knowledge of the world and its mores and morals were enhanced by much more than the newsreels. Subtly, but incisively, the films themselves changed us far more than we ever realized. Well beyond wanting to be able to draw a gun as fast as John Wayne or look as glamorous as Joan Crawford, we were unconsciously acquiring the social graces and manners of Hollywood.

After watching Cary Grant (always referred to as GARY Grant in our circle) or David Niven stand for the twentieth time when a woman approached their table, we started doing the same thing. Even more striking were the moral lessons taught directly by Andy Hardy's parents when he forgot his manners, and since he was one of "us," they carried a lot more weight. In those innocent days before films were rated, the Hays Office made sure that crime didn't pay and that justice always triumphed. It may have been only celluloid, but in a true sense it was our real world. When the screen reinforced what we were being taught at home and in school, it made a lasting impression. There weren't any lurid love scenes back then, but regardless of how suggestive they might have been, they were of absolutely no interest to our ten and twelve-year-old minds. What we wanted was action and plenty of it. Hollywood never disappointed us, and I recall acting out huge chunks of "Gunga Din", "Drums along the Mohawk" and "The Charge of the Light Brigade," in the empty lots of Unionport. The trick was to position yourself on the side of a hill so that when you were "shot," you could roll over and over just like on the screen of the Castle Hill theatre.

As a mesmerizing device, movies had no equal. Unlike today's diminutive multiplexes, one forty-foot screen riveted your attention. The darkness was almost Stygian. During the chapter or the adventure flick no one talked or moved. Little boys could sometimes be observed furiously wiggling their legs so they wouldn't have to go to the Men's Room and miss any of the good parts. The same picture was shown again, but it meant sitting through another three hours of news, cartoon etc. Often, an older sister or worn-out mother would instruct the senior child going to the theatre. "Don't bring them home until 5 P.M." One of my best friends, Henry Schwartz, was so taken with "Stanley and Livingston," that he not only sat through two afternoon shows, but also hid in the Men's Room during the break and watched it again at seven o'clock. Unfortunately, he neglected to inform his mother of his plans and she had half the police in the 43rd Precinct were out searching for him!

By the late afternoon the floors would be sticky from gum and awash in candy wrappers. In my time there was no soda or popcorn, just candy. Most of us carried enough rations from home, however, to support Admiral Byrd's expedition to Antarctica, and the theatre soon reeked with the overpowering aroma of tuna fish and peanut butter.

Moving up the scale but not yet venturing into Manhattan, we could enter a Bronx "Arabian Nights" by taking the trolley car to the Loew's Paradise on the Grand Concourse. From its glittering entrance with huge columns that seemed to reach into the stratosphere, to the fountains and gargoyles along the upper terraces, this was a never-never land come true. When we thought we'd seen it all, we were literally floored upon entering the main auditorium where we were greeted by a ceiling of deep blue sky studded with twinkling stars. For my family, when it came to "movie palaces," Radio City took first place in our dream of the perfect theatre. A visit there would be an all-day outing, complete with dinner at some restaurant on the style of Toffanetti's. In most cases our venture into Manhattan would be linked to their Christmas or Easter spectacles where the stage show never varied. For me, the parade of wild animals was always the highpoint; I was still too young to appreciate the Rockettes. Regardless of what was on the stage or the screen, it was the building itself that left the most lasting impression. Resembling a huge cathedral, we were overwhelmed by its sheer size. Best of all, no matter where we sat, there were no pillars or posts to mar our view. During the intermission, a mighty organ poured out deep resonant sounds that literally froze the audience in place. The very floor beneath us trembled and the vibration seemed to make every bone in my body tingle. In such an intimidating atmosphere, there was no need for matrons. Everyone dressed to the "nines" in keeping with the dignity of the house, and I can never recall anyone speaking above a whisper. Right down to the reading lights installed in the back of every seat, Radio City Music Hall was a class operation.

All that splendor aside, our little local "Pits" or "Itches," if nothing else, held more opportunity for adventure. When only one of us could come up with the twelve cents needed for a ticket, a favorite ploy would be to send him inside while the rest of us positioned ourselves just outside the fire exit. Once inside, he'd open the door and the rest of us would quickly scamper into some empty seats before the overtaxed matron caught up to us. Other times, after 6 P.M., we'd have to find an adult to buy our ticket. If you asked politely, invariably an older man would take you in. You never asked a woman: she'd want to know if your mother knew you were out, along with your whole life history.

Our local theaters all followed the same pattern: the big film and its accompanying Boston Blackie or Charlie Chan second feature ran Thursday through Monday, with the middle of the week usually devoted to a western and another "B" movie. There were always Coming Attractions, the only real intermission in those days, and usually welcomed as an opportunity to visit the facilities. But missing a few minutes of anything was rarely a problem since the plots were simple. Unless it was a murder mystery like the Thin Man series that was best followed from the beginning, people would walk in whenever it was convenient. When two-and-a half-hours had elapsed and the same scene reappeared, one person would turn to the other and say, "Let's go. This is where we came in." Most families went to the movies at least once a week, on a Friday or Saturday. My father would often go on Tuesday since it was rarely crowded. I always had to have my homework completed before being allowed to accompany him, so I'd tackle it as soon as I came home from school. My Aunt Anna, on the other hand, was an absolute fanatic and would go every day if she could, often traveling great distances by trolley car to other theaters.

Everyone in my family had their favorites and would literally spend hours defending their heroes or heroines. My Dad's big heartthrob was Ida Lupino. Whenever someone raved about a rival's performance, his ready reply would be, "She's good, but she's no Ida Lupino!" His other top choice was Margaret Sullivan. My sisters Dot and Rita loved Brian Ahearn, Tyrone Power and Lana Turner. (After seventy years of fascination, Dot still looks as though she could pass for Lana's understudy!) For my mother, Clark Gable was always Mister Right, and her view was probably shared by half the country. Loretta Young was my heartthrob, followed closely by Paulette Goddard and Carole Lombard. In those halcyon days, the performers were bigger than life and all remained on the scene long enough to almost resemble family. While the censor's hand was very much in evidence, my sisters were always obsessed by who was the better kisser on the screen. That difference would dominate their whole conversation on our walk back home. At that time kissing was too far in my future for me to catalog, but I well remember watching Paul Henreid simultaneously light those two cigarettes and then offer one to Bette Davis in "Now Voyager." Once I started dating and smoking, that feat became my trademark as well as that of most of my friends.

If the Hays Office wasn't bad enough, the Catholic Church went one step further with their Legion of Decency. (I often wondered who dreamed up that title.) All the movies were rated in the CATHOLIC NEWS with such commentary as: Suggestive Situations, Glorifies' Divorce, Objectionable In Part, or Condemned. A precious few were deemed suitable for family viewing. Unfortunately for the Legion, slotting these movies produced just the opposite effect by raising our curiosity. (One of my friends remarked that it would have been far simpler to allow us to only see films beginning with the letter "B:" "Boys Town," "Bernadette [Song Of]" and "Bambi!") The category CONDEMNED invariably attracted our virgin eyes, but alas, these Occasions of Sin were usually foreign films only shown in some remote art house buried deep within the city. "Ecstasy" was always at the top of the list; it supposedly contained a nude scene with Hedy Lamar. But none of us ever found out for sure. I only knew Hedy from her big line in "Strange Cargo" ("I am Tand-elayo") and in my book she couldn't touch Loretta Young. But then, my love for Loretta was so pure I couldn't even imagine her taking a bath without being fully clothed!

Once a year in the middle of Sunday Mass, everyone was made to stand and solemnly repeat the long Legion of Decency oath after the priest. When we walked out of church suitably chastened, no one even dared to glance at the "Condemned" heading in the CATHOLIC NEWS for fear we'd be sent directly to Hell right along with Hedy!

CHAPTER SIX

WAR

Ration Points

La Guardia Airport opened when I was ten, but even then there were so few aircraft that the sight of one often brought all activity to a halt. Everyone followed the silver plane's journey across the sky. None of us knew anyone who had flown—it was a mode of transportation strictly reserved for movie stars and the very rich. However, that did not stop us from dreaming about planes morning, noon and night. We built scores of balsa models and hung them from thumbtacks in our ceiling. The sweet scent of "airplane glue" permeated many an apartment. Once smelled, it was never forgotten. I built a replica of Lindberg's "Spirit of St.Louis," along with a Stinson "Reliant." Our newspapers kept interest at a fever pitch with the likes of Smilin' Jack and Terry and the Pirates.

September 1939 brought the onset of World War II, only it wasn't called that yet. It was just the European War. Except for some heated arguments among those who were born in Germany or Ireland and who were rooting against the British, the struggle could have been taking place on another planet. The Atlantic Ocean seemed to be infinite, relegating continental problems to the inside of our newspapers.

Three years earlier Spain had been embroiled in a terrible civil war, but the issues were too vague for our ten-year old minds to grasp. Our parents were similarly confused and tended to ignore it. There were just too many problems right here. It was the prevailing opinion that the continental war would be over in a few months. In our wildest dreams no one ever imagined that we would not only become involved, but would be the deciding factor in its outcome.

Subtly though, things were changing. As one country after another fell to the Nazis, more and more uniforms appeared on the streets. For the first time in our history, a peacetime draft went into effect, albeit for only one year. Junior military groups sprang up overnight and all of us desperately longed to sport khakis or dress blues. Every kid wanted to tote a rifle, even if the firing pin had been removed. All at once, the Boy Scouts went out of fashion. Along with several of my friends I joined a junior naval group: the American Bluejackets. Wearing dress blues, we drilled weekly in public schools, marched in every parade, and held military reviews in the cavernous armories dotting the city. We didn't know it at the time, but it was a forerunner of things to come.

The widening European war took center stage in our lives as the British navy rescued their expeditionary force from the jaws of the German army at Dunkirk, and France collapsed a few weeks later. Suddenly the menace was a lot closer. A great debate ensued between the America First isolationists and those that wanted to render all aid to Britain short of war. Soon it became a dinner table topic in every home in the Bronx. In school, geography took on a greater respect. As part of our study, we often had to draw maps of foreign countries, vividly illustrating their products by gluing a gasoline ad or a rubber band on the nation's location. So we learned, for example, why the Japanese might want to conquer the Dutch East Indies or the Germans—Romania. As a budding history buff, I was captivated by the struggle—devouring the newspaper and avidly listening to every commentator's analysis. My schoolwork took second place.

Most of my friends tended to take the same side as their parents in this ongoing debate, but the movies, subtly, but effectively, began to influence our thinking. A whole slew of adventure films extolled British history in the most favorable light. THE CHARGE OF THE LIGHT BRIGADE, SEA HAWK, FOUR FEATHERS, SPITFIRE, GUNGA DIN, and

IN WHICH WE SERVE, always championed the English cause. Hollywood chimed in with THE FIGHTING 69TH. Regardless of where your parents' sympathies lay, it was pretty hard to root for the Germans when Pat O'Brien, Errol Flynn and James Cagney were on the other side.

Aside from parades and our weekly drilling in public schools, as members of the American Bluejackets we were often taken on field trips to West Point and sporting events in the city. One Sunday in early December 1941, about a hundred cadets and their parents went to Madison Square Garden to watch the New York Rangers play the Maple Leafs. It was my first experience with hockey, a fast-moving sport. Halfway through the game the PA system crackled with announcements asking various military officers to call their bases. Finally the action was halted and we heard an official speak from the middle of the ice, "Ladies and Gentlemen: We have just heard over the radio that the Japanese have attacked Pearl Harbor in Hawaii. All leaves are cancelled and all military personnel are to report back to their ships and posts immediately." It was a stunned and sober crowd that filed out of the arena.

Soon after Pearl Harbor food rationing went into effect and books of stamps were distributed to every family. We were envied because we were a family of five, as each person counted as an adult in the allocation of meat and vegetables. My mother often gave stamps to my oldest aunt who was childless. We had more than enough stamps, but rarely enough money.

My friends and I were 12 and 13 when we entered the war, but that wasn't too young to feel that we couldn't have a real effect on the outcome. We gathered newspapers, old pots and pans (some not so old when our mothers were out of the house), dismantled abandoned cars for scrap metal, and collected fat for munitions. In our spare time we memorized the photos of the Axis aircraft, just in case some of them should get through to New York. We prayed for our soldiers and sailors, and my older sisters wrote to them or attended USO dances. We all purchased 25-cent War Stamps that we religiously pasted in a book (much like Green Stamps) until they reached a value of $18.75. Then the book was magically transformed into a War Bond. Just holding that certificate in your hand made you feel like J.P. Morgan!

A few months into the war New York's Great White Way became a memory as the city implemented a "brownout." This government enforced program resulted in a sharp reduction in the collective outdoor lighting that was causing a glow along the coast, silhouetting our ships and making them easy targets for U-boats. Then there were air-raid drills with wardens who blew whistles at any crack of light from a window. It was all very exciting to a budding teenager, watching the darkened Bronx from a fifth-story window.

The Electric Boat Company made submarines at Groton, Connecticut. Their Life magazine ads portrayed action scenes of subs at war printed in brilliant color. A tiny notice indicated that reproductions could be had free of charge just by writing to the company. Soon the kitchen alcove that held our table and chairs was covered in these posters. I didn't expect to be allowed to hang these illustrations, but most of the renderings were done by well-known artists, at least well known by my dad. At one point he remarked that he felt that he should be wearing a life jacket when he sat down in the evening.

For the most part, though, life went on not too differently as before. Not owning a car, we weren't inconvenienced by gas rationing, and there was always plenty to eat. In one stroke, the war wiped out the Depression, and my father returned to full time work. In spite of some shortages, most people were far better off than they had been during the thirties. Ironically, just when money went back into people's pockets, there was little to buy. Factories that once produced automobiles and household appliances now built tanks and guns.

In spite of the lack of consumer goods, the war brought an excitement missing in the previous decade. Great things were happening and we were intimately involved in them. Everybody was working, sometimes holding down two jobs, desperately trying to recapture some of those "lost years." My sister's social lives went into high gear. Rita graduated from Cathedral High School in 1942 and began to work in the city. On weekends she attended dances for servicemen at the "Y" and the USO. Dorothy was already employed by AT&T on lower Broadway. She was engaged to Johnny McDonald, who worked for Western Electric. Later, when he was drafted, this experience enabled him to be assigned to the Army Signal Corps.

Closer to home my friends and I were actively involved in scrap metal drives. We'd scour the neighborhood gathering discarded auto-mobile parts, rusted bicycles, and broken buckets. Once we came upon a partially wrecked car and spent more than week dismantling it. We became caught up in a patriotic fever that consumed us. For the first time we felt that we were directly helping our war effort.

One of the places that thankfully remained the same was the corner candy and stationery store. Aside from selling magazines, ice cream, candy, and soda, it was the dispenser of all the daily newspapers. In the 1940s there were a number of evening editions in addition to the morning papers. Awaiting the Journal-American, the World Telegram, and the Post, neighbors tended to congregate just before the delivery truck dropped off the heavy stacks of papers. Satisfying the curiosity of the older men who were primarily interested in the results at Aqueduct and Belmont Park racetracks, these late editions provided us with the final baseball scores. Nearly all the games were played in the afternoon. Magazine racks were stacked with comic books, creating a temptation to browse that was hard to contain. This always brought forth a cry from the owner behind the counter, "Boys, This isn't a library. Either buy the comic book or put it down!"

For the most part, the candy store became a hangout, a place to meet friends, find girls, or talk away a summer night. For some this would be their regular social hall, to kibbitz or follow the course of the war. Their offerings never changed. Egg creams (a soda concoction made with chocolate syrup, seltzer, and a little milk—sorry no eggs!), thick milk shakes, simply known as "malteds," and frozen Milky Ways. The latter must have been a favorite of all the dentists as it consisted of a caramel bar covered in chocolate that tended to stick to your teeth like glue. Frozen, they seemed to last forever.

Another popular item was an ice cream roll encased in two paper strips. Sugar cones were shaped to accept these frozen cylinders, and the vendor could separate the two paper tabs and allow the ice cream to drop freely into its receptacle. It was trademarked "Mello-Roll."

Ice cream was such a big part of our lives that most evenings ended over a sundae or ice cream soda. Every drug store boasted a gleaming marble counter with high round leather stools where serving banana splits was a specialty. For us, the arrival of Howard Johnson's on the scene a few years earlier was as epoch-making as D-Day. This was our introduction into the world of pistachio and chocolate chip. The sole Ho Jo's (as it was popularly known) in the Bronx was situated on the approach to the Bronx-Whitestone Bridge. The bridge's opening coincided with the inaugural of the first New York World's Fair in Flushing, just across the sound. All the luminaries gathered for this historic event. A parade of automobiles carried, among others: President Roosevelt, Governor Leheman and Mayor La Guardia. In our eyes, all these events paled next to the grand opening of this small elegant building with an orange roof. Inside they served the best hot dogs we'd ever eaten, and featured some exotic items like salt-water taffy. But nothing in the Bronx (or New York) matched their munificent array of ice creams, no less than twenty-eight flavors. Could heaven be far behind!

I managed to visit the "World of Tomorrow," the 1939-40 World's Fair only twice; once with a school outing. There were just too many images to absorb in a few hours. So I came home with a jumble of memories: the General Motors Motorama that predicted gorgeous freeways and concrete overpasses (always with few cars!), mixed up with the tiny ceramic Heinz Pickle, that I carried around for some months afterward.

The death of F.D.R. and the end of the war signaled a sea change in our lives. For the first time new cars began to appear in showrooms, nylon stockings and other lingerie in ladies shops, and all restrictions were lifted on popular cigarettes. The twin plagues of the Great Depression and World War II had ended, and a curtain was rising on a new era. It was as if the long-awaited consummation of a national marriage was at hand and the promise of America was at last being fulfilled.

Some customs lingered for a few more years, but there was no doubt that a significant social alteration was in bloom. Soon it was clear that nothing would ever be the same again.

The war's end and those first exciting months of the new peace coincided with my passage from childhood to young adult, locking those years forever in my memory. The country and I were both "growing up" and irrevocably changing.

CHAPTER SEVEN

96*th* STREET

As most of my earliest excursions from the Bronx were to my mother's parents, I remember this flat as if it were yesterday. Their living quarters were on a second floor of an ancient brownstone gained by ascending a dank, dark staircase that creaked and groaned with each step. Two apartments shared this level and their only light emanated from windows in the front and rear. For this reason, the parlor that faced 96th Street was called, appropriately enough, the "front room." Furnished with two stuffed chairs and a small wooden table, its other attribute was an entrance to the hallway.

The second doorway admitted one into two bedrooms that led to a large kitchen facing a courtyard. "Large" doesn't do this space justice since it could easily hold a table capable of seating ten adults. Overlooking and dominating everything else in this room, was a huge coal stove and oven venting into a massive galvanized flue that disappeared into the wall. On those lazy Sunday afternoons when I went visiting my grandparents, this is where I spent most of my time. Since I was much too young to go outside on my own, I would spin away the hours playing dominos with my grandfather, a game he taught me. Crafted from ivory, the pieces were a prized family possession. The walls displayed his handiwork, finely wrought plaster brackets, resplendent in gold, each one holding an exquisite porcelain figure. I imagine the figures were a gift from a client. A series of Civil War prints completed the decoration.

Other than those Union soldiers, my six-year-old gaze was focused on those tall rear windows in another string of railroad flats overlooking the courtyard. During the summer many of the occupants could be seen perched on the fire escapes, taking the air. Poking up from the shadows, the branches of the tallest trees reached out close to the wash lines that crisscrossed over the whole yard. On Sundays, these lines were empty, but when we visited during the week it was a rainbow of whites, reds, blues and yellows. Scores of men's trousers, work clothes, "long-Johns," and shirts, vied for attention with row upon row of colorful dresses and underwear. This scene always reminded me of the fluttering signal flags on a warship. While all these people were desperately poor, everyone took pride in wearing an array of different fabrics, colors and styles. (Curiously, today, in spite of a prosperity undreamed of then, nearly everyone wears the same dreary denim. Up until the nineteen sixties, that material was strictly reserved for laborers. I never understood the allure.)

On the biting cold Sundays of winter, I passed the time reading the NY Journal-American, a paper we didn't get at home, while stuffing myself with sugar-coated crullers from the marvelous bakeries of Yorkville. Around that huge kitchen table sat various aunts and uncles, telling and re-telling their sad plight of trying to survive in the bitter days of the Great Depression. I was too young to appreciate the enormity of their problems, but even I could sense that things were not going well. But I don't want to get ahead of myself. I always had enough to eat and a roof over my head, and my five-year old mind didn't dwell on such adult concerns. When the conversation got too heated, my grandpa Ludwig would grab my hand and say, "Come on, Jackie, Let's take the radio to the front room and listen together." In the summer there was a baseball game; in the winter a concert. Radio never failed to fascinate me, and by the time I was six I'd memorized my favorite stations and times. My grandfather was everything my father wasn't. He spent time with me, taught me how to play dominos, rummy, and later to swim and float, climb hills and pick berries.

Sometimes my great-grandfather, John Martin, would capture my attention with stories of the Civil War. One of his tales involved the siege of Vicksburg. (I had no idea what Vicksburg was. I wondered perhaps if it was where they made Vicks Vapor Rub, a vile smelling cream that my mother would liberally coat on everyone's chest who even had the hint of a sniffle.) Martin was part of a Union Army artillery battery. They subsisted on bread and the contents of a barrel of molasses. When they finally reached the bottom, there was a dead rat! I don't know if the story was true, but it sure added a lot of spice to his telling. It may seem odd, but in the early thirties' there were still a number of veterans of the GAR (Grand Army of the Republic) around. John Martin was over ninety at this time.

But my most lasting memory of 96th Street was not of war, my grandfather, the kitchen, the front room, or the back yard; it was that dark and evil-smelling communal toilet in the hallway. A horror I never used except when it was absolutely necessary. Awful.

By far, the best part of going to my grandparents was the memorable journey on the Lexington Avenue subway. Technically, the train was elevated for about half the trip, but no one ever called it anything but the subway. To me, there was only one place to ride: the first car. Here, next to the motorman, I shared his unobstructed view of the gleaming rails and stations. Just before entering the tunnel at Hunts Point, the tracks crossed a high trestle above the Bronx River. In the eyes of a five-year-old, a whole new world was unfolding. On a clear day one could see half the county, and an unobstructed vista downtown to the gleaming spires of Manhattan.

Entering the tunnel, the crashing sounds exploded, coming all at once, and blotting out everything else. I became temporarily in a state of shock. The close proximity of the walls made it seem as though we were traveling a hundred miles an hour. Hurtling through this black void, the rushing noise, the flashing lights and the sudden appearance of another speeding train going in the opposite direction, literally took my breath away. Secretly, I hoped that someday I could be a motorman. I couldn't imagine a better job.

CHAPTER EIGHT

GERTIE

Gertrude Ludwig as a young girl, with her future husband, John Sauter.
With that bathing suit, it must have been true love!

The second Ludwig daughter was Gertrude, my mother, who was born on July 18, 1901. More than any other person, she shaped my life. Perhaps only a Thomas Wolfe could have done her justice, choosing a dozen adjectives to describe her.

None of us ever called her "mother." It was always "Ma" or "Mom." Whatever we called her she was a no nonsense parent. Standing five foot, three inches, and tipping the scales at 180 pounds (or more!), she was a formidable figure. Among her other qualities she was a loving wife and mother, a no-nonsense cook, a fierce patriot, a true friend, and a singer of some volume. Subtlety was not her forte. Like her singing, what she lacked in finesse she made up with lusty enthusiasm.

To the weak and oppressed, she was a champion. One of my earliest and fondest memories was watching her cajole a subway seat for a tired woman or a mother with child in a crowded train. She'd position herself in front of a likely candidate, and if a series of insulting remarks about "gentlemen" didn't achieve the desired result, she'd start leaning against his newspaper. If all else failed, she'd "accidentally" step on his feet with all 180 pounds. Her record was perfect.

Watching a parade when the American flag passed, God help the bystander who didn't remove his hat fast enough. With a sweep of her arm she'd knock it off, loudly denouncing this hapless creature and making him feel like some latter day Benedict Arnold. "What are you, some kind of Bolshevik?" And no one ever survived jumping in front of her on a movie line or other queue. She'd often just reach forward and grab the offender by the collar and drag him out of the line. Gertie never cared how big he was. No one ever challenged her, but standing there next to her I would be dying a thousand-deaths. I was certain someone would shoot her! If she had nothing else, she had presence.

Once, sometime before I went to school, she showed that she was someone not to be trifled with. She was ironing in front of the kitchen window, overlooking the empty lot in front of Westchester Square Hospital. This space, later my favorite playground, was always a hangout for the kids of the neighborhood. On this day, one of them had come across a large mirror, apparently put out with some garbage. Spying my mother at the window, he thought he'd have a little fun by shinning the sun's reflection in her eyes. She thought it was a passing moment, but he kept it up, trying to force her away from the window. Unplugging the iron she took me by the hand. "Come with me, "she said. Down the five flights we went and in a few moments confronted this 14 year-old boy. "Thought you were having some fun at my expense, you little runt? " With that she reached out and grabbed the mirror. The boy tried to hold it, but he was no match for the strength in my mother's arms. She used to tell us how she carried heavy loads of coal and groceries up three flights of stairs when she was growing up on 96th Street. With one motion she lifted the mirror over her head and flung it to the ground, breaking it into pieces. Then she turned and took me home. The boy hurled insults and threats after her, but my mother ignored him.

We weren't home more than a half-hour when there was a knock on the door. Visibly agitated, a short Italian man stood there. He shouted something, half in Italian, half in English that I couldn't understand, but I got the message. He wanted to be paid for the broken mirror. I was ordered to remain in the kitchen, but I could hear the exchange very vividly. Not only wasn't she going to pay anything, but if he didn't get out of her sight she'd pick him up and throw him down the stairs. Since we were on the fifth floor that was no idle threat. Her closing remarks I recall with exactitude. "And if your miserable son tries that trick again, I'll personally break the mirror over his head. If you interfere, I'll break your head as well. Now get the hell out of my sight before I lose my temper." He ran down those steps two at a time!

These were no hollow warnings. Whenever a screw topped bottle or jar resisted opening after everyone in the family had given it their best, Gertie would reach over, grab the bottle and with one turn open it. If the grooves were rusted shut, she'd strip it. In spite of this withering mien and the thrust of her manner, she never took advantage. She was fair, but she wasn't about to be short-changed.

I rarely, if ever, felt her wrath. She had great plans for me, but like most kids, my mind was in the funnies. I had to excel. When I was four she taught me the alphabet, and a few words. I longed to learn the meanings of the words. I can still recall her reply when I pleaded for help. "You've got brains. Use them! You can do it. Look at your sisters. Do you want them to be better?" She did her best, reading to me from some of the stacks of books all over the apartment. I loved those stories and couldn't wait until I could read them myself.

Her finest hour came in 1937, when the Great Depression was at its worst—at least for us. The family savings, what little they were, had long disappeared. My father hadn't held steady employment for close to six years, and was desperately seeking any job he could find: Fuller Brush man, part time accountant, giving art lessons. But precious little money was coming in. Soon it was apparent that we couldn't meet our basic obligations. There was rent to pay and food to put on the table.

My mother had been looking for permanent work, but had not yet been successful. She'd been with the fledging Social Security Administration in the city, but that was short lived. Finally things came to a head. One night a family council of war was called and a group of Ludwigs met in our kitchen. We weren't supposed to be privy to these stormy adult discussions, but my sisters and I were deeply concerned about our future. My mother's mother suggested breaking up the family, parceling out my sisters and me to various aunts and uncles. Ensconced on a couch in the living room, I was supposed to be asleep, but the conversation became quite agitated, naturally so. We could clearly hear my mother's voice ring out over all the others. "Nobody's breaking up this family! I don't care if I have to scrub floors from morning till night, we'll stay together." They were some murmurings after that, which I couldn't hear too well, but my mother's point had been well taken and accepted. When she made a statement, it had conviction. We'd remain together. We were witness to many fragmented families, and wanted no part of that.

CHAPTER NINE

POP

My father couldn't have been more different, physically and temperamentally than my mother. While he was well proportioned, he was in every outward appearance, small. I wore his suits, shirts and shoes when I was ten and eleven. Like all his brothers and sisters, as well as his father, he stood about five foot five. His trim frame never carried more than 110 pounds. In his youth he had been a gymnast of some note, and well into his forties he could still bend backwards from a chair to retrieve a handkerchief from the floor—a feat he would demonstrate with little encouragement. Inside that compact body was an array of muscle. I never saw him engage in any athletic activity, but he always walked at a blistering pace, leaving everyone behind him. He kept this up until the last two years of his life when a weakening heart slowed him down.

Like Mom, we never called him anything but "Pa" or "Pop." We heard that some kids addressed their fathers as "Sir," but we only saw that in an occasional film. In contrast to my mother, he preferred to remain in the background. He shunned controversy, and would never engage in a shouting match or an argument on the street. One of the rare times I saw him lose his temper was the day my sisters decided to rearrange the living room furniture without informing him. They weren't home when he arrived from work, already to settle into his favorite easy chair. Not bothering to turn on the lamp he promptly fell on his behind. I learned some new words that night!

I saw little of his emotional side, but he was very attached to his mother, visiting her without fail every Sunday. Women were easily drawn to him and he enjoyed their company. Whatever romantic involvements he had remained a mystery, only surfacing some years after his death. But some of my earliest and most pleasant recollections were of him and my mother embracing in our apartment. They were among the most treasured images of my childhood. At five or six, one feels very vulnerable, and nothing is more reassuring than the sight of your parents reaffirming their affection.

Wedding picture June 1919

When I was a kid, I used to love to tell people my father was an artist. I still do. Some of my most rewarding memories were waking up to the smell of paint: a distinctive scent that permeated every corner of our apartment. While there were stacks of canvases and art books, I mostly remember stepping over a big compressor in my parents' bedroom. My father used this for his air-brush work.

Strangely, I don't recall my mother or my two older sisters getting too upset over all this clutter. The thought of having to make their way around an easel, a drawing board, and a compressor, would have driven most women crazy, but my mother was a woman of infinite patience. Married to an artist, she had to be.

Sometimes his avocation would result in interesting companions. Much to my mother's chagrin, he'd bring home fellow artists, always down on their luck for supper. There was a Mr. Waldron, who kept us at the edge of our seats with his stories of traveling in places we never dreamed of. He was a small lively man, over-brimming with ideas, whose personality resembled a charged battery. His clothes were threadbare, his hair never stayed in place, but he had a wealth of knowledge and was a painter and writer of great talent. Nearly every time he visited, he'd fall asleep in my father's easy chair after supper, causing no end of consternation as the family tried to decide to wake him or not. My father would be long asleep at this point. Other times my dad would invite a Negro artist and my mother would worry about what the neighbors would think. Ralph was much younger than Mr. Waldron and was a rare introduction into the real lives of blacks. This experience completely changed my attitude toward them.

Tall and heavy, Ralph had smooth dark skin that glistened in the light. His stories revealed a hard scrabble early life. Born and raised in Alabama, he exhibited an early talent in drawing and painting. Since there was no opportunity for a Negro in his home state in the 30s, he was encouraged to move to New York City to study.

In 1935 he embarked on the only mode of transportation available—the freight train. Some of his tales were harrowing. "I decided to hop a train when I was 18. My family was literally starving and I was just one more mouth to feed. I went down to the yards and waited until I met a few other men with the same idea. It was very common then. Don't forget there were few highways at that time. I remember that I had exactly sixty-two cents and two apples. Well I jumped in this open freight car and found myself in the company of about a dozen men of various ages. Nobody seems to care that I was a Negro. I covered myself with some newspapers that first night and nearly froze to death from the cold. Every time the train stopped or slowed near a town, some of us would jump off and tried to scrounge some food—fruit, bread, anything to keep body and soul together. One morning I discovered that one of the "men" was actually a woman in disguise. I grew up fast on that trip."

"The railroad police were very tough. Some of them wouldn't hesitate to shoot you on sight. But I was lucky. The more experienced hobos showed me how to jump off before the train reached the yards to avoid the cops. In New York I had the address of an uncle who was a porter

for the phone company. He told me about a scholarship program at the
Art Students League. I applied and was accepted. I was on my way. I was
one of the few lucky ones."

My Dad Painting

At first we were all rather tongue-tied in the presence of a black person.
We were afraid we'd say the wrong thing and offend him. But Ralph put
us all at ease when he related a story that God in creating man had left
white people half-baked!

Although my Dad had studied art at Cooper Union before he was
married, he never made a living from his paintings. Rather, they were
a labor of love. When he was employed (which, during the Depression
wasn't very often), he worked as an accountant and was a stock analyst.
In the first ten years of his married life which turned out to be his golden
age, financially speaking), he worked for some of the largest brokerage
houses on Wall Street. By the time I arrived on the scene in December of
'29, his glory days were coming to an end. Within a year, he began what
would be nearly a decade of unemployment.

In 1935 he came up with the idea of painting portraits to supplement his meager income. One of his first subjects was his younger brother Willie. (Oddly, his five brothers, who never saw the inside of a college, worked steadily all through the Depression.) Every Sunday morning, Willie would arrive about ten o'clock, and sit perfectly still for an hour while his likeness took shape. He sat patiently for three sessions. I don't know if he had another Sunday job, or if the tedium of remaining immobile for a solid hour finally got to him, but he didn't show up for the next two weeks. When he finally reappeared my Dad was out, so he flipped through a stack of unfinished canvases searching for his painting without success. Not long after he left, my Dad returned and my mother related what had happened. Without batting an eye he said, "I told the stupid bastard he had to be here every Sunday. I ran out of canvas and turned him into a horse!"

There are some memories I keenly recall. I was only five or six, but I remember him as if it were yesterday, seated in front of his easel with total concentration. He never knew I existed. I was terrified of him, and it took years to develop enough nerve to even open a conversation. I sometimes wondered if he regretted having me. Certainly the timing of my birth couldn't have been worse—arriving only a few weeks after the Great Stock Market Crash in October. Surrounded by adults who must have appeared as giants, I was wrapped in the insecurity of childhood. On top of this, my father's silent treatment was devastating. I couldn't begin to imagine what I'd done wrong. Later I discovered it wasn't just me. When he was working nothing else existed. The apartment could have been ablaze, but I doubt if he would have missed a brush stroke.

Strangely, he never painted a portrait of any of his other brothers or sisters, or even his mother, but he did a masterful rendering of his father in the late 'thirties. Later, much later, nearing retirement, he did some vivid watercolors of my niece and nephew, but he never captured my mother or any of his own children on canvas. I always meant to ask him why in one of the many letters we shared when I was in the Navy, but somehow the subject never arose.

Those letters, written when I was in my early twenties, provided the first major crack in this formidable barrier that had separated us all those years. We began to open a dialogue just before I entered the Navy, but it was rather limited in scope. Writing to him, however, I could explore subjects that somehow would have been impossible to utter face to face. Maybe it was just that natural reserve between parent and child, I don't know. Now, we could discuss history and books and music, and just plain "growing up." What a revelation it was to discover this man whom I hardly knew (at this stage of my life), and to experience a sharing of ideas on almost equal terms. (Although, I wonder if we ever achieve "equal terms" with our fathers.) Exchanging a stream of letters, I treasured his. At last, we were bridging the gulf that had separated us for so long. In the end, the real discovery was that he was a man just like me; a man whom I had first feared, then respected, and finally, at this late hour, learned to love. That correspondence made up for a multitude of things we didn't share when I was growing up, and coming when it did, I was probably better off for it. A spontaneous breakthrough at the advanced age of twenty-one was far more meaningful than all those missed afternoons of playing catch. In contrast, most of my friends and their fathers were, during this same period, clashing.

I was far too young at the time to understand what the Depression was doing to him. Looking back, it must have been devastating for my dad to watch my mother and sisters provide most of the financial support for the family. My mother said that he was a different man before the crash and it took years for him to recover. I often think it was his painting that kept him sane during all those lean years without permanent employment. I couldn't begin to understand his struggle until my own son was born some twenty-five years later and I put my Dad's ordeal into perspective.

When my son, Keith came along, my aunt reminded me that my father was exactly my age when I was born (I was following in his footsteps, having had two daughters first). From that time on I compared his early life with mine.

My 'thirties were salad days and my business took off. Every once in a while I'd stop and try to imagine what it must have been like to endure even a fraction of my father's long suffering. For the first time, I began to understand his mysterious detachment. He hadn't purposely ignored me: he just had too much to cope with.

Keith didn't have to wait twenty years to approach me, but it wasn't instant recognition either. Every person has his own inner defenses, and between fathers and sons these instincts may be among the strongest. While many fathers are criticized for not communicating, one must be careful not to smother a good friendship in well-meaning possessiveness. Each person needs his own space. Happily the last decade of my father's life brought a strengthening of the bonds we'd forged with all those letters and I finally came to understand him as much as it's possible to understand anyone. He's been gone these past twenty-five years, but there's hardly a day when I don't think of him. His legacy is everywhere. I'm lucky to have a score of his paintings in my home—I'm literally surrounded by them. I can't imagine a better gift. Among them are some unfinished canvases, which strangely, hold more of my interest than the others. They reveal, like nothing else, the blood and sweat that went into each creative effort.

Painting and reading were his main passions, and although he didn't shun company, it had to be on his terms. He didn't suffer fools gladly. While his language was well spiced with the rough and tumble of the Bronx and Wall Street, he could hold his own on any subject, whether it was Chinese philosophy or American literature. He was a voracious reader, averaging a book a week. In his early twenties, while attending Cooper Union, he struck up a friendship with the great novelist, Thomas Wolfe. He made a series of sketches of the hulking writer, some of which surfaced upon Wolfe's untimely death.

His reading nurtured an intense interest in the world around him. He yearned to travel, but raising a family and later the Great Depression put all those dreams on the back burner. He never forgot them though, and he sparked scores of conversations with imaginary trips to California. It got so he nearly convinced us. Like some latter day pioneer, he was going to drive across country, visiting all the national parks. Later, when he became gainfully employed he began to formulate some plans. My sisters and I reminded him that he had no driver's license, never mind a car. Trying to goad him into a closer destination, we'd make fun of his grandiose plans. We said we'd believe him when we saw the tickets.

In the early fifties he made some astute stock choices, raising enough money to seriously contemplate long-distance travel. In the end he and my mother opted for Europe rather than the West Coast, making several tours encompassing most of the continent. A few years before he died he took a six-month freighter voyage around the world, satisfying once and for all his insatiable wanderlust. Watching him eventually achieve his dream was one of the most rewarding experiences of my life.

Among his catalog of talents, he had a flair for writing. I'm told that he used to entertain the office girls in his Wall Street firms with serial romances— one chapter a week. Ghost writing an essay in a New York City Fire Prevention contest for my sister Rita garnered first prize. But I only have the memory of his letters to go by.

Unfortunately, during a housecleaning my mother threw out my collection of his correspondence, and none of his stories survived. In spite of his creative ability, he made his living in the financial world. Most of his life was spent on Wall Street as a stock analyst. He had an uncanny ability to pick some winners in the early fifties that not only changed his life, but the lives of many others. Aside from stocks and bonds, he was an accomplished accountant.

How I would have reveled in all this knowledge of his early years when I was growing up, but it was only revealed to me years after the fact, along with some other far more intimate details. .

When we did spend the rare afternoon in the Zoo, the Bronx Botanical Gardens or the canyons of Wall Street, it was always a history lesson. What could put a more forceful imprimatur on the lesson than to be reminded of the impact of "flesh and blood" events on the actual ground it took place? None of this "history" was taught in my grammar or high school. Under my father's tutelage, Peter Stuyvesant, George Washington and Robert Morris, became alive and immediate. More important, leading by example, and on rare occasion by a long conversation, he instilled in me the merits of being my own man. Among his precepts were that most people never dig any further than the headlines of the front page or some windbag on the radio. The true answers always lie deeper. "Always go back to the source material," he cautioned. "In politics that's the U.S. Constitution. Few Americans take the trouble to read it. If you don't know the New Testament, how can you call yourself a Christian? It's a difficult, but very rewarding path." He was the personification of that concept in everything from his choice of friends and reading material, to his ardent passion for art and painting.

On another plane I inherited his inquiring mind, and with it a fierce thirst for knowledge. More like buckshot than a high-powered rifle, I was interested in anything and everything. It would have been a distinct advantage had I channeled my curiosity, but that wasn't in the cards. Once I cracked the door to a subject, be it deep-sea diving or the history of the American Revolution, I had to know everything about it. Of course, most of the research material was either right in our apartment or a few blocks away at the local public library. Once absorbed, it seemed to stick like glue. When it came to history, I obviously excelled.

There were times when I felt I was living through the pages of a current history book. Certainly, a great deal of immense importance was going on right under my nose and I often imagined that I was playing a part in it. On occasion I'd say to myself: Jack, you must remember this! While I relished these opportunities, it often set me apart from my friends. One of my classmates' fathers took me aside one day and said, "Jackie, you're a nice boy, but I think you march to the beat of a different drummer." I didn't immediately grasp his meaning, but he was right.

CHAPTER TEN

HOME, SWEET HOME

My mother in the kitchen. Note the drying rack on the ceiling.

Wrapped in a warm cocoon of love and affection, my mother read me endless stories. I can still recall whole sections from an illustrated Dickens and Washington Irving from our own collection. Even if times were hard, one thing we didn't lack was an ample supply of reading material. Many of the stories brought tears to my eyes. I later learned that my father's library had once been formidable. Only their constant moving had whittled it down to something that would fit comfortably into the confines of a four-room apartment. There appeared to be stacks of books everywhere. As a teenager, he'd befriended many of the wealthy families who occupied the mansions in what would later become Pelham Bay Park in the northeastern part of the Bronx. When they had to relocate just before the First World War, they offered him a significant treasure of books from their vast private libraries. With my father at work and my sisters at school, my mother and I shared an intimate partnership with books all the way to my first day of school.

Certain images stand out in a blur of memories. Every morning, I'd leap out of bed and in my pajamas run into the living room. Jumping into my father's easy chair, I'd push my nose into the thick fabric, trying to recapture the darkness of sleep so recently lost. Occasionally, I'd be repelled by the strong, pungent scent of vanilla and bolt into the kitchen, trying desperately to get that smell out of my nose. There I'd usually find one of my father's brothers who worked in the "plant," a chemical laboratory on Starling Avenue, where one of their main products was vanilla extract.

Although it was seventy years ago, I can remember each and every detail of that first apartment, my mother's kingdom, where she reigned unchallenged.

We didn't have television, but often the kitchen window offered far more arresting sights. Scarcely a block away stood Westchester Square Hospital, its view unimpeded by the handful of one story homes in its path. The Operating Room was on the same level as our apartment, and after dinner we'd often turn off the light and watch the medical drama unfold. Although we had an old pair of binoculars, we didn't know who was on the table, or what was being removed. Somehow, just witnessing that real-life struggle was exciting enough. In some ways this scenario could have been the makings of another Hitchcock's "Rear Window."

My father had early eating habits. It was coffee and toast for breakfast, a quick bite he ate in silence before making a dash for the subway. Although it would be some years before I had lunch with him, we knew he sat down at 11 A.M. At the end of the day he wanted his big meal hot and on the table at 6 P.M. Our kitchen table became the focal point as we ate together and exchanged all the gossip of the day. In my "time machine" the kitchen of 1940 is coming back into focus. A combination oven and gas stove filled one corner and a porcelain sink and its counter, adjoined them. On the opposite side stood the icebox. Without electric appliances (at least of the kitchen variety), our morning toast was made by utilizing the open gas flame of the range. Two shelves in the cupboard held our favorite foods. Among them were: Wheaties, Aunt

Jemima Pancake mix, Log Cabin maple syrup, Ovaltine, Heinz catsup, Gulden's mustard, 8 O'clock coffee, Boston baked beans, Green Giant Corn Niblets, Philadelphia brand hash, and a variety of Campbell's soups.

The icebox possessed a life of its own. Depending on the season, the ice had to be replenished anywhere from two to four days. Tony, the Ice-Man came by every day chanting, "Ice, Ice, Ice," in a musical tone and intensity that never varied. He also sold coal. I often wondered how they came up with that combination. Why not ice cream or bottled soda?

When my mother needed ice, she'd shout, "Ice, 57!" (That was our apartment number.) Calling out a price like 25 or 35 cents, she'd indicate how much ice she wanted. The deal made, Tony would climb up on his open truck, remove the heavy insulating tarpaulin, and cut out the proper size. Lifting it out with his huge tongs, he'd swing the block up on his shoulder and carry it into our basement. There he'd place the ice on the dumbwaiter and climb the five flights of stairs to our apartment. Meanwhile, we'd have removed the remnants of the old ice and any food from the compartment.

Arriving at our place a little out of breath, he'd haul up the dumb-waiter to our vestibule and deliver the ice to our chest. Sometimes he'd have to trim the block to allow it to fit snugly into our compartment. Tony would then take out his ice pick and wielding it with the dexterity of a sculptor; he'd deftly shape it to size. "Mrs. Souza, Howsa you lika dis ice? She's h'ok. Yes?" That exchange never varied. Cleaning up any ice shards and water, he'd then and only then accept payment from my mother. My mother always inquired about the health of his wife and five children, all of whom seemed to flourish on those 25 and 35 cent pieces of ice.

Aside from ice, another familiar tradesman was the Crystalline Man. Crystalline, a clothes- washing product, was made by mixing raw-bleach with water. It was delivered in gallon glass containers. The vendor would stand in the courtyard in warm weather and shout "Crystalline!" Upon hearing this clarion call, housewives would call down to order. In the winter the "man" would work his way down the five floors, again calling out at each landing. Everybody knew him. Socializing with business was a familiar pattern that was woven into the fabric of our lives. The butcher, the grocer, the baker, the corner stationery store, and all the other tradesmen were literally extended family. When I accompanied my mother on the rounds from store to store, we'd learn all the neighborhood gossip. Many of the shops offered credit and there was never an extra charge or an interest payment. This was simply the way business was done.

All the store names ring out through the passage of time: DeLayo's Grocery, Angelo Terio, the shoemaker (whose daughter later taught me French at Fordham University), Simelson's Pharmacy at Westchester Square. Then the two bakeries; Daylight, on Tremont Avenue for everyday, and Weigand's on Zerega for Sunday mornings, and finally, Olga's beauty parlor on the corner of Seddon and Tremont. Closer to my heart were Tony's candy store on Zerega just off Buck Street where I bought my favorites; Hooten's chocolate (for 2 cents) and "Dots," a bean-shaped delight that came attached to long paper rolls.

Then there was Sal, the butcher, who always gave me two slices of liverwurst. An A&P, our only concession to an "all in one" store, was no doubt a few cents cheaper, but it was a half mile away, too long a distance to carry heavy bags. We, like most of our neighbors, had no car. Personal shopping carts were unknown. If one really had a heavy load of groceries to transport, a baby carriage would be pressed into service.

When there was "serious shopping" to do (although with our meager finances, there was precious little of that), it was the trolley that we used most often. A trip to Fordham to Alexander's would require two trolleys, with a change at West Farms. All the routes were identified by a large letter on the face of the car. For example, the Tremont Avenue line carried a "T." Cross-town trolleys were all identified with an appropriate "X." Streetcars ran on tracks laid down in the middle of the road. They were powered by a long pole reaching electrified overhead lines. The operator stood up front, collecting the nickels in a metal cash box. A bell rang as each coin was deposited. If you didn't have a nickel, the operator would make change.

For older boys, the trolleys provided an unlimited opportunity for mayhem. One of the most popular tricks was jumping on the back and removing the power bar from the overhead wire. The trolley would of course come to halt and the operator would have to reset the bar. More adventurous types would hitch rides on their bicycle by holding on to the side. This could be quite dangerous if your wheel became locked in another rail and you fell off, since the trolley was in middle of the traffic flow.

Much like the subway, the seats were made of wicker, and similar to railroad cars, they could be turned around depending on the trolley's direction. Windows lined the side. In the summer the glass enclosures were removed and replaced by eisenglass or rubber curtains that could be lowered in case of rain. Then the sides were covered in a steel grill, allowing fresh air to circulate. The faster the speed, the stronger the breeze. Being electric, they didn't pollute the air with motor exhaust, and their tracks allowed the traffic to pass them without concern that they might move to the curb as the buses did. By the late forties they were very modern—fast and quiet. And they went nearly everywhere. Sadly, just as they reached their pinnacle of speed and stability, they disappeared— replaced practically overnight by buses. These vehicles were not nearly as fast, and they polluted the air with their diesel exhaust. But the bus manufacturers had more money to contribute to the politicians and the trolley became a memory. (The Europeans were more far-sighted and I still enjoy riding the trams in the cities of Germany and Austria.)

Returning to our kitchen, there were other distinctive qualities. One contraption that used to decorate the ceilings of thousands of cooking areas was the portable clothes dryer. No fancy electric device, this invention was energy friendly. It encompassed a bedspring-like frame that held six metal bars with clothespins attached. After the laundry was washed and rinsed, my mother would squeeze the excess water either manually or through a metal wringer and hang the clothes on this dryer. Then it would be hauled back up to the ceiling with a length of wash-line. On occasion, a pair of say, thick, heavy, corduroy trousers would still be wet and they would drip on you while you were eating or doing your homework. When the weather was clear and sunny, my mother would use the wash lines on the roof. Then she was glad we lived on the top floor.

The most lasting "one-and-only" remembrance I have of that kitchen was the skull-shaped indentation in the plaster wall. This was referred to as "the timely reminder." At some point before I had recall, my mother had asked my oldest sister Dorothy a question, and received what she perceived to be a "snotty answer." In a reflex action that would have made Joe Louis proud, her hand struck out and caught my sister's head, leaving a lasting impression in the kitchen wall. Whenever one of us started to get out of line, my mother only had to point to that spot to bring my sisters and me back on course.

My mother was a "meat and potatoes" cook. By the time I was ten, she worked more or less full time. When she arrived home there wasn't time to prepare anything fancy, even if she had the inclination. Chops were a mainstay; lamb or pork, or my favorite, veal cutlets. If money were tight, as it often was, our fare would be potato pancakes with applesauce or spaghetti with meatballs. Friday, there was always fish on the platter in spite of my father's objections. He was raised Catholic, but somewhere along the way he'd become disenchanted with anything to do with Rome and incense and monthly collections. However, in the end my mother prevailed, and our plates would be filled with fishcakes and spaghetti.

Saturday evening's meal was the least elaborate of the week. It featured cold meats, fried spaghetti and whatever leftover was in the icebox. A mainstay was mashed potatoes, and as an accompaniment anything that had survived a week next to the ice. Often this meant a solitary meatball or a fishcake. The whole batch would be dumped into a skillet and fried, filling the kitchen with a variety of smells that would defy a gourmet cook.

Sundays the pattern changed. Most of the time my mother accompanied my sisters and me to the 9 o'clock Mass at St. Raymond's, a few blocks away. While we were absent, my father would take this opportunity to make his regular weekly visit to his mother. He was the oldest, and invariably, she made a fuss over him.

After Mass, we'd dutifully pick up the Daily News outside church. It seemed that every Catholic Church had an open-air newsstand outside, and in addition to the local New York papers, the religious press would be hawked. With the meter of a rosary and the sing-song chant of an auctioneer, the boys shouted, "Catholic News, Brooklyn Tablet, Social Justice," (the latter being the infamous Father Coughlin's yellow journal). Afterward, we'd walk down to Wiegand's bakery on Zerega Avenue. As if set in stone, my mother always bought the same things: hard seeded rolls and crumb buns. The crumb buns were a particular favorite of my father and he never failed to criticize the paucity of the Wiegand family and how they had systematically reduced the number of large crumbs through the years. "Old man Weigand must have a barrel of money stashed away from what he's saved on crumbs all these years." Breakfast would be a long, leisurely affair with eggs, toast, butter, jam and coffee. There was always a coffee pot on the stove, and my Dad would have a cup next to his easel in the bedroom all morning and afternoon.

Brush and canvas would command his attention from the last crumb bun until the setting sun cut off his light. Sunday dinner, our main meal of the day and the most elaborate family gathering of the week would provide his only break. Roast pork or roast chicken were the most common entrees found on our table. We'd sit down just after noon, (my Dad made a concession on Sundays to eating an hour later than his usual time) and the meal and lively conversation stretched into the early afternoon. My father often had wine, not as an extravagance or primed by any superior attitude, but purely to show us that in spite of being raised around goats and horses, he had some class. No one we knew, either family or friends, ever drank wine. He'd encourage us to try some in portions half cut by water, and on occasion we would. I thought it tasted awful. (Later I discovered he had a fondness for dessert wines: Muscatel and Sauterne, and that they were a disastrous choice to drink with pork or chicken. Twenty years later wine would become a mainstay at all my meals, so in spite of my early turn-off, I learned thankfully, to give the grape a second chance.)

It was at this table that my father spoke most of what he had to say all week. Although he was extremely well read, his language was that of the rough and tumble Bronx and Wall Street. His sentences were full of "joik" and "woik," but what I enjoyed the most were the colorful expressions I heard nowhere else; couplets like, "shit-healer," piss-poor runt" and "cute-mug," the last being his highest accolade. And he never failed to have some choice remarks about my mother's side of the family. "If the Ludwig girls had brains as big as their asses, they'd all be Einsteins!" Then my mother would chime in with, "John, the children!" rolling her eyes in her inimitable way of showing displeasure. My Dad would only humorously reply, while looking at us for approval, "For Chrissake Gertie, it's true. Just ask them." Enveloped in laughter, the ice would be broken.

Expounding on anything and everything, it often seemed as if he was just rambling, but once in awhile he'd hit upon a truth that we wouldn't appreciate until years later. Food was a favorite topic and he had some pet theories; one being that white bread caused cancer. Everyone laughed, but just after he died scientific research revealed that some of the chemicals in bleaching flour contained carcinogens.

Among his less than common beliefs was the medicinal benefit of gunpowder, which he regularly ingested in small amounts. He avoided most sweets and was essentially a "meat and potatoes" man. In all the years I was growing up, I never knew him to be sick a day. His bank employer rewarded punctuality and unbroken service by awarding "honor days" –extra time off. My dad capitalized on this benefit and always garnered enough extra days to stretch his vacation by a week. Walking at a blistering clip was his main exercise and he went at it with a passion. He set a feverish pace that would later be termed "race walking." As a result his weight never varied more than a pound a year.

With this kind of diet and regimen he should have lived to be a hundred, but it was his passion for tobacco that did him in. Standing in front of his easel or reading a book, he was always enveloped in a ring of smoke. He was wedded to tobacco. Not one to play favorites, he enjoyed his pipe, his cigars and more than a pack of cigarettes a day. Early on, he developed emphysema, but he kept it hidden from the family until well into his sixties when he caught up to him with a terrible vengeance. Sometimes he'd cough so hard he'd turn red in the face, but he brushed off our concerns by calling it, his "bronical" (sic) cough! Of course this put a strain on his heart and that's what eventually killed him at 68.

Sometimes after dinner, one of my sisters would be attempting to finish a crossword puzzle and she'd be stuck for an answer that required an author or book title. Invariably, my father would come up with the correct name. He was a whiz at this—a veritable storehouse of knowledge. How I envied him. His level of learning appeared unattainable. After the dishes were cleared, we'd sit around the table reading the Daily News and discussing the latest scandal. Most of the lurid events involved some actress who was being divorced, a big deal in those days. Of the scores of relations and friends my parents knew, I can only recall one neighbor, Tess Horton, who was a divorcee. She appeared to be a pleasant enough lady and always invited me into her apartment for a jelly-bread sandwich whenever we met on the stairs. But I kept a wary eye on her, half expecting to see horns sprouting! Her son was in my class and it seemed odd that although his mother's name was Horton, his was Donovan.

Our main source of entertainment was the radio and on Sunday morning it was always playing. Seemingly locked on one station, I loathed it. It was the Major Bowes Amateur Hour sponsored by the Horn and Hardart restaurant chain. Their dreary theme song was "Less work for mother," and there was no escaping the Major for at least two hours each and every Sunday.

After lunch the Major was thankfully replaced by Sammy Kaye whose romantic melodies kept my sisters enthralled. This was easy music to either listen to or ignore with a minimum of talk. My favorite was Bing Crosby whose mellow voice was both appealing and infectious. Later I'd become a devotee of the New York Philharmonic broadcasts but I never tired of Bing.

Several neighbors had pets. Dogs were the most popular—whatever canine was being featured on the Hollywood screens was in abundance. Rin-Tin-Tin produced German Shepherds galore, but for apartment dwellers terriers took prominence after "Astor" starred in THE THIN MAN. I wanted a dog (I would have settled for a cat), but my mother vetoed anything with four legs. She was raised in a two-bedroom apartment with seven siblings. Where would they fit a dog? On the other hand our photo albums were replete with pictures of my father embracing goats, ponies, horses and dogs. In the allotment of family responsibilities the apartment was exclusively my mother's domain. No dogs or cats. My father breached this unwritten agreement by bringing me two reptiles: a good-sized box turtle and a chameleon. I already had some baby turtles—they were sold in the five and dime, but this huge box variety was something else entirely. Maisie, as I immediately dubbed her, was amazingly perceptive for a reptile. She would come to me if I jiggled keys. My mother had no problem adjusting to this unique and slow-moving creature, which often occupied the bathtub, but the lizard was something else entirely. Whenever he got out of his enclosure, my mother wouldn't go to bed before tying her nightgown around her legs!

We were by all accounts a remarkably healthy family. I never saw the inside of a hospital after I was born—all ailments being treated at home. On occasion we'd see Doctor Thron, the physician who delivered me, and who also brought my sisters into the world. He was, in the best sense of the word, a "family doctor." His office was only a few blocks away. It was always crowded with people waiting, often for hours. Some would sign in and then go out to shop.

Years later, he delivered my two daughters, and expressed disappointment that I'd opted for another doctor, closer to home after we'd moved away. He once related that he had more than 12,000 active patients. He described an "active patient "as one he saw at least every two years. Thron was a Bronx legend, living to his mid-nineties. After his wife died, he married her two younger sisters.

I made it to age 62 without undergoing anesthesia, keeping my appendix and tonsils. I never saw a dentist until we moved to Gleason Avenue where one resided and had an office. There was no money except for fillings and extractures. This lack of preventative therapy later accelerated the movement of my incisors due to a congenital bone loss. Fortunately, my sisters didn't inherit my problem and their teeth remained fine. How I hated that drill! Before the development of water injection, the friction would generate an uncomfortable heat along with that terrible grinding sound and vibration that seemed to reach right into your brain.

My mother, who reined over all family illnesses from the flu to chicken pox, usually rendered all the basic treatments. She was a great believer that the body, given a chance, would usually heal itself. We discovered that bed rest and plenty of liquids cured most sore throats and running noses. It didn't take a Pasteur to figure out that most colds came from the crowded classroom rather than running around without a hat. Gargling with salt water and sweating it out under innumerable blankets worked miracles. Aspirin was the only drug I took until I was fifty.

In spite of, or perhaps because of this lack of medical attention, our family was remarkably fit through my childhood and adolescence.

CHAPTER ELEVEN

RADIOACTIVE

Radio program guide

"This is London!" Across the broad Atlantic came the never to be forgotten voice of Edward R. Murrow, speaking on short wave radio. Was there ever a more modulated and authoritative voice bringing "live" history into our living rooms?

Recently I was doing some research for an article on the liner NORMANDIE, and I unearthed some of my yellowing newspaper clippings from 1943. The date on the Daily News centerfold (those were the days when the word "centerfold" had a totally different meaning) was

August 8th, 1943. Just after the war began, the NORMANDIE was being converted to a troop transport at her pier when, through sheer negligence, she caught fire, burned and capsized. After lying on her side in the mud of the Hudson River for eighteen months, the great French liner was finally stirring in answer to the Navy's Herculean salvage efforts.

As historically fascinating as these dramatic ocean liner photos were, it was the reverse side of the clipping that captured and held my interest. Bordered by some fascinating ads like 35-cent music lessons and Brioschi for "the morning after," was a complete radio listing for New York City.

In lieu of some magical elixir, I can't imagine any single page that could have jolted my memory bank more thoroughly than that extraordinary schedule. This clipping was nothing less than a modern day Rosetta Stone holding the key to untold riches.

Scanning slowly down the page, nearly every listing interrupted my task. The floodgates opened and a myriad of treasured recollections surfaced. I could almost hear the strains of Rossini's "William Tell" Overture, as the announcer intoned, "Out of the west came the thundering hoof-beats of the great horse Silver," followed by that familiar cry, "Hi Ho Silver, Away!" Silver Cup Bread was their sponsor. In spite of the passing decades, that recollection was just as secure as if it had occurred yesterday. Much like Proust's Madelines, every time we crossed the Queensboro Bridge around midnight, returning home from an opera or concert, the penetrating aroma of that baking Silver Cup bread from their nearby plant was powerful enough to stir long-forgotten memories. Even today, close to seventy years later, I can reel off the sponsors of practically every program. What would an ad agency give today for such product identification?

Jack Armstrong—WHEATIES, Captain Midnight—OVALTINE, The Shadow—BLUE COAL, Fibber Magee and Molly—JOHNSON'S WAX, Bob Hope—PEPSODENT TOOTH PASTE. Of course some sponsors made it easy by tying their product's name to the show: LUX RADIO THEATRE, KRAFT MUSIC HALL, LUCKY STRIKE HIT PARADE, to name but a few. Can anyone recall who paid for I LOVE LUCY, or JACKIE GLEASON, or ALL IN THE FAMILY on television?

There were kids in my First Grade class who couldn't tell you who the president or mayor was, but could instantly relate what Tonto called the Lone Ranger—"kemosabe," or the name of the Green Hornet's faithful servant—"Kato." In this "theater of the mind," those aural images were indelible and stayed with you for a lifetime.

For just about everyone, the radio was our initial exposure to the outside world. Long before we could read, those half-hour serials stretched our imaginations. LITTLE ORPHAN ANNIE, THE SHADOW and SUPERMAN could paint far more brilliant "pictures" than anything we read in a comic strip. At our age the spoken word was always superior to the written one. Hadn't our mothers and fathers read to us long before we could pick out those symbols on a page? Anthropologists record scores of tribes whose history was kept alive solely by storytellers. Now that little box was fulfilling the same purpose.

I grew up with radio, and radio grew up with me.

The medium was less than a decade old when I came of age. Like sound movies, it revolutionized nearly every facet of American life. At the height of the Great Depression when even the price of a magazine was often hard to come by, the entire family could be entertained and brought into the daily events of the nation and the world, with no additional cost.

Similar to the phonograph, the cabinet housing the receiver could be as simple or as ornate as the family budget allowed. In the early days most of the cost was contained in the "furniture" rather than the electronics. In fact, the very word "electronics" didn't exist until well into World War II. My godfather, who was well fixed, boasted a huge Atwater Kent that dominated his living room. Curiously, in spite of the fact that this medium was transmitting only sound, listeners tended to crowd around and stare intensely at the cabinet. When smaller table models appeared on the market, this gathering dissipated, and the little Bakelite (plastic was still in its infancy) boxes were soon accepted as no more unusual than a toaster. Portability had the further advantage of allowing the housewife to do her ironing while being totally engrossed by YOUNG DOCTOR MALONE. For many "shut-ins" or people living alone, the radio provided that priceless comfort of another human voice, speaking or singing.

The first "set" we had was a General Electric table-model that my parents bought sometime around 1937. It had the added advantage of employing an open turntable on the top. This innovation was eminently practical as we, like most families had record collections that stretched back into the twenties. We'd inherited a few dozen 78-RPM disks from my grandparents with music solely on one side. The voices of John McCormack, Enrico Caruso and Henry Burr often filled the apartment. These primitive devices were far from "high-fidelity," another term that hadn't yet made it into the vocabulary. Shellac records, while easily cracked or broken, had sturdy grooves that could apparently adjust to any stylus to produce sound. If one couldn't locate a needle, a hairpin or nail would often substitute very nicely.

Sure, there was "needle-noise," but this came with the territory, and our ears made the proper adjustment. After all, we fully accepted black and white movies, even though our "real" world was in color.

In my apartment it was my sisters, Dorothy and Rita, who called the tune (no pun intended), so our record collection reflected the current popular singers of the day. Bing Crosby towered over a platoon of crooners and warblers that included Connie Boswell, Buddy Clark, Vaughn Monroe, Kate Smith and Tony Martin. As young people needed dance music at their parties, many disks were primarily orchestral: Glenn Miller, Tommy Dorsey, Paul Whiteman and Eddie Duchin, to name but a few. These ensembles all played ballads and the newer Lindys and Big Apples. Most vocalists made their initial appearance with these big bands, and many became icons on the weekly radio shows. Jack Benny introduced Dennis Day, and later Frank Sinatra made his debut with Tommy Dorsey. The Saturday night "Your Hit Parade" resembled a mini-Academy Awards for the top songs of the week.

I was very fortunate in that my adolescence coincided with remarkable advances in sound reproduction. Many of the electronic inventions in World War II carried over after the conflict into what was then known as "high fidelity." The British were pioneers in this field.

In many respects the improvements had to proceed on a multiple front, similar to the growth of the automobile industry in the early 20th century. Then, everything had to be developed simultaneously: engines, batteries, gasoline, tires and roads. With sound reproduction, this meant amplifiers, turntables, heads, styli and speakers, not to forget the records themselves.

By 1946, English Decca, also known as London FFRR (full frequency recording), began to produce recordings that were a quantum leap over anything heard before. These were still 78-RPM disks, limited to four-minute sides, but that was a minor concern. Never before had we heard such clarity in recorded sound. The next big breakthrough was in the turntable—more commonly known as the record changer. Garrard, another British company, came out with a popular-priced unit that swept the market. Diamond needles soon followed. Improved loudspeakers made their debut and the industry was off and running. Good quality amplifiers had been around for awhile—many made here: Scott and Fisher come to mind.

For the first time I could hear tympani and real piano sound, along with woodwind solos that had been buried in needle noise. The results were breathtaking. All these changes were geared to the classical music audience.

The long-playing record: 33 1/3 RPM was the next big step forward and that revolutionized the recording business. For the first time one could listen to a complete symphony with only one interruption. Each side contained twenty to thirty minutes of music. Columbia pioneered this major step forward in 1948. Stereo recording completed the transition in 1958. It was tantamount to moving from the biplane to a jetliner in a 12- year span! For someone devoted to good music, it was an exciting time to be alive.

Whenever my sisters weren't around (and sometimes when they were) my mother would add her powerful, if not very mellifluous voice to a current melody. What she lacked in finesse, she made up in volume. My father on the other hand was completely tone deaf. He'd be whistling along totally oblivious to the fact that his efforts bore little if any resemblance to the song or melody being played. I was born with a good "ear," and reveled in listening to any and all the music on the radio.

How different our choices were from today's television. I don't know if there is an easy answer to this question about the "dumbing" of America (I think most of it is all too true), but we were certainly challenged far more extensively in the 40s and 50s than we are today. Perhaps rock and an overexposure to TV had something to do with it, but I grew up with jazz, swing, crooners and be-bop, and there was still plenty of room for very good music on the dial—all of it in "prime time," and sponsored by the cream of corporate America.

The New York Philharmonic was broadcast live every Sunday afternoon from 2 to 5 P.M. (Many people can still recall that program being interrupted for the news of the attack on Pearl Harbor). Its sponsors included the US Rubber Co. and US Steel. Sunday evenings boasted the NBC Symphony from 9 to 11. Also live, and featuring the great Arturo Toscanini. It was David Sarnoff, the founder and head of RCA who was instrumental in bringing Toscanini over from Italy and creating an orchestra for him.

They never lacked for sponsors—General Motors being one of the longest.

Saturday afternoons were highlighted by the Metropolitan Opera broadcasts from December until April. Incredibly, even today in the new millennium they still retain the same corporate supporter—Texaco; a relationship that began in 1940! (Sadly, the sponsorship ended in 2004 when Texaco merged with Chevron.)

On a lower scale, but still quite sophisticated musically were the Longines Symphonette, the Bayer and Firestone Hours, and the Bell Telephone program. All featured top vocalists and instrumentalists. It wasn't unusual to hear such eminent singers as Jussi Bjoerling, Ezio Pinza, Robert Merrill, Jan Peerce, Eleanor Steber and Lily Pons. Popular melodies were interspersed with operatic arias. This was "crossover" at its best. As many of these arias were already familiar from those 78-RPM records, it wasn't a great leap for most listeners. Pianists and violinists whose ranks included Heifetz and Rubenstein brought non-vocal music into millions of living rooms. These programs spawned many a life-long love of good music.

Realizing that their public image would be greatly enhanced by their support of higher art forms, corporate advertisers actively supported these programs. Rather than cater to the least common denominator, they tried to raise the level of popular entertainment. They knew full well that they were, in the end, using a publicly owned medium to sell their products. That "social contract" was controlled by the government through the F.C.C, and had the wondrous effect of producing programs on the level of Information Please, The Hallmark Hall Of Fame and I Can Hear It Now.

Nowhere was this seen to greater advantage than the network attitude towards news. In the mid-thirties' CBS and NBC sent reporters overseas for the first time to cover the story of Edward, Prince of Wales as he renounced the throne in favor of an American woman. A few years later foreign radio correspondents came into their own as H.V. Kaltenborn covered the Munich crisis from a cramped hotel room in Germany filled with transmitting equipment. Relaying these electrifying events, he ad-libbed for four days, sleeping on a cot in the corner. For the first time the American people felt that they were witnesses to world events. That voice over the airways contained the most essential ingredient—believability.

In that same decade we were blessed with a rare group of marvelous political speakers. Regardless of their philosophy, each and every one could hold an audience spellbound. Churchill, Roosevelt and even Hitler became familiar through their radio addresses. While most of us couldn't understand German, Hitler's sinister ranting sent chills up your spine—a fear only intensified by the eerie rising and falling roars of his Nazi followers over the undulating short wave signal. But no one, not even that master of the medium, Winston Churchill, used radio to a greater advantage than F.D.R.

His "fireside chats" brought him right inside your living room. One felt that he was talking to you and you alone. Taking you into his confidence, those sonorous tones washed away all your anxieties. Here was a father speaking to his children; a teacher to his class. "Yes", he would say, "Things are very difficult now, but we're going to come through all right." He was so persuasive that even his enemies were afraid to listen to him.

Part of his great success was his ability to communicate with us on our level; not down, not lofty, but right on target. A Harvard educated patrician; Roosevelt used the simplest examples to get his point across. When Great Britain ran out of money in the midst of the blitz, F.D.R. had to find a way to continue supplying them with war material without appearing to be giving the store away. The isolationists were very powerful at the time and were waiting for any opportunity to label Roosevelt a "warmonger." When the president proposed what would become known as Lend-Lease, he didn't get carried away with trying to explain the geopolitical reasons for supporting the British. Instead he used the example of a neighbor whose house was on fire and wanted to borrow your garden hose. He didn't want to buy it, Roosevelt explained, he just wanted to use it until the fire was out and then he'd return it. Everyone in the country could understand that reasoning and the bill passed through Congress. Without it, Britain would probably have collapsed.

His chats were so popular that during the dark days of 1940 and 41, many movie theaters changed their opening times so as not to interfere with the broadcast.

Those voices had a distinctive timbre that was as recognizable as Hitler's mustache or F.D.R.'s cigarette holder. The vigorous tones of Roosevelt's voice effectively transmitted a sense of well being rarely matched in any man. When Truman took his place, this marked difference in speaking was one of the major obstacles to his general acceptance. Harry made very good sense, but that flat, Middle Western delivery derailed him before he left the station. In spite of his tremendous post-presidential popularity, for most of his two terms he suffered from this marked comparison with his predecessor.

There were no "talk shows" as we know them today, but there were newspaper columnists who had their own programs in prime early evening time. Walter Winchell ("Good evening Mister and Mrs.America and all the ships at sea"), Drew Pearson and Louella Parsons had tremendous followings. Following closely on their heels were the pure radio commentators like Gabriel Heatter, Raymond Graham Swing and Jimmy Fiddler. But the best "newscasters" were those men who had just witnessed the momentous events first hand and brought the experience to you unalloyed by sponsor pressure or audience appeal. Such men rose to the tumultuous times and became icons of broadcasting. Others became outstanding historians.

William L. Shirer, Edward R. Murrow, Robert Trout, Howard K. Smith, Charles Collingwood, Waltern Cronkite and Lowell Thomas led a stellar group of reporters whose voices became as familiar as the members of our family. Some of them hosted documentaries such as The March of Time. As I recall, these newscasts were provided without commercial interruption.

But radio was large enough to encompass many viewpoints—some right off the wall. Father Coughlin was just as mesmerizing as F.D.R. for an entirely different audience and was extremely effective. Mixing a virulent hatred of Jews, the New Deal, England, and recent immigrants (Irish excluded), he stirred up a violent stew among his stalwarts. In the south Huey Long followed the same formula, only in his case he included Catholics and blacks.

More conventional religious programs crowded the airways. I do not have very fond memories of being forced to listen to the Catholic Hour where the rosary was recited endlessly. Other faiths had their moments with such features as the Lutheran Hour, Norman Vincent Peale, and the Voice of Prophecy. Sundays carried many services live directly from the church.

On a less contentious level major league baseball filled the afternoon airways. The voices of Mel Allen and Red Barber came to epitomize the New York national pastime. For me, the most fascinating part of the game was the play-by-play rendering of the out of town games where the information was relayed to New York via Western Union Teletype. Real fans would remain glued to their sets listening to the click, click, click of the Teletype key as the announcer tried desperately to instill some drama into this distant relay. This exercise carried the "theater of the mind" to greater heights than one could imagine. In later years some enterprising station came up with the idea of "re-created" games—canned fan response included—that were broadcast during the supper hour. At that time most games were played in the afternoons.

Each of us had our favorite programs. My sisters were entranced by the dreamy melodies of Sammy Kaye, while my mother enjoyed Kate Smith, along with most other musical shows. While all of the above appealed to the older members of my family, I was only concerned with the prodigious adventure fare offered up by nearly every station. These programs were at various times: terrifying, dramatic, breathtaking and suspenseful. "Dick Tracy, Jack Armstrong, Captain Midnight, the Shadow, the Lone Ranger, the Green Hornet, the Witches Tale, Superman, I Love a Mystery, Inner Sanctum"—the list goes on, endlessly and gloriously. What mind of man could have created a more delicious bill of fare for a young boy's imagination? For a couple of hours every evening we were all transported to another world. In a family of five I was by far the lowest on the roster, and yet no one ever tried to interfere with one minute of my precious slate. How many hours did I sit perched in front of our radio, with a Captain Midnight decoder in my hand, hanging on every clue? Boy, did I drink a lot of Ovaltine for that privilege!

Ordering that decoder introduced me into the magical world of the U.S. Postal Service. I was eight when I wrote my first real letter. It was addressed to General Mills, the company that made Ovaltine. That breakfast drink sponsored Captain Midnight, one of my favorite programs. It seemed that they were always running promotions. This time they offered a secret decoder for ten cents and the tinfoil from the top of the can of Ovaltine. I recall composing this, my baptism of communication, and not a school exercise. "Gentlemen: Please find enclosed…" I was elated when, in due course, the package arrived with everything I'd ordered. It instilled in me a lifelong respect for the postal service and the mastery of the written word. In grammar school we learned how to compose simple letters, always placing our address in the upper right hand corner and always using a colon after the greeting. It was one of our first English lessons.

Letters have a wondrous enchantment lacking in other forms of communication. As one of my chores, I'd often be entrusted with the tiny mailbox key. "Christmas morning" is the way I approached the mail in our brass box in the vestibule of our apartment building. The only thing missing was the red ribbon, but who needs a gift-wrap with all those gorgeous stamps decorating the missives? It didn't take long for me to identify the sender by his or her handwriting. It became a matter of pride to tell my mother whom the letter was from without reading the return address. Everyone's florid script made it appear as though they were all direct descendents of John Hancock.

But in my eyes, letters paled next to the riches available just by turning a small dial. I had schoolmates who were convinced that radio was the real world and everything else pure fabrication. After a few hundred hours of being immersed in this wonderland, it wasn't hard to fall under its spell—the theatre of the imagination. The beauty of course was that each of us created our own mental "picture" of what Captain Midnight or Superman looked like. This image was shaped mostly by the timbre of their voices. Every once in awhile a newspaper would show us a photo of the "real" radio actor and it was terribly disappointing. These people could only truly exist in a never-never land that was uniquely ours.

Enlightening America's youth was hardly the purpose of network radio, but subtly, this is exactly what happened. Living in the Bronx, we had an extremely limited knowledge of wildlife, but radio, in the guise of "Renfrew of the Mounted," taught us to recognize a wolf's call. (Many young girls in the Bronx didn't need to tune in to learn this phenomenon). A myriad of serials proved that "crime does not pay," and one learned early on not to stand in close proximity to Fibber Magee's closet!

Fully aware that just about every family sat down to dinner at six o'clock when the father returned from work, the networks cleverly scheduled our programs from 4 to 6 P.M, Monday through Friday. This neatly avoided any possible conflicts for every member had his or her favorites. But for the most part the evening fare was designed for the entire family. Among these stalwarts were Bob Hope, Fibber Magee and Molly, Fred Allen, Jack Benny, Amos and Andy and Bing Crosby. Long running series included Death Valley Days, Lum and Abner, the Goldbergs, Easy Aces, the Answer Man, Mr. Kean, Tracer of Lost Persons and the Lux Radio Theater. The latter was one of my favorites, but I had to have all my homework completed to be able to listen in to this 9 P.M. show. Cecil B. De Mille was the host, and I can still hear his resonant voice proclaim: "Lux, presents Hollywood."

Radio gave me an object lesson in the difference between the sexes. One could practically underline those programs that were the sole property of my mother and sisters, and those that were only found in my father's realm. I quickly learned that women were primarily concerned with "human interest" scenarios. Tales of romance, family conflict, love in all its forms and foibles, and most popular, a show called, Mister Anthony.

Mister Anthony was an early male form of Dear Abby, where the most excruciating domestic problems were aired live, tears and all. After listening to this unbroken catalog of misery for ten minutes, Mister Anthony would come up with what was generally pretty sound advice. What I liked best was his admission that some family problems were intractable. One time a poor wife related that she'd just discovered her husband had three mistresses, one of whom was pregnant, and that he was supporting all them from embezzled funds from his company. In spite of this, she still loved him and wanted to know how to get him back! Often my mother and grandmother would be into their third handkerchief hanging on every word. For them, the best part was the commercial pause between the end of the problem and Mister Anthony's solution. This gave all the women a chance to come up with their own answer. There were no prizes, except the satisfaction that you could read a heart just as well as a radio psychiatrist.

My father on the other hand, had no use for these "soap opera" type programs. He loved mysteries—"The Shadow, The Witches Tale," and all the radio dramas. Keenly interested in politics and history, he devoured the news broadcasts, and especially enjoyed those commentators who gave an in depth analysis of the day's events. This often kept him up past eleven, the witching hour in the Sauter household and most others. I slept on the living room couch at this time, so I was privy to the same late night programs that he enjoyed. I became very familiar with John W. Vandergrift, Lowell Thomas and Major George Fielding Elliot, who had a voice like broken gravel. In between all the commentary, my mother's Kate Smith voice would ring out, "John, are you coming to bed, it's after eleven!"

When it came to question and answer programs, he was a past master. His knowledge of books and authors was truly remarkable. While he loved to tune in most nights, radio barely put a dent in his steady diet of a book a week. He read everything from "Random Harvest" and "Northwest Passage" to the writings of LinYutang.

On Monday evenings it was an "off station" that brought us to one of the most enjoyable hours of the week. Broadcast directly from the stage of the cavernous Fabian Fox Theater in downtown Brooklyn, it was the one and only Fabian Fox Amateur Hour. Carried on WMCA, Joe

O'Brien was the host and his droll manner and delivery never varied. Every contestant was called "old chap" or "old girl," and the downtown, rough and ready Brooklyn audience often seemed but one step from a lynch mob. Getting up in front of that raucous group required the fortitude of the Christians entering the Coliseum. But for many, the Great Depression was still very much in evidence, so that $25.00 prize loomed large.

Each contestant had to sing a song to the accompaniment of the theater's pianist. The problem was the pianist would ask the trembling vocalist what key he or she wanted. Most of these people had no idea what he was talking about, so they left it in his hands. Bad choice! To get rid of them in a hurry, he'd begin in a high register that only a Lily Pons could navigate. Once the singer faltered, even slightly, the crowd would begin popping paper bags and whistling. If the poor guy or girl stopped, a siren would sound and a long hook appeared pulling them from the stage. With their exit Joe O'Brien would walk up to the mike and in his most sympathetic voice intone, "Too bad, old chap, but better luck next time." Everyone in my family had some input, so this was as close as we ever came to interactive radio. My mother became quite proficient in predicting the end of many singers purely by listening to the opening chord of the pianist. "She'll never make it," she'd say. One of the most popular vocals was "Cheri Beri Bin," which had some very high notes near the end of the song. Completely unrehearsed, the Fabian Fox Amateur Hour remains the highlight of my youthful radio memories.

During a newspaper strike in 1945, there was another unrehearsed program, this time featuring Mayor Fiorello La Guardia reading the Sunday comics. Talk about an astute politician! He broadcast over the city station: WNYC, and not only read the blurb, but changed his voice for each character and added sound effects. He had a rather high-pitched, squeaky croak that once heard, was never forgotten. ("Flat top is trying to escape, but Dick Tracy is right behind him! 'Watch out, Dick, he has a gun!'") The most beloved mayor New York ever had, he knew his worth and once exclaimed, "I could run on a laundry ticket and beat all these bums!"

I should mention that with the exception of a few stations such as WNEW, WMCA and WNYC, the networks ran the show. Oddly, they weren't identified by their corporate logo, but by colors: Red and Blue. The sole exception was Mutual (WOR). The primary stations also had different call letters than we're used to today. WNBC was WEAF, WABC was WJZ and WCBS was called WABC. If anyone is interested, all stations east of the Mississippi used "W" as the first call letter. Those out west used "K." Don't ask me why.

In between every program (with the exception of our city station, WNYC and WQXR, a classical music outlet, we were not so subtly introduced to a new form of advertising—singing commercials. Compared to today's high decibel approach, these messages were subdued, but quite effective. Most of us can still recall the jingles: "Rinso White, Rinso White, happy little washday song, Pepsi-Cola hits the spot. Twelve full ounces, that's a lot. Twice as much for a nickel too. Pepsi-Cola is the drink for you, Don't despair, use your head, save your hair, use Fitch Shampoo." and the male chorus that sang "L-A-V-A, L-A-V-A" introducing "Gang Busters," a police drama. While not musical, cigarettes weren't far behind with: "Chesterfield's, they satisfy, L-S-M-F-T—Lucky Strike Means Fine Tobacco, I'd walk a mile for a Camel, and Lucky Strike Green has gone to war!"

For my twelve year-old friends and me perhaps the most endearing moments were those spent listening to the terrifying moments of "Inner Sanctum." A squeaking door introduced the narrator, Raymond, who had the perfect manner and voice to scare the living daylights out of us. To show how brave we were, we'd often turn out the lights and gather close around the radio.

Looking back, the writing was on a very high scale. One of the most difficult things to create is a half-hour drama with a beginning, a middle, and the perfect climax. Talk about composing a sonnet! Alonzo Dean Cole, an outstanding short-story writer, created "A Witches Tale," among other shows, and collaborated on Sanctum. Many of today's playwrights—Neil Simon comes to mind—cut their creative teeth in radio.

Radio-Plays were a staple. Again, the skill employed to compress a three-act drama into an hour (cut by commercials) was hard to appreciate. Among our choice spots were First Nighter, I Love a Mystery, the Philco Playhouse and the fore-mentioned Lux Radio Theater. All these hour shows featured the cream of Hollywood stars. Radio money was very good and far easier to earn than making a movie. If an actor or singer could snare a long-term contract, he or she could retire in a few years.

Bing Crosby dominated the airways for all of my early life—an astonishing 15-year run, from the early thirties' until just after World War II. That he pulled off the same feat with movies and hit records placed him in on a special pedestal in the history of 20th Century show business. During this period he had more than twice as many recordings in the top ten: year after year, than his nearest competitor, Frank Sinatra, and his record, in spite of Elvis and the Beatles, still remains unmatched.

One of the major differences between today's songs and those of my youth was the nearly universal appeal of the musical output. There was no generation gap. My grandparents embraced the same songs as the teenagers, and we sang their favorite melodies of the turn of the century at our parties. Standards like "Mary," "When You Were Sweet Sixteen," Margie, "When You Wore a Tulip," and "The Band Played On," transcended age. They were national treasures to be enjoyed by everyone. On the contrary, it seems that today's songs are not meant to be sung.

When my interest in girls moved beyond Little Orphan Annie, and a darkened room signaled more promising results than an installment of "Inner Sanctum," radio again came to my rescue, much like a trusted friend. That swelling music accompanying a passionate couple on a couch was no longer the sole property of Hollywood. Those love songs pouring out of that little box put us on a par with a Paul Henreid or Clark Gable. "I'm in the mood for love…" If a couch wasn't available, the front seat of a parked car would do just as well with all that misty music at our beck and call. When we were alone, how comforting it was to know that in the middle of the night we only had to flip a switch to hear a song or the reassuring sound of another voice.

Just after the war ended, we were introduced into a new medium: FM. FM stood for Frequency Modulation. That definition went a long way to understanding why it took forever to catch on. Unless you were an electronics engineer, the words, "frequency" and "modulation" meant little. Few listeners were even aware that they were listening to AM— Amplitude Modulation. The spectrum or more simply, the span of the stations utilized a much greater range with FM than AM—millions of cycles rather than thousands. Because there was more "room" between the stations, interference was eliminated. More importantly for the average person, static was no longer a problem, not even in the worst electrical storm. Because of this limited appeal, however, the networks had little interest. The early stations were experimental, playing, to my delight, only classical music. To give you an example of how low key it was, WABF, an early entry, ran a five-hour evening program devoted to symphonic music. Initiating a program, the announcer would say, "Bloomingdales is proud to present five-hours of good music." Period.

No more announcements. Very few radios carried FM, and if I mentioned it to my friends, I was usually met with a blank stare.

Television came on the scene just as I was outgrowing those afternoon serials. But by the time the tube began to elbow out the prime time radio programs, my interest in classical music had taken precedence over everything else. Like most people, I was initially captured by the video medium itself— "movies" brought into your living room! But in spite of some marvelous programming that's now considered to have been the golden age of TV broadcasting, I missed that "theater of the mind." Once the initial glow of those flickering images wore off, the level of quality on the screen decreased sharply and the commercials got longer, sillier and louder. I retreated to my record collection, which by now had grown considerably along with the good music stations: WNYC and WQXR. For lighter fare, I still enjoyed Martin Block's Make-Believe Ballroom on WNEW, and shows like Dinah Shore, Perry Como and Arthur Godfrey.

For many of us, radio became our best friend, and that friendship has lasted to this day. Stay tuned.

CHAPTER TWELVE

READING

With the Sunday dinner dishes cleared away, my sisters disappeared with their friends and my mother would take a nap. Strong, steady breathing matched the brush strokes on my father's canvas, and soon became the only sound in our apartment. I'd curl up with the news part of the paper, the comics having been disposed of earlier. At six or seven I didn't understand half the words, but there were lots of pictures and the New York Daily News was primarily aimed at an audience intellectually not much further advanced than me. This is in no way a criticism, since looking back, the paper was very well organized with punchy writing and an easy narrative flow. It was no accident that it was the most popular newspaper in New York and probably the country.

How that paper fed my fantasies! I imagined myself a sailor doing brave deeds and attracting scores of friends— something I desperately needed. In those days the featured stories concerned the Spanish Civil War, the only war we had in 1936-37. The Daily News photos were of ancient tanks and Loyalists firing rifles over the carcasses of dead horses. I had no idea what the fighting was about (it later developed that neither did most of the adults) but to an eight-year-old boy, any war is better than no war. Although the pictures and stories gripped my imagination, the conflict was never discussed at our dinner table. Spaniards were in short supply in the Bronx at that time, and the only link I had to that country involved some movies about the Spanish-American War. But my memory of that conflict was a jumble of Teddy Roosevelt, Yellow Fever, Admiral Dewey and Cuba. It was all too complicated for me to sort out and hardly seemed worth the trouble.

Reading the Daily News, I discovered early on that in spite of its bulk, most of its pages were filled with ads for dresses, underwear, hats, coats, ties and an infinite variety of food. (No automobiles or appliances!) I looked at the pictures, but I didn't have a clue what it took to earn $4.75 or 79 cents. My brush with economics was limited to buying ice cream from the Bungalow Bar truck that was designed like a white house on wheels, and candy from Dominick's on Zerega Avenue. My pencils and notebooks were purchased at Woolworth's "five and ten" at Westchester Square, known also to my grandmother as "the village." Before the Bronx became part of New York City in 1903, she'd spent much of her life in the "wilderness" of Pelham or Throggs Neck.

Between our kitchen and living room was a small alcove that held the door to the dumbwaiter on one side and a huge mahogany bookcase on the other. Here on six sturdy shelves stood the family's supply of good and not so good reading and my father's art reproductions.

One day, when I was twelve, running out of reading material, I decided to explore these volumes. They were, without a doubt, the largest and heaviest books I'd ever seen. Groaning under the weight, there was nearly an entire shelf of these, all with brilliantly colored velour dust covers. Collections from the masters filled most of them, but one contained an array of "art" photographs. Up until this time my exposure to the female figure was limited to underwear ads, most of which resembled women clothed in armor rather than lingerie. I was flipping pages when all at once my eyes were riveted to a full-page image of a young woman completely naked! It had an immediate effect on me. Electrifying in its impact, that book answered more questions than I could imagine. (At the same time I had a whole new set of mysteries to tackle.) It was akin to discovering a whole new world. I was very careful to replace the volume in exactly the same position I'd found it. It would be my secret. I never again doubted the power of books.

Most of the books in the apartment, aside from school textbooks and the occasional trashy novel, belonged to my Dad. When he wasn't painting, he was reading. Three or four volumes were always stacked on an end table next to his living room easy chair. At that time John Steinbeck, Kenneth Roberts and Pearl Buck were among his favorites. While we didn't get regular magazines; I guess our limited budget couldn't handle it; we did receive some Reader's Digests and The Saturday Evening Posts in the form of hand-me-downs. LIFE was too recent to have made an impact on our family and it wasn't until the European war started that I began to see it on a regular basis. Then it dominated my reading for its superb coverage of international events and its outstanding photography.

A few years earlier, magazines entered my life in a different way. I got a job delivering the Saturday Evening Post. In the infinite wisdom of the distributors, one had to develop a clientele, before he could begin to deliver their product. This was my first lesson in salesmanship—more easily translated into: which sucker in the family can I call on first? This of course was my Aunt Irene. She not only signed up, but also conned a group of her neighbors and friends to do likewise. If one sold x-number of subscriptions, he would win a bicycle. Alas, I never moved beyond a certain fixed number, as early subscribers would drop out just as I ensnared new ones. Stuck in place, I figured I'd be married with a family long before the Curtis Publishing Company endowed me with a Schwinn three-speed!

Our living room held my Dad's easy chair with an accompanying floor lamp, a China closet and a sofa bed, along with two small cabinets. Completing the furniture was a magazine rack, a huge ashtray and a footstool. When I was three or four, the latter was my favorite since turned upside down it became in my imagination a "lifeboat." Grasping the two front legs I could rock myself across the trackless seas of my mother's dark green rug. (I still have that small bench in my home, the sole tangible link to my childhood.) The sofa bed also doubled as my bedroom since my sisters rightfully occupied the smaller of the two sleeping quarters.

One bathroom completed the flat. It held at any given time: my father's shaving cup, his razor and Gem single edge blades, bottles of Mercurochrome and peroxide, a roll of bandages, Band-Aids, a supply of bobby pins, curlers, Kotex, lipstick and face cream. Resembling nothing so much as Spanish moss, silk stockings, garter belts, panties, brassieres and girdles, hung from the shower curtain rack. All of them belonged to my sisters. My mother changed and kept her underwear in her bedroom, no doubt because there just wasn't enough room. On the other hand, my initial sight of my father heading for the bathroom early in the morning clad in "long-johns" was a bit of a shock. He wore this heavy underwear from December until April. Later I was forced to wear this uncomfortable garment while I was in the early grades of grammar school.

We were in the best of my memories, an easygoing family. To be sure, there was an affectionate discipline, and while it was rarely enforced, its subtle presence was never questioned. My mother only had to raise her eyebrows to show her displeasure. It never failed. My sisters and I were, in the true meaning of the word, "good" kids, and never gave my parents any cause to worry. Trying our best to live up to the lessons dispensed by the nuns and brothers of the Catholic Church, we in effect, made her job easy. Whatever money we made from our jobs, no matter how small, was turned over to her, for she held the keys to the family treasury. If she or my dad needed something from the store and asked one of us, there was never an argument. In spite of the five flights both ways, we unhesitatingly did their bidding. (Taking the steps two-at-a-time, all this climbing no doubt helped develop my leg muscles and stamina). My father stood aloof from all family disagreements, only stepping in at the last minute if things were getting totally out of hand. This was usually a rare occurrence.

I had my heart set on a bicycle and one day I saw a used two-wheeler in a neighborhood shop. I carried groceries from the A&P for scores of women, who paid me ten or fifteen cents for each trip. I earned every nickel. It took me a couple of months, but I finally reached my goal. My mother was against the whole idea from the start. She'd read in the Bronx Home News that some boys had been killed riding bicycles in traffic. I prevailed, but a few weeks later I had a flat. That was the opening my mother was looking for. She brought my pride and joy back to the shop and got the fifteen dollars back. It went into the household "kitty." End of bicycle quest.

And so we ate more spaghetti and noodles, placed cardboard in our shoes when there was no money for the shoemaker, and made do or do without. It was tough, but we had a lot of company. And we had faith that better times were ahead. In these four rooms, on the fifth floor of 1704 Seddon Street, five people lived through the Great Depression.

CHAPTER THIRTEEN

THE SAUTERS

John and Anne Sauter, grandparents

When I was six, the Depression was just a word. Never associating with anyone my own age that wasn't living under the same conditions, I had no point of reference. There is nothing about poverty in itself that makes it disgraceful, and I noticed that my friends and classmates did not feel humiliated by it. We all felt that this was the way the world was, and it was not until I reached adolescence that I became aware that people were divided into the rich and the poor. More than anything else it was the movies that demonstrated a totally different world than we were living in. Even Andy Hardy (a teenager we could readily identify with), lived in a comfortable home and had his own car. His society, while not wrapped in affluence, was certainly one where want never raised its head. Just about every home had a maid or a cook, and no one appeared as if they were wearing hand-me-downs. In their milieu, the word "depression" was unknown.

Later, I noticed that one of my classmates, Bobby Mack, always looked a bit better set out than the rest of us. Not markedly, to make him stand out, but subtle aspects of his clothing and the fact that his family took him to Canada or Bermuda on vacations. Their home was just across the street from our apartment, but the only similarity was its proximity. It could just as easily have been set down in fashionable Bronxville or White Plains. It took me some time to notice this, but inside it resembled, more than anything else, the home of Judge Hardy—Mickey Rooney's film father. Bobby's dad had a seat on the New York Stock Exchange.

As I moved through grammar school the Depression was a constant subject, not only in the newspapers and the radio, but also at every dinner table. Every editor and politician had a prediction about when it would end. Having known no other existence for my entire conscious life, I found this discussion a mystery. Wasn't it always like this? My friends and I had no other recollections. I'd often hear my parents and my older sister, Dorothy, speak longingly of the better days they had enjoyed before I arrived on the scene, but for all the difference, it could have been a scene from a movie.

In spite of living very close to the edge, on occasion my mother would surprise us. If she were a few dollars ahead she'd think nothing of hailing a cab if she was tired and faced a long walk. I think she did this to demonstrate that she was at least partially the master of her fate. From the look on her face, I could see that it brought her great satisfaction. Living as we did, there were few opportunities to splurge, even in the smallest way.

A child's sense of time is very restrictive. We measure happenings or expectations in days and weeks, rather than years. The day after your birthday was not a happy time—364 days remained until the next one, and the weeks stretched interminably. Being born on December 15th, I was doubly cursed because of the proximity of Christmas to this event. My Godmother had great fun teasing me when she'd give me a faux birthday present of a pair of socks on December 15th. Inside the box was a note: "The left one is for your birthday, the right for Christmas!" (She always came through with a real gift.)

The only relatives who lived markedly different from us were my father's parents.

The senior Sauters always occupied huge houses. With the number of children they had to cope with they had no choice. My grandfather was quite adept at buying large, rambling older houses in need of repair and thoroughly refurbishing them. Once updated, he'd sell it at a handsome profit and move into another. Coming from our small alcove, I always felt as if I were exploring some grand castle with long corridors and countless high-ceilinged rooms. I learned early on that my mother was not overly fond of my father's side of the family. This distressed me no end, since all my male cousins close in age were attached to this branch, and were logical playmates. At that time I never quite understood what had caused this gap between mother and mother-in-law, but luckily this hostility didn't carry over to my sisters or me. We literally had cousins by the dozens and the big house always rang with the cries of countless children of all ages.

My paternal grandmother, Anna Sauter, had twelve children (nine lived), and later adopted an infant who had been orphaned in the great influenza epidemic of 1917-18. All the children married and had offspring except George who lived at home and remained a bachelor.

The Sauters had a mixed heritage with roots in France and Germany as well as New York. My father's grandmother, Mary Oberle, was born in Alsace, France She emigrated to the U.S. as a young child and married Joseph Hemmerich who was born in New York. As a young man he served in the Civil War. My dad's fraternal grandmother came from Baden-Baden, Germany. His father was the only child of her second marriage. A widow, she later married for a third time, bearing three more children. A busy woman! (One almost needs a scorecard to follow all these relatives!)

The progeny of my uncle Joe and my aunt Anna provided me with two boys and a girl who were close to my age and lived nearby. Joey, my uncle Joe's son was three years my senior, a great barrier at my tender age, but Anna's oldest son Matthew (who was forever known as "Sonny Boy") became my closest friend. He had two sisters, one the age of my sister Dot, and the other a year younger than me. Both were pretty as a peach. I loved this easygoing family and secretly wished I'd been born into it.

Grandma Sauter had been married at sixteen, and my father, the oldest, was born in May 1899. She had her last child, a daughter, in

1922. This girl was born about a year after my oldest sister Dorothy, so my sister in effect had an aunt younger than she was. That might have seemed odd enough, but there's more to the story. For reasons known only to my grandmother and God, she named her last child Dorothy as well. Of course they both attended the same school and the presence of TWO Dorothy Sauters must have created endless confusion.

In those days my mother possessed what was commonly referred to as "delusions of grandeur." I never knew where she acquired these ideas, because while I attended St.Raymond's we were just about hanging on by our fingernails. Perhaps it stemmed from two things: my father, prior to my arrival on the scene, had been something of a financial success. He was also the only Sauter who'd seen the inside of a college, studying art at Cooper Union in his teens and early twenties. My mother's father Charles had been a craftsman, fashioning fine furniture. But that was all in the past and both of them were suffering along with most of the rest of America.

Oddly enough, my father's side of the family whom my mother held in some distain, were all prospering either in plumbing, (my grandfather's trade) or working in the neighborhood chemical plant. I don't know what they made, but whatever it was, it smelled for blocks around, and was apparently much in demand because they operated full blast all through the 30s and 40s. My grandfather had some connections there and it seemed he could always find a job for his younger sons when they came of working age. Raymond and Harold stayed there all their lives and later employment was found for Matty, Sonny Boy's Dad.

On occasion, (much to my delight) my mother would swallow her pride and we'd all go over to Grandma's for dinner or a party. The dinners were monumental affairs with much eating, drinking, laughing, shouting and everyone (except my mother!) having a marvelous time. Everything the Sauters did was on a grand scale. In the cause of peace, my mother suffered through these afternoons in silence since she considered the antics of my grandfather and my uncles more than a little uncouth. Their favorite adjective was "shit," and it was sprinkled liberally throughout the conversation. I, of course, relished every minute of it for only sailors cuss more than young boys! They didn't own cars; they drove "shit-wagons," and Mayor La Guardia or any other politician was a "shit-heeler." I never quite understood the latter expression, but it made for a colorful exchange. In my young eyes, these were real people, full of life.

My grandfather was an extremely gregarious man. He loved to tell stories. Short, and stocky, with a shock of pure white hair, he had the power and stamina of a bull. Years of carrying iron bathtubs up flights of stairs had given him strength far beyond his small frame. His diminutive stature was a marked advantage in a profession that was spent in tight corners. Well beyond his skills with plumbing, he was an astute salesman. While replacing a bathtub or repairing a broken pipe he'd keep his customers enthralled by his endless and engaging patter. They'd feed him tea, and cake and sandwiches, and he soon became their family "plumber." Recommendations followed and he was never idle.

This Sunday gathering of the Sauter clan was seemingly set in stone. Because my mother was committed to her family, we probably joined them about once a month. Everyone sat down at a massive table that appeared to expand to any size to accommodate this platoon-sized group. My grandmother was a cook of some note and had the time and wherewithal to create some memorable dishes. She thought nothing of preparing a feast for fifteen or twenty sons, daughters and various offspring. In those days, no one lived more than a mile or two away, so there was no excuse to miss one of these hearty affairs. For some suffering under the economic turndown, that Sunday dinner was often THE main meal of the week.

That solid walnut table was always filled with succulent roasts or fowl, with giant mounds of mashed potatoes and fresh vegetables grown on their own property. Anna was a prodigious baker, and mouth-watering cakes and pies emerged from an oven that never seemed to cool. Her delicious pies were deep conceptions, with flaky crusts and thick chunks of apples, cherries or peaches. Beer was always on the table—never wine, and mixed drinks were enjoyed before and after dinner.

But it wasn't merely the food that caught my attention. In the living and dining rooms were strange accouterments I'd never before laid eyes on. A huge fireplace dominated one wall, and deer and elk heads gazed down on us from the others. Examples of my father's artwork were arrayed along another wall. Newspapers and magazines were strewn everywhere, and the whole place reeked of tobacco smoke. More than anything else, the entire interior wrapped you in a comfortable lived-in atmosphere. Usually I was ill at ease in new surroundings, but here I felt instantly at home.

Later, when the adults sat back, loosened their belts and lit up their cigars and cigarettes and settled in for an hour of coffee and small talk, my cousins and I would roam the house. Each corridor opened to room after room where strange and exciting magazines lay waiting to be devoured. POPULAR MECHANICS and FIELD AND STREAM were totally new to me. On Sundays the senior Sauters bought different papers than we did; the Mirror and the Journal-American. Twice the size of the Daily News, the Journal had a completely different set of comics and equally as good. I was entranced by Mandrake the Magician, Prince Valiant, the Phantom and the Katzenjammer Kids.

Running out of reading material, we'd explore the backyard and garage where a jumble of cars sat parked and unlocked. (I don't recall ever coming across a locked car during the Depression, nor did I ever see one broken into or vandalized) Sonny Boy and I, and on occasion Walter Heinbuck (another cousin, who was my age but didn't visit as often), would sit in these marvelous creations of the thirties' and imagine ourselves driving along Tremont Avenue without a care in the world. All the vehicles were suitably equipped with a clutch and shifting gears became a great pastime. Escaping the sentinel eyes of a mother or older sister, we'd repair to these hiding places and exchange those close confidences that only ten or eleven-year old boys possess. Other times we'd climb up to a huge attic filled with every manner of furniture, trunks, clothing, books, magazines and linens—a veritable treasure trove.

My older cousin Matt reached an age where he became very curious about the opposite sex. One day roaming this attic he discovered a small opening just over the bathtub ceiling light that gave him a partial view of the area below. Frustrated by his lack of a clear field, he began to enlarge the opening. Fortunately for him, whoever he was watching had just exited the room when a huge piece of plaster became dislodged and fell with a crash into the bathtub. He said he just barely kept himself from following it, and he made his ignoble escape before anyone came up to investigate. Once he came into the possession of what were referred to then as "dirty pictures." The images were blurred and dark, but I could just make out what the people were doing. "Jackie, you want to see how people make babies?" I thought he was crazy. I looked at those pictures and told him in no uncertain terms, "My parents would never do anything like that!"

Sonny was always crazy about horses and spent all his free time helping out at a riding academy. Often he'd show up at my apartment on a Saturday morning mounted on a big stallion, surrounded by every kid for blocks around. My mother always frowned on our friendship, and sometimes with good reason. Once, when I was thirteen, he told me that he had discovered an abandoned rowboat and that we could take it for a sail out on the Sound. For someone enthralled by the sea and the navy, this sounded like a terrific idea and off I went, trailing along as usual. It was April and the shoreline was deserted. There were a number of boats laid up for the winter, but my cousin zeroed in one lying just above the high water line. He discovered a set of oars in a nearby shed, and after pushing the boat for a few yards we were afloat. I assumed that he knew the people who owned these boats, and that they'd have no objection if we took a short ride in one of them.

About fifteen minutes after we launched our rowboat and were about five hundred yards from shore, we heard some shouting from the beach we'd left. We couldn't make out what they were saying, but it didn't sound very friendly. Facing the shore, I could see two men shaking their fists and waving their arms. Their intentions were unmistakable: return that boat NOW! "Just ignore them," my cousin said, but this time without his usual confidence. "We're not going to be out long anyway."

At first I believed him, but then things took a turn for the worst. Launching their own boat, they each manned an oar. They moved a lot faster than we could. I offered to take an oar, but my cousin said it would only slow us down. Soon they were narrowing the gap and began to hurl dire threats. Calculating my chances of making it back to shore without a life jacket in water that was probably below fifty degrees, they didn't look good.

All at once they were alongside and each of them menacingly held an upraised oar as a weapon. "Out of that boat, you goddamn thieves," they shouted. Now I knew we were in real trouble. My cousin's bravado evaporated. He stood up and started to make his case, but one of the men jabbed him with oar and into the Sound he went with a mighty splash. Then they turned to me. I tried my best to explain that I was just a victim of circumstance, but they were in no mood for explanations. "I hope you both drown, you thieving bastards. It'll teach you a lesson."

My Guardian Angel must have been working overtime that morning because out of nowhere appeared a Coast Guard powerboat who hailed us. "What's going on here? Put down that oar," one sailor shouted. They maneuvered the boat close by and hauled my cousin out of the Sound. He was shaking uncontrollably, barely able to speak. A crewman wrapped him in a blanket and took him below. Then they pulled me aboard. "These two hoodlums were stealing our boat," one of our pursuers yelled. A Coast Guard Chief in khakis stepped out from behind the bridge-screen and glowered down at these two. With a .45 Colt pistol strapped to his waist, his words carried more weight. "Are you guys nuts, or what? They're only a couple of kids. I have a good mind to run you in for endangering the lives of minors." They began to reply and he cut them short. "There's a war going on and you two spend your time beating up a couple of boys. You call yourselves men. If you want to mess it up with somebody your own size, I'll be at the Coast Guard station at the end of City Island, and I'll be glad to accommodate you. And incidentally, why aren't you two in the army? I think you're a couple of goddamn draft dodgers. Now get the hell out of here." With that the chief pushed the throttle and the boat leaped forward.

In a few minutes we were at the Coast Guard station on the tip of City Island where my cousin was placed in one of the beds in their quarters. Sonny Boy was given some brandy and wrapped in blankets. They told me they were going to keep him in bed until he could be checked out by a hospital corpsman that they had just called. He was expected in about a half hour. I was welcome to ride in one of their boats out to Oyster Bay where they were to pick up some supplies. Would I like to come along?

So I got my boat ride in the Sound after all, and in style. My cousin wasn't doing too badly, pampered by a half-dozen sailors and being fed a hot turkey dinner, but I had one of my best days ever patrolling the Long Island Sound with armed sailors making sure that no U-Boats had slipped through the submarine nets. I don't know what we would have done had we seen any subs, but I was having the time of my life. I couldn't wait to get back to school to tell all my friends. But upon reflection, I decided to keep all of this under my hat. If my mother discovered just how close I'd come to drowning, I'd never see my cousin again. And I couldn't wait to see what new adventures he had up his sleeve!

Every family has their "crazies" and we had ours. My father's brothers were either very wild or totally benign. Joe and Harold were the real nuts and no one could imagine planning a party without them. Joe was an alcoholic, but it was often hard to tell. No one ever knew what his normal behavior was. One of his favorite tricks was jumping on my mother while she was taking a nap. This would bring forth screams from her and shouts of joy to everyone else. He usually drove a truck delivering some provisions, and since my mother was one of his favorites, he'd often appear unannounced at all hours to drop off a "souvenir" from the back of his truck.

I remember one night in particular when he rang our bell about 10 P.M. He'd obviously been drinking and when my mother suggested he go home to his family, he tried to defuse her by telling her he had some great salami downstairs on his truck. My mother said she'd make him some coffee and off he disappeared down the five flights of stairs. When he didn't return for some time, she thought he'd forgotten about her and off she went to bed. After a while we heard some furious shouting in the hallway and my mother recognized Joe's voice. She followed the echoing sounds and walked down two flights where Joe, with a massive salami under one arm, was holding our quiet Swiss neighbor, Mr. Loeffler, by his bathrobe lapels screaming, "What have you done with my sister-in-law!" Joe had miscounted the floors, something easily accomplished in his condition.

Willie, a little younger than Joe, and a totally different personality, was married with two girls and lived on the ground floor of our apartment building. After a year or two he moved a few blocks away to St. Raymond's Avenue and we rarely saw him except at parties and the regular Sunday afternoon gatherings. Quiet by nature, one could easily overlook him. Once, however, he became the central character in a family comedy right out of Mack Sennett.

During these lean years when my Dad worked sporadically, he hit upon the idea that he could supplement his income by painting portraits. There was little doubt that he was an accomplished artist and our walls were covered by his canvases. One of his first subjects was his brother Willie.

I've already related this story of how Willie sat immobile Sunday after Sunday while his image took shape under my father's hand. But he failed to show up for three weeks, and needing canvas, my father turned Willie into a horse! Willie of course was forever linked with those four-legged creatures and never lived it down. Although my Dad's reputation for being his own man was enhanced, Willie never held it against him and they remained close. He and George were as quiet as Harold and Joe were wild.

In contrast, I knew little of my mother's brothers. The two oldest, Joe and Charlie had died from rheumatic heart disease in their early twenties', a few years before I was born. Raymond married a Czech woman, and they always appeared to be perched at the edge of the family. He had two daughters whom I never knew until after I was married. The fourth son, John, was also rarely seen, but for an entirely different reason: he was a career Navy man. Johnny had enlisted in 1926, after having engaged in a "wild" youth and some brushes with the law. The Navy was thought to be a steadying influence on him. I don't think it worked, as he was always a mutinous maverick, all too quick with his fists.

One of my earliest recollections of him was at a time when the fleet was "in". It was a common practice during the twenties' and thirties' to bring major units into New York for a few days, anchoring in the Hudson and having an "open house" for the public. Johnny was serving as a water tender onboard the huge aircraft carrier LEXINGTON and the entire family went onboard one Sunday in 1933 for a visit. I was four at the time and what I recall most was watching a cook stir a massive pot of mayonnaise with a shortened oar!

While exploring this monstrous flat-top (at that time the largest warship in our Navy), I became separated from my mother. This set off a vigorous search and after a few minutes I was found on the flight deck surrounded by a group of sailors who paid me a nickel every time I repeated a phrase they'd taught me. "The captain is a sonofabitch!" They were delighted.

Johnny had a long and varied career. Between the wars we were always involved in military actions in Central America. Basically, our government was making the world safe for companies like United Fruit who were exploiting the native population, but the press never portrayed our actions in that light. It was always labeled, euphemistically—"protecting American interests." As a result Johnny took part in suppressing various revolutions that went under such titles as the Second Nicaraguan Campaign and the Haitian Insurrection. Years later, coming home on leave from the Pacific, he was arrested in Grand Central Station by two MPs who charged him with wearing unauthorized service ribbons. He was fortunate that there was a senior officer who was old enough to recall those military actions back in the early thirties'.

He seemed to live a charmed life in the Pacific. He'd been in the engine room of the heavy cruiser VINCENNES for more than two years, but in July 1942 a recurrence of malaria he'd come down with years before blossomed, and was sent ashore to a hospital in Noumea. Less than a month later the VINCENNES was sunk with heavy loss of life in the Battle of Savo Island, off Guadalcanal. No one in his Engine Room crew survived. Later he was serving onboard the carrier SUWANEE when she was struck by a kamikaze, but he came through unscathed. My mother's other brother, Raymond, was torpedoed off Australia and spent two days in a life raft until he was picked up.

Johnny's domestic life was hardly more tranquil. For reasons known only to he and my aunt, (who was just out of the convent!) they married and had four sons. Every time he came home on leave she got pregnant! Luckily, the war ended or they would no doubt have had a dozen children!

CHAPTER FOURTEEN

GRAMMAR SCHOOL

In September 1935, in spite of the fact that I wasn't six years old, my mother wheedled me into the first grade at St. Raymond's School. This was of course completely against the rules, but my mother always felt that there wasn't a rule made that could stand up to her power of persuasion. The school practically had our name on it. My aunts and uncles joined my sisters in this St. Raymond's "alumni." When I started, Rita was in the fifth grade. In the normal course of events our paths would never cross since the school was strictly segregated by sex. My older sister Dorothy had preceded me by nine years and was already in high school. I guess my mother wanted me out from underfoot so she could go to work, and she convinced the principal that I was ready for the first grade.

I recall being terrified at first because I wasn't used to being surrounded by thirty-five other boys. For someone who never had a brother and a father who stayed in the shadows, it was an abrupt transition. But I soon discovered that most of the other kids were just as numb as I was and friendships were born out of necessity. Our main concern was this black ogre with the huge rosary beads. She towered over us with an all-powerful presence. Her formal name was Sister Bernadette and she was a Sister of Charity.

Sister Bernadette turned out to be a sweet young thing not much older than my sister Dot, and probably on her first teaching assignment. Destined to live a celibate life, she reveled in having not one, but 35 five and six year old boys to guide all day. She of course, never revealed this to us, but in later years confessed this to my sister Rita.

Poor Sister Bernadette! I'm surprised she still had some good memories of me after what I did to her one morning in the spring of 1936. I must have been cutting up in class because she singled me out. "John, go outside and stand in the corridor. Perhaps you'll pay more attention and stop talking to your neighbor." I don't remember what I was saying, only that I didn't think it warranted that kind of punishment. The more I stood there and thought about it, the angrier I got. I finally decided to take things into my own hands.

Without so much as a "bye your leave," I descended the back stairs to the street level. Since everyone was in class, no one saw me. Crossing Castle Hill Avenue, a main thoroughfare, I walked the three blocks to home. It must have been about 10 or 11 A.M. when I surprised my mother who was ironing in the kitchen. I made up some story about being let out early and she accepted it. Soon I was busy with a game, completely forgetting my brief adventure. About an hour later, my sister Rita, out of breath from racing up the five flights of stairs, asked frantically, "Is Jackie here?" When my mother said yes, Rita sank utterly relieved into a kitchen chair. My disappearance had hit St. Raymond's School like a thunderbolt.

About a half-hour after sending me into the corridor, Sister Bernadette went out to fetch me. I was nowhere to be seen. At first she thought I'd gone to the Boys Room and sent one of my classmates to check. "John's not in the Boy's Room, Sister." Hearing that, her heart sank and she rushed to Sister Natalie, the principal. I can imagine the scene when Bernadette announced that she'd "lost" one of her pupils! The Lindberg kidnapping was still fresh in everyone's mind. The chief intermediary with the ransom was "Jaftsie" Condon, the principal of P.S. 12, located not half a mile away, and St. Raymond's cemetery was the drop point for some of the money.

Someone suggested calling the police, but before taking that drastic step a detailed search was made of every classroom, lunchroom, boiler space, toilet and closet—-but no Jackie Sauter. They were no doubt agonizing about how to explain to a mother that her only son had disappeared from under their noses in broad daylight, when someone recalled that I had an older sister in the sixth grade. They called Rita in. No, she hadn't seen me since breakfast, but she'd be glad to run home and see if I was there. And there she found me, blissfully unaware of all the havoc I'd caused. Needless to say, I was never put outside a classroom again, at least by Bernadette.

We always used the back staircase while going to and from assembly or lunch. As the school was about thirty years old, photos of every graduating class (male on our side of the building) were positioned all along the walls. It didn't take long for me to pick out my uncles. I always felt as if I had some relative keeping an eye on me.

Settled in Seddon Street, we were surrounded by my mother's sisters. Irene lived on the first floor of our apartment building and Florence occupied the lower level of a two-family house on Dorsey Street, a block away. Flo, my Godmother, had a son, Jimmy, four years my junior, but Irene was childless. Regardless, she soon became a surrogate mother to all of us and I spent many happy hours with her and her husband, Charlie, who was also my Godfather.

CHAPTER FIFTEEN

IRENE AND CHARLIE

Irene and Charlie just after they were married

I f there was ever an odd couple, it was Irene and Charlie. A giant of a
man, tipping the scales at better than three hundred pounds, Charlie
worked as a paper-handler in a large printing press in Hoboken. His
plant produced such publications as the Sunday supplement of the N.Y.
Daily News, and a variety of what passed for "girlie" magazines of that
era. The Police Gazette was their biggest seller. By today's standards, it'd
be on a par with the Saint Anthony Messenger, but in the late thirties
in didn't take much more than the sight of a black garter and a few
inches of thigh to turn men on. At the time I couldn't understand why
anyone would spend good money to look at something he could see
for free at any beach. I wasn't old enough to understand the underwear
connection. Women and girls were far from my thoughts. I was far more
interested in the adventures of Don Winslow of the Navy.

My Uncle Charlie had two passions (three if you count Irene, but
I guess no one was counting): stamp collecting and horseracing. Not
content to place individual stamps in an album, he was a serious philat-

elist, always acquiring First Day Issues and sheets of postage. Often he'd let me accompany him, and I'd cringe as he'd tie up a long line in the post office examining the sheets to see where the margins were. I never understood the significance, but if it wasn't just right, he'd return it and make the clerk dig through seemingly endless stacks of stamps until he satisfied my uncle's wishes. Tying up the window for an interminable period, no one ever raised a voice in anger or frustration. Charlie was built like a defensive end. Little did they know that underneath all that bulk was the world's biggest cream puff.

American stamps were his exclusive enthusiasm. When a mixed bag arrived from one of his innumerable suppliers, he'd bestow the balance on me, instantly turning me into a fellow collector. Early on he bought me a Scott stamp album and I was on my way. Learning of my interest, my father had the mailroom where he worked save the cancelled stamps, and soon I was buried in likenesses of Hindenburg and George VI. With a multitude of stamps, I soon devised my own war games, each stamp representing a soldier. The long airmail numbers were officers. With American, German, British and French postage in preeminence, I commanded "battalions." I'd line them up on a blanket with appropriate "fortifications" and drop clothespins as bombs. In addition to providing me with an endless pastime, I also had an object lesson about the terrible German inflation when each of their stamps cost a million marks! In addition to learning the word for "postage" in several languages, I probably could recognize George VI and Hitler long before anyone else in my class.

But there was no sharing in Charlie's other pastime, and it was more than a little strange. His interest in horseracing bordered on being an obsession. The Green Sheet, the Racing Form, and half a dozen other turf magazines were always in evidence in his dining room. One of my chores nearly every night (for which I earned a nickel) was to walk up to Tremont Avenue at 8 P.M. to collect the "late" papers. In those days, the raison d'etre for a final edition was not the news, but rather what happened at Belmont, Aqueduct, and Monmouth Park. Appearing with the Journal-American or the World-Telegram, Charlie would often grab it from my hand and quickly turn to the right page, intoning, "That's a winner, there's another."

Imagining him a racing wizard, I often wondered why he didn't drive a big car and sport a diamond ring. It took me some time to discover that in spite of an uncanny ability to pick winners, he never bet a nickel!

I don't know if it was his decision or if Irene forbade it, but I never asked. In any event, Charlie was so set in his ways that I don't think he'd know what to do had he won a million. He'd probably continue to trudge to the subway at the crack of dawn and work every Sunday they'd let him. He never owned a car, and if he had more than one blue suit I never saw it.

But he was as good-hearted and generous as they come, never refusing me a nickel when the ice cream truck made its' daily appearance on summer nights. His deep pockets were always filled with a vast assortment of coins and his meaty hand would scoop up a batch and hold it out to me. "Get me a Chocolate Pop and a Buttered Almond for Aunt Irene." If I had friends who were bereft of funds, he never failed to play Mr. Bountiful. Aside from the track, he also enjoyed the midget auto races that were held regularly at the end of Castle Hill Avenue, just off the Long Island Sound. I often accompanied him and reveled in the wild melee of spinning cars, smoke and shattering noise.

My father and Charlie once had a great friendship, or so I heard. Among other ventures they were partners in a 36-foot motorboat that they often sailed to the Jersey shore. But something occurred before I was born that irrevocably destroyed their relationship. Whatever it was, I was never privy to the cause and my father, resolute in his contempt, went to his death never uttering a word to either my aunt or my uncle. Our close proximity often made this painfully difficult, and I didn't learn of this state of affairs until I was much older. This may seem odd, but my father rarely spoke to me, and these family strains were never discussed when I was around. I couldn't imagine not speaking to anyone who lived that close and was a relative besides. I was far too young to understand the peculiar adult world of intrigue and grudges. Not even Charlie's demise from brain cancer many years later could ease this strain. When I told my father that Charlie had died, his reply was, "Charlie died thirty years ago, but he was too dumb to lie down."

Fortunately, I wasn't expected to join in this "silent treatment" and neither my mother nor my sisters altered their close relationship in any way. It was a singular and unrelenting vendetta.

My Aunt Irene was the strangest and at the same time the most lovable of all my relatives. In an age when conformity ruled, she did her own thing. She was the living embodiment of what would be later labeled a "hippie."

The month she died was a bad time for the very old: those special people among us who reach ninety. In the course of a few weeks we lost, Lillian Gish, Helen Hayes, Marion Anderson, and then Aunt Irene. It may seem odd, linking her with those notable women, but in her own indomitable way she left a mark every bit as lasting as they did.

She was so many things to so many people that it's difficult to know where to begin. That she was unique goes without saying, but she was more than that. A person of immense joy and warmth, she radiated a friendliness and charm that touched every person she met, and left them better just for knowing her.

From a historical perspective, she was our last contact with a world and a family that we only know from books and fading photo albums. Who'll tell the new generation about Grandpa Martin and Uncle George? If there was ever someone whose wonderful memory should be preserved in print and stone, it's George. And who'll relate what it was like to grow up in a cold-water flat on 96th Street at the turn of the century? Raised with seven brothers and sisters, plus a grandfather and an uncle, one wonders where they stacked them all! For any of the younger generation, the apartment in that marvelous movie "A Tree Grows in Brooklyn," will give you a fair idea of what 96th Street was like: right down to the long wash lines hanging in the back courtyard.

New York, the country, and the world were so different when Irene was growing up, it's nearly impossible for us to visualize. Queen Victoria, Kaiser Wilhelm, and Czar Nicholas were all on their thrones, and William McKinley was in the White House. McKinley? Most people today have a hard time remembering who Gerald Ford was! Born before the famous flight at Kitty Hawk, she lived to see spacecraft zoom past Jupiter and Mars, and men walk on the moon. Irene didn't straddle the twentieth century; she embraced it.

As interesting as it is to look at the long shadows of her life, it's far more fun to recall her close up, the central figure in so many family anecdotes. I guess everyone has a favorite Aunt Irene story, and I'm no exception.

CHAPTER SIXTEEN

THE STORY TELLER

One Aunt Irene story I always savored, but which may not be so familiar, concerns Uncle Johnny who was a career man in the Navy. Returning to his ship anchored in the Hudson, Irene rode down to West 72nd Street to see him off in the liberty boat. Once it left shore, she started waving and screaming as only she could. Her voice had both the cutting edge of Ethel Merman, and the power of Niagara Falls. Half way to the cruiser, one of Johnny's shipmates remarked, "Say, John, isn't that screaming woman a friend of yours?" Without turning his head, my uncle replied, "I never saw her before in my life."

Another gem involves the time Irene was 13 or 14 and she went ice-skating in Wilson's Woods. (She always called it Woodsy Woods). The elastic in her long drawers snapped and they fell down to her ankles, causing her to fall along with about a dozen others. Listening to her describe how she scooped them up, all the while diverting her boy friend's attention, was a story all its own!

It wasn't until I entered the insurance business that she related a story concerning my younger Aunt Flo. The local Met Life agent made a living selling hundred and five-hundred dollar polices for literally pennies a week. Just about every family bought one. Essentially, they were bought for burial expenses. When my Aunt Flo reached the age of five my grandmother inquired about a policy on her life. A neighbor cautioned her that since Flo suffered from a rheumatic heart, she'd be ineligible. However, my grandmother was, if nothing else, tenacious. She paid a neighbor's daughter, who was the same age, to take the medical in Flo's place. Strangely, that young girl died at thirteen from diphtheria, while Flo, who began smoking two packs of Camels a day at twelve, lived to be seventy-eight!

At a time when most people lived very orderly lives, Irene made Aunty Mame look like a Carmelite nun! Years before Mame was invented, she spouted her philosophy, which proclaimed, "Life is a banquet, and most poor sonsabitches are starving to death!" My earliest memories it seemed were of her and her long-suffering husband, Uncle Charlie. She appeared in so many pictures with me before the age of six, that friends looking at my family album thought she was my mother. In a way, I guess she was. Having no children of her own, she was a mother to us all.

As we had no phone, Irene became the conduit of countless messages—mostly from young men to my older sisters. She'd lean out the window (she lived on the 2nd floor-we the 5th.) and shout up to Rita or Dorothy that one of their heartthrobs was on the phone. So many images come back at a time like this: my calling out, "Aunt Irene, the Bungalow Bar man is here," and out from the window would drop a couple of nickels just like in the Automat. Lying sprawled under the kitchen sink with both of them in a darkened room, watching the Lionel trains they just bought me for my birthday go round and round. And who can forget those icy fingers reaching under my warm blankets on a winter Saturday morning, imploring, "Hurry up and get dressed, we're going to Radio City." (It was 35 cents before 9 A.M.)

While she was loved by everyone, it was the children who held a special place for her in their hearts. Irene possessed this amazing openness, completely without pretense, that said, "This is me. What you see is what you get!" She was of course the eternal child, refusing to take on those nasty habits we acquire in later years. Once, in the late sixties, we asked her to baby-sit while we attended a weekend convention. Our car had no sooner pulled out of the driveway than she turned to my daughter, Karen and said, "Let's have a party tomorrow night." Naturally, none of them tried to talk her out of it. Saturday night, with a dozen kids for an audience, she put on a show they still remember. She danced to "Ba Ba Ba Ba Barbara Ann" until 1 A.M., and for an encore proudly showed all-present her scar from a recent skin graft. I'll leave what part of her anatomy to your imagination! As great a performer as she was (and she was always on stage), I'll always remember her talking in her famous non-stop delivery. For hours, she'd weave tales of her childhood, what my parents were like long before they got married, and her fledgling days as an information operator for the telephone company. It was probably here that she developed her superhuman memory. Irene never needed an address book, or a telephone directory for that matter.

If everyone had been endowed with the same gifts, I.B.M. would have had no market for their computers! She not only knew addresses, but all the birthdays and anniversaries, right down to how many years it was since uncle so and so had died. (While most of the long deceased relatives she spoke of were completely unfamiliar, that never seemed to slow her down). Every time she spoke to you on the phone, (enabling AT&T to declare a special dividend) she'd pepper her conversation with all this family flotsam and jetsam, and make all those distant names somehow seem like real people.

Once, I was about to accompany her to a Good Friday service on the last seven words of Christ. When my father discovered where I was going, he said, "It's lucky she wasn't standing at the foot of the cross, or He would never have gotten them out!"

Her generosity was without peer, and she was truly a Lady Bountiful if there ever was one. Whether I was selling chances or a subscription to the Saturday Evening Post, Irene was the first sucker I'd hit. Only God knows how many coats, shoes, suits, and dresses she bought for nieces and nephews, and in later years a great deal more. Sad to say, a few took advantage and barely acknowledged her kindness, but she was, if nothing else, a sharp judge of human nature. Reminding her of someone's lack of gratitude, she just smiled and said, "Remember, only one leper came back."

Irene's life seemed to be totally without direction. Childless and never employed after she married, she involved herself completely in other people's lives. Except for rising every morning for six o'clock mass, the clock meant nothing to her. Engrossed in shopping or gossiping with a neighbor, she'd completely forget about my uncle's dinner. When my sisters or my mother reminded her about the time, she'd just laugh and say, "He'll never miss a meal." And she was right. Charlie would never complain. Finding her out of the house and no food prepared, he'd open the icebox and polish off an entire cake or a pie or whatever was handy. And that wasn't hard for him to do.

Actually when she put her mind to it, she was an excellent cook. My sisters and I loved to be asked for breakfast. "Asked" is the wrong word. All we had to do was ring her bell around eight A.M. on weekends to be invited in for her famous scrambled eggs. No one ever made eggs as she did—even the best restaurants. I'd have to travel to France years later to finally find an equal. Her eggs had a perfect consistency and color—never burned or runny. Later, I discovered that her marvelous cast iron pan had a great deal to do with the quality of her dishes. The heat was uniform cross the entire surface.

She was a perfectionist—very slow, but sure. Nothing was left to chance. The toast was always uniformly browned, and she used a whipped butter that never adorned our icebox. As a result the butter wasn't hard, as ours was, but soft and easily spreadable. Her cocoa was prepared from scratch—no instant Nestles powder. And she added cream, not water. All of her culinary efforts bore the same stamp of originality and perfection. Mashed potatoes, veal cutlets, biscuits—whatever it was was memorable.

Irene didn't limit her love for food to the table. Traveling with her to Water Witch, my grandparent's bungalow on the Jersey shore, she'd pack enough food to last a week. I can happily recall her opening a can of peaches on the Jersey Central train, as well as a thermos of hot chocolate. Of course she always carried the right dishes and utensils. At the end of the meal, one could be sure of a packet of Drake's cream-filled cupcakes.

Their first-floor apartment always resembled a place where the moving man was about to arrive—momentarily. When my daughters, Karen and Laurie were about six or seven, they returned from a visit to Aunt Irene, commenting: "You never told us that Aunt Irene was moving." We tried to explain that that was the normal look of her home. Cartons of canned goods and toilet paper that she'd found on sale were stacked in the foyer, and every pullout shelf was overflowing with letters and countless cards of Christmases past. Charlie followed directly in her footsteps. His corner of the dining room (I don't think anyone ever ate in that room during the 50 years they lived there) was filled with cartons of Camels, stamp collections, and scores of magazines. One had to navigate this area with all the skills of traversing a minefield. Nothing was ever thrown out; it simply disintegrated. If there was ever a couple perfectly suited to each other, it was Irene and Charlie.

Among other attributes, Irene was the dispenser of an endless supply of family lore. She seemed to have a new story ever time she saw me. It was she who introduced me to Uncle George long before I met him in the flesh. George was my maternal grandmother's first cousin. Unmarried, he was content to live with his single sister, Kate. Never holding steady employment, he supported himself doing odd jobs for the family and some neighbors. More than anything else, he had a flair for getting into mischief. Two stories about George were told and retold until they became part of the Ludwig family tradition.

My grandparents had a bungalow built on the New Jersey shore, near Highlands just before I was born. It had no bathtub or shower. Times were hard however, and the Ludwigs were ecstatic to have this summer get-away, only a few steps from the beach and about an hour and a half commute by train to Manhattan.

Coming into the possession of a large bedspring, my grandmother asked George to bring it down from the city to the bungalow over the weekend. As it was the height of the summer, George decided to take the excursion boat down rather than the train. Mixing business and pleasure, the following Saturday night he took the moonlight sail departing New York around 9 P.M. He carried his mattress spring up to the top deck where there was a breeze and settled down for a pleasant sea voyage of two hours.

Hearing dance music, he made his way down to the main deck where a band was banging out the popular tunes of the day. A dancer of some note, he soon found himself a partner and whirled her around the deck. Enjoying the music and his partner, he lost all sense of time until he felt the ship coming into the Atlantic Highlands pier. Then he attempted to make his way to the gangway with his oversized spring so he could exit and catch the train that was waiting. But the crowd on the dance floor was steaming, and they rapidly surged upstairs to the open deck. George struggled with his cumbersome "furniture," but it was a losing battle. Since most of the passengers were onboard solely for the dancing, the ship's stop was brief and they were soon underway back to New York's Liberty Street with George and his bedspring still onboard.

Now he was deposited back in the city at midnight. No one in the family had a telephone in those days, so he had no way of reaching my grandmother. When he didn't appear on the late train it was assumed he'd had a change of plans and everyone went to bed. (I was in attendance that summer.) He trudged back to his sister's apartment on Elizabeth Street and banged on the door. "Who is it," she cried out. "Your brother, George. Let me in." he responded. Kate replied, "My brother is in New Jersey. Whoever you are, go away." So he carried the bedspring back downstairs and slept on a park bench. The next morning, Sunday, he caught the early boat to Atlantic Highlands.

We were just getting ready for dinner when my grandmother came in and said," There's a peddler coming down the street. Everybody inside and don't make a sound or he'll be here all day." I looked outside through the window and saw this strange man coming down the street with a gigantic contraption on his back. Surrounded by a dozen kids, who were laughing and taunting him, he dominated the street. Suddenly he stopped in front of our house and began to bang on the screen door. "It's George, George, Annie, open the door!" At last he was admitted and the more he looked for sympathy the more we laughed as he recounted his tale of chaperoning a monstrous bedspring three times across New York harbor.

Another time my grandmother asked him to dispose of an old feather mattress at the sanitation dump, some distance away. Always looking for an easier solution, he carried the mattress up to the roof where he cut it open. The strong May wind soon carried off all the feathers turning 96th Street and 3rd avenue into a veritable blizzard. Spying him on the roof, the local cop walked up the three flights where he collared him. He was going to charge him, but my grandmother interceded. The cop told him he had to clean up the mess, or else. George picked up a bucket and mop and spent the rest of the day trying to corral the errant feathers that were now dispersed all over Yorkville.

Like many people unburdened with the chores of raising children, he had a natural affinity toward them. Finding a cheap glass ring in a flea market and a fine felt jewelry box to mount it in, he'd present it to my sisters as the real McCoy, sending them into ecstasy.

Irene was a natural wordsmith. To her, the English language was merely a vehicle to make everyone laugh. Admiring a new baby boy, Irene would look intensely into the crib and make a dramatic announcement. "I just noticed something about him," she'd say, focusing everyone's attention. "He resembles his mother around the eyes, but he looks more like his father around the thighs! "When someone was confused about the spelling of a word, she'd pipe up, "You must remember that the "P" is silent, just like in "swimming." Then there was the tale about the newly married couple that wrote to their friends "We're sorry we can't see anyone now. We're still putting our things together!"

One of my all time favorites was an expression used by Irene, but not exclusively in the family. "If Aunt Maggie was alive today, she'd be spinning in her grave." Whenever someone made a gaff, she'd say," He's going to be marked lousy on page four." I never understood what 'page four" was, but in the end it became part of the Ludwig lore.

She would have been a natural on the stage. Whether she was talking about someone who had just been married, or how cold it was that morning, her every gesture and word had the quality of a Sarah Bernhardt. Her descriptions could have been composed by a novelist. "Succinct" was a word that had never made it into her vocabulary. If you made the fatal error of asking how she was in passing, you kissed your day goodbye.

CHAPTER SEVENTEEN

FIVE-STOREY WALKUP

Our initial apartment at 1704 Seddon Street was a microcosm of the 1930s Bronx. Since almost no one moved unless they died or were dispossessed, most of the characters remain etched in my memory.

Irene's next-door neighbor was Tess Horton, the divorcee. I remember her most for her son Jimmy, who went to St. Raymond's with me. I also remember that he had only one eye. He'd lost it when another boy hit him with a stone. Learning that, I never threw a stone at anyone again. I was always haunted by the terror of causing someone to go blind. I couldn't imagine a worse disability. Jimmy's lack of two eyes didn't appear to pose any serious problem for him however. He was a good student and adjusted better than most to school.

Across the way from Tess lived the sole bachelor in our building: Mr. Hall. That he'd spent some years in the Navy earlier in his life was evidenced by a series of exotic tattoos on his muscled arms. He was a foreman for Blue Coal, a company with a plant on Westchester Creek, near Westchester Square. Towering a hundred feet over the Westchester Creek, their huge storage facility was a landmark in our part of Unionport. If nothing else it resembled one of those impressive grain elevators we often saw in the movies. One day we met on the stairs. "Jackie, how would you like to climb to the top of the tower?" Would I!

Standing on the ground looking up to that unimaginable height, I began to have second thoughts, but I was too timid to back down. Mr. Hall positioned me in front of him on the ladder and up we went, rung by rung. "Don't look down—only up." I needed no convincing. Every few minutes he'd tell me to take a break. When I stopped I'd feel his hands clasp my waist in an iron grip. There was no way I was going to fall. Higher and higher we climbed. Looking to my side I could see a great distance. Even St. Raymond's church and school stood out clearly, well over a mile way. I began to feel like I was Jack scaling the beanstalk!

1704 Seddon St.

Reaching the top, I was astonished to discover how small the roof was. And there was no guardrail. Mr. Hall pointed out Fort Schyler in the distance and the Whitestone Bridge. It was an exhilarating experience. Relating my adventure gave my standing a major boost among my friends, but my mother came down hard against anymore lofty jaunts.

On the second floor lived the Johnsons, a Swedish family; mother, father and two sons. A quiet quartet. Old man Johnson had gone to sea in sail around the turn of the century, and he kept me on the edge of my seat with tales of giant waves and fierce gales that snapped the masts like matchsticks. Sailing around Cape Horn, a mountainous sea lifted him from the deck, presumably to certain death, but the next wave re-deposited him back onboard only a few feet from where he'd been standing. He reeked of tobacco, snuff, and whiskey. Matched with a weather-beaten face, his aura lent credence to his stories, and the infinite detail he could conjure up kept us mesmerized for hours. The only thing he lacked was a peg-leg!

The Johnson's sons, were both single and in their thirties. They were subdued in that uniquely Scandinavian way, but Ben, the youngest, had a terrible weakness for alcohol. When he drank he'd rant and throw things until his parents called the police. Once in an uncontrollable thirst, he drank a can of varnish and he came moaning to our apartment door pointing to his mouth. I was terrified, but my mother opened two cans of peaches that Ben swallowed with one gulp. I didn't know it, but the varnish incident was the beginning of the end for poor Ben who died less than a year later of alcohol poisoning.

Mr. Rooney, who lived on the same floor shared a drinking problem; one that was quite different than Ben's. He was like a volcano: dormant most of the time, but nearly causing an earthquake when he got drunk. A neat man, I always recall him in his subway conductor's uniform, which he wore with deep pride. I never saw him dressed in anything else except on Sunday when he donned his black suit and highly polished shoes. Every time I'd meet him he'd say with that brogue, "Jackie, keep your shoes polished like this and you'll go places." I don't know if he was grooming me for a job on the Pelham Bay Local, but it was good advice.

Rooney was the ideal husband and father until he drank which fortunately, wasn't too often. Then he'd become so violent that his wife would come running into our apartment for safety. She'd bang on our door, shouting, "Please, Mrs.Sauter, let me in. Mike has the devil in him and I fear for my life. Put the chain on your door." I was glad my father didn't have a problem with drink. He'd enjoy a Scotch or two after dinner and occasionally brought a bottle of some vile-tasting wine to the table. That was it. When he was at a party at my grandmother's, he could apparently enjoy himself all night with a glass in his hand, but he could hold his liquor and was smart enough not to mix his drinks.

The Schneiders were the only other family of German decent on our side of the building. Having no children they of course, "adopted" me. I was a regular and welcome guest of theirs at dinnertime. Gus was a career postal worker, so the Depression had no effect on him. His wife introduced me into a new dish—potato pancakes, as well as some luscious homemade cakes and pies. One night when I guess I was about five or six, I must have committed a breach of table etiquette and they quickly corrected me. "Gentlemen don't eat like that. I replied, "My father says gentlemen are bullshit." They loved it.

There were two Italian families on the fourth floor and they pretty much kept to themselves. One of them, the Gentiles, had a son, Gaetano, who was in my class at St. Raymond's. As all the teaching Sisters and Brothers were Irish, poor Gaetano suffered terribly at school. There wasn't much Christian Charity among those Sisters of Charity and the other religious who should have set a better example. Gaetano was a Samaritan in a world where no one believed in following that famous parable. His parents didn't speak much English and all communication was done through their children. At the time my family (like just about all the other Anglo-Saxons), thought Italians were greatly inferior, probably due to their inability to assimilate rapidly and because of the smells of olive oil and garlic coming from their quarters. This was particularly noticeable during the summer when all the apartment doors remained open. My father, in their defense, often remarked that the Irish had no reason to put down the Italians. "After all," he'd remark to anyone within earshot, "these people had a magnificent civilization when the Irish and English were running around in bearskins!" I couldn't verify that, but I loved the cooking smells emanating from their apartment. Every floor had its own signature aroma, and everyone knew what everyone else was having for dinner. In those lean years there weren't too many steaks and roasts—it was more often spaghetti, stew, potato pancakes or soup. Sometimes at mealtime, I wished I belonged to another family since some of the mothers were far more imaginative cooks than my own.

I often relate this story. When I was in the Navy, the first time I went on liberty in Memphis and was looking for a meal, I came across a restaurant with a huge sign proclaiming, "Meals just like your mother used to make." I walked right by.

CHAPTER EIGHTEEN

TEACHERS

There may have been great events taking place outside our neighborhood in the late thirties, but nothing matched the building of Parkchester. Constructing these great apartments, capable of housing more than twelve thousand people, not only irrevocably altered my neighborhood, but also the character of the entire east Bronx. The vast tract of land upon which it was built extended west from Castle Hill Ave. to White Plains Road, and south from East Tremont to Westchester Ave. It was owned by the Christian Brothers. The bulk of this space was virgin forest, little changed from the time of the Indians. On the northwestern corner however, there stood a great stone pile called the Protectory. Inside these walls were housed homeless boys up to the age of eighteen, and what we'd refer to today as juvenile delinquents. Rising menacingly out of the giant elms and oak trees, those dark gray prison-like walls struck fear into the heart of every young boy. Capitalizing on this image, our parents cleverly employed the Protectory as a subtle method of keeping us on the straight and narrow. "If you're not good, we're going to send you to the Protectory!"

In the late thirties, a deal was struck between the Christian Brothers and the Metropolitan Life Insurance Company to transfer the land for $4,000,000. The paper was hardly dry when the Protectory was demolished. That removed the greatest threat our parents could hold over us, but this destruction paled against the effect of the felling of hundreds of huge oaks to make way for the construction of the apartments.

These trees provided all the boys with a nearly unlimited supply of ammunition in the form of acorns, which we shot at each other day and night, at home and in school. As we still wore knickers, every kid had a perfect storehouse for these early guided missiles. With an infinite storage capacity: immies, milkies, aggies, koboloas, bottletops, pennies, tooth-picks, and hard candy found its way to our kneecaps, sloshing around when we walked. For months the floors of St. Raymond's seemed to be inches deep in shells, and I can still recall the crackling sound underfoot as were made our way from class to class.

Back in school, I left Sister Bernadette for one of the Leahy sisters. These two spinsters spent their lives teaching at St. Raymond's. Catholic schools paid lay teachers so poorly that they no doubt only survived because there were two of them and they shared expenses. One taught the Second Grade, the other the Fifth. They'd been part of the scenery for so long that even my oldest uncle remembered them. If for no other reason, their physical appearance made them memorable. I never figured out who was the oldest, but one was tall and thin and the other was so small she was practically a midget. As short as she was, Miss Leahy, the Lesser, knew her stuff. No one was left back in her class. She was particularly good at arithmetic and English and I enjoyed my year in the Second Grade under her tutelage.

My uncle recalled a humorous incident that occurred some time before I met her. In his time pupils were left back regularly if they couldn't grasp the material in the allotted time. It wasn't uncommon for a slow student to remain mired in one class for two or three years. No doubt it was a convenient way for some parents to warehouse their kids while they were at work. As a result, some of the older Italian kids were shaving before their received their grammar school diploma! One day one of these older boys was disciplined by Little Miss Leahy. He gave her some gruff and she came down hard on him. In spite of her lack of stature, she had a sharp tongue and a quick hand, bringing up many a taller boy who tried to take advantage of her. But that day her size and temper brought her to grief. It was the last class and the older student retaliated by lifting her up and hanging her by the back of her jacket in the coat closet. Miss Leahy made a lot of noise, but those classroom doors in St. Raymond's were designed to hold off the Visigoths. She wasn't discovered until hours later by the janitor.

Sister Eugenie was my next teacher, and quickly became a favorite. I don't know where they got their names from, but I'd never before run into any Eugenies or Bernadettes for that matter. (This was before Franz Werfel's bestseller was made into a movie, generating literally thousands of Bernadettes.) Older than Bernadette and a lot more experienced, Eugenie knew how to employ absolute control over forty, eight-year old fidgety boys while hardly raising her voice. Swirling by in that floor-length black habit, with her rosary swinging on its giant crucifix, she left a lingering scent that was never forgotten. An incongruous mixture of soap, ammonia, and mothballs, it unmistakably identified every member of the clergy. We found it hard to imagine that they once had other lives. Because of the length of their habit, we rarely, if ever laid eyes on their shoes. Since they appeared to glide silently across the floor, there was a story making the rounds that they never wore shoes; they had rubber rollers attached to their feet!

Eugenie was a dominating Mother Figure and was treated as such. Assignments were always handed in on time, not so much out of fear, but simply because one just couldn't imagine not doing her bidding. Her ability to answer any question gave her a reputation equal to radio's Answer Man. In every home where my classmates lived, "Sister said," brought all arguments to a quick end. She had a way of getting the best out of us, and neither my friends nor I had any problems. My faded third grade report card reveals only nineties and gold stars.

The fourth grade produced the only "bomb" of my grammar school years: Miss Flynn. She was typical of the lay teachers hired by the church in that era: a dried up spinster who smelled awful and read the lesson in a monotone. God only knows what they paid her. Probably not much more than the nuns and they'd taken a vow of poverty! Recalling her five decades later, my cronies remember only that she used to sit with her legs spread apart at an open faced desk. I don't know if she thought she was giving us a thrill (we were all light years away from thinking about girls), but I doubt if anyone was sorry to see the class end in June.

CHAPTER NINETEEN

BOOKS

Geography was one of my favorite subjects. Our massive atlas provided me with fantasy travel to far away lands. Spending hours poring over each page, I often wondered what it'd be like to live in Timbuktu or Bali. At that time most of the mapmakers color-coded the holdings of the various empires: British, French, Dutch etc. Great Britain of course dominated the world and their vast red areas seemed to encompass the globe. Canada, Bermuda, most of the Caribbean, Gibraltar, Egypt, Kenya, Somaliland, South Africa, Rhodesia and sundry other huge chunks of the "dark continent." Then there was India, Burma, Ceylon, Australia, New Zealand, and vast chains of islands in the Pacific. All this sprawling area was part of a colossal empire ruled by a tiny country off the continent of Europe. It was staggering.

Sometimes, lying in my bed in the early hours, I'd listen to the bells of St. Peter's a few blocks away, and I'd be carried on wings of dreams to some of the exotic locales in my atlas. There was a big world out there, but mine was framed within a few square miles. At the time it seemed big enough. I was only fair in arithmetic, but generally enjoyed the rest of the schoolwork. Being a big reader helped immeasurably.

When I was six, my mother took me down to the Westchester Square Public Library about a half-mile from our house and enrolled me. How proud I was to have my very own card! Suddenly I had the world's riches at my fingertips. There was a children's section, but no one particularly cared if you roamed the aisles as long as you treated the books with respect. I treated them with reverence.

There were plenty of words I didn't understand at first, but for many the meanings revealed themselves by their place in the sentence, and I didn't have to refer to a dictionary. With each visit more and more of this vast world of literature opened its doors and I was hooked for life. This was the first time I'd ever been given the freedom to do anything on my own. It was a heady feeling. Taking as much time as I wished at the reading table, I could browse two, three, or four volumes. There was a tremendous satisfaction to be at last considered old enough and responsible enough to handle some of the most valuable properties of our society. Saturday mornings brought readings of popular stories by a librarian in the upstairs meeting room. Here I was introduced to Paul Bunyan, Davey Crockett, Roosevelt on San Juan Hill, Admiral Byrd, and "Lucky Lindy." Every young boy needs heroes, and the imposing white brick building under the Westchester Square subway platform supplied them in spades.

Westchester Square library

By the time I was eight or nine I was taking home two and three books a week. The First World War dominated my interest at this time, but strangely there was very little on the shelves about it. Instead I settled for sea stories, especially tales about submarines and deep-sea divers. Submarines were no doubt the most exiting of all warships, and the thought of living below the surface of the water was beyond belief. I devoured Jules Verne and later became introduced to Edward Ellsberg, a US Navy Commander who directed the raising of the sunken submarine S-51 off Block Island in 1925. This true-life adventure was far easier to relate to than the fantasy of Captain Nemo. I soon focused my attention on non-fiction.

Each book, it seemed, cataloged the further published writings of the author, and I worked my way across the shelf of Ellsberg. As the Commander was a prolific writer with many interests, this in turn introduced me into other subjects beyond submarines and diving. He'd written a fine biography of John Paul Jones, called CAPTAIN PAUL, and this account led me into the Revolutionary War. I didn't know it at the time, but I was practicing early networking at its finest. As I immersed myself in each story, I could see all the action in my mind's eye, fueling an already over-active imagination. Among my early favorites were TREASURE ISLAND, SWISS FAMILY ROBINSON, WE, BEAU GESTE, and anything by Edgar Allen Poe. Some of the narratives were rather dense for my limited vocabulary, but I always ploughed on, finishing every story.

Living in Gotham, we could often broaden our horizons without the benefit of books, for in a very real sense the city itself was our "library." A nickel subway ride could transport us to the site of Nathan Hale's execution, where he uttered those famous words, "I regret that I have but one life to give for my country." A little further south we could follow Washington's footsteps as he made his way to BOTH his inaugural addresses. Revolutionary battle sites were seemingly everywhere in the boroughs— from Brooklyn Heights, to Throggs Neck. At the tip of Manhattan, there was an apex of riches. What other city could offer wondrous views the Statue of Liberty, Wall Street, the Stock Exchange, the great harbor, and if one was really lucky, perhaps the liner QUEEN MARY moving impressively out to sea? History was soaked into every sidewalk. Looking east, three monumental spans arched the river, the closest and most memorable being the Brooklyn. Like an Italian restaurant, the city smothered you with spectacle. Gotham possessed the tallest buildings, the longest bridges, the most lavish museums, libraries and concert halls. If that wasn't enough to impress the most jaded out-of-towner, there was a railroad beneath the streets that carried more passengers than all the rest of the trains in the country combined.

Growing up in the Bronx, we didn't encompass everything, but just knowing it was there made us proud to be a New Yorker.

In 1939, my father's uncle, learning that I had a passion for nautical subjects gave me a copy of Fletcher Pratt's THE NAVY: A History. It changed my life. I began to read everything on the shelves related to the Navy and began to plan a career in this service. My mother's younger brother was a 30-year man, having enlisted in 1927. His stories while home on leave only fueled my obsession. During the war my models became warships rather than planes. Christmas 1942 brought me a copy of JANE'S FIGHTING SHIPS, and soon I was absorbing great gobs of detail about the warships of every navy. Later, while a senior in high school, I took the test for NROTC, but my weakness in math did me in. Entering college and embarked on a teaching course, I forgot my earlier infatuation. But as so often happens in life, the seed had been planted and it would blossom just at the outbreak of the Korean War.

CHAPTER TWENTY

GODLINESS

St. Raymond's Church and School

It was in the second grade that I prepared for my First Holy Communion, and that remains uppermost in my recollection.

The taking of this Sacrament was a major event. Day after day we were drilled endlessly in learning the proper prayers and in preparing for our first confession which preceded the taking of the host. I don't recall how many sins I had to confess; I can't imagine doing anything worse than talking in church or answering back my mother on occasion (but not often if I knew what was good for me). Sex could have been on the dark side of the moon for all the difference it made in our lives, so our time inside that stuffy dark box was very short indeed.

St. Raymond's church was cavernous with six confessionals located next to the side aisles. The priest sat inside an enclosed space, about the size of a closet. Adjoining were two other musty alcoves, concealed by heavy drapes. His only access to the dark chambers holding the sinners was a sliding wooden panel. Kneeling uncomfortably in the dark, one could just barely hear the mumbles of the other penitent. The heavy curtains made these quarters nearly soundproof as well as airless. Once the panel opened on your side, you were barely inches from your confessor. Instantly, you knew if your priest was a drinker or what he enjoyed for lunch.

"Bless me Father for I have sinned," was our opening line in this terrifying dialogue. To relate your inner most and embarrassing secrets to a stranger, even if he was God's messenger, was deeply disturbing. Each clergyman was different in the dispensing of penance—usually a string of "Our Fathers" and "Holy Marys," so there was always some jockeying for an easy mark. Once we had an ancient visiting mission priest who must have been over eighty. The older boys figured he wouldn't be able to hear much so they lined up outside his confessional. They were right. His hearing was poor, but he compensated with a booming voice that could have been heard across the street. I watched a 15-year old boy enter and shortly afterward heard this stentorian voice, "You say you were with a girl? How old was she? Was she married? Are you married? What were you doing? Speak up?" I never saw a line of boys melt away so quickly. The poor sinner came out of the confessional with his head down and looking for all the world like one of those criminals on the courthouse steps about to be arraigned.

To be fair, as I got older and had more substantial sins to tell, I always felt immensely relieved when I walked out of the church after confession on Saturday. It was the cheapest therapy ever devised. Much later, when I was in the Navy, I attended nearly a year of aviation schools in Memphis. This being our first strange city, our primary aim was trying to determine the best way to meet girls. One shipmate had a novel approach. He'd station himself near the back of a Catholic church on Saturday afternoon and wait to see which girl spent the longest time in the confessional. He'd engage her in conversation as she was leaving and it was all downhill after that.

The big First Communion Sunday finally arrived, and the faded black and white photos in the family album show me suitably attired in black knickers and jacket, with a huge white bow wrapped around my left arm. On that May Day, the church was filled to overflowing with beaming relatives, and although I was only one of over a hundred boys and girls, I guess nobody will ever forget me.

For some reason, which I've never been able to fathom, I wouldn't open my mouth when the priest came by with the host. For some long seconds he stood there imploring me to cooperate and stick out my tongue as I'd been drilled over and over, all to no avail. One of the nuns came up and tried to gain my confidence, but no go. Meanwhile my mother was dying a thousand deaths in the pew near the front. Agonizing over my behavior, she shredded three silk handkerchiefs. Everyone else had received the host without incident and there I was, kneeling alone at the altar rail, every eye in the church riveted on me. Finally, they called up my mother. She gave me the kind of special look only she could beam, and with the pressure of sundry members of the clergy, I relented. I'd completely purged this incident from my memory, and it obviously wasn't something the family wanted to remember. I only heard the story from my sister Rita when I was 64 years old!

Later, when I easily accepted the host, it always seemed to become stuck to the roof of my mouth. Then, for the balance of the Mass, I'd furiously maneuver my tongue trying to dislodge the gummy mass. Communion brought other problems. Back before Vatican Two, all Catholics, except the very elderly, had to fast from all food and drink from the preceding midnight before receiving Communion. I may have had a low blood sugar level, but nobody thought of those things then. As a result, I'd be standing for the gospel one minute, and awaken on the front steps a few minutes later in the company of a couple of ushers. My mother was obviously aware of this, but she didn't appear to be too concerned. Just like a number of other afflictions, we were told that we'd grow out of it. When the doctors couldn't diagnose some illness, they'd label it "growing pains." Nobody in our society was ever known to question a doctor.

One of the less desirable results of close contact with forty other bodies in class was the spread of infectious diseases like impetigo, ringworm, and lice. Many of my classmates were first generation immigrants and their hygiene left something to be desired. I vividly recall my mother shampooing my hair with scalding hot water, but the worst torture was submitting to the fine comb running through my scalp, trying to pick up those little devils. Eventually the school nurse started to examine the heads of all the students and later arranged to speak to the parents of the worst offenders and prescribe treatment. The problem disappeared as quickly as it had started.

I studied Religion, English, Arithmetic, History, Penmanship, and Geography. History and Geography were my favorite subjects. I can recall poring over maps in our set of encyclopedias at home for hours on end, totally fascinated by the strange sounding names. My father had a complete 1905 edition of the Britannica and all the place names were pre-World War I. Thus, I ran across vast forgotten areas such as German East and West Africa, and found that the Ukraine was once a separate country. (Nearly a hundred years later it reverted to its original designation.) The world had changed so dramatically in those thirty-odd years that I often thought I was living on another planet.

Discipline in the classroom was strict, and punishment was swift and often brutal. Both the nuns and the brothers were quick to slap your face or pull your ears if you weren't paying attention. I was terrified most of the time. On the other hand I had some teachers (Sister Eugenie was one) who were almost gentleness personified. Standards were high and nearly all the teachers, lay and religious, took their calling very seriously.

Brother James, the boy's school principal, was over seventy but he still had a bit of the sadist in him. If you were sent to him for punishment he'd break out a vintage bamboo rod that was taped on one end. He'd order you to hold out your hand, palm raised, and told you that if you flinched you'd get double! On occasion he'd whip down the rod and stop just an inch short of your hand. Then he'd shout with glee, "You flinched. I caught you, you flinched!" There was no recourse.

A few years later in the seventh grade, Brother Peter discovered a condom in one of his student's wallets. Wildly incensed, he started beating my buddy Red unmercifully up one aisle and down another. Peter only stopped when five boys and another teacher constrained him. An inescapable religious atmosphere pervaded every moment of our existence. For seven hours a day we were under the direct control of the sisters and brothers. All classes started and ended with prayers, and a crucifix hung prominently in every room. Every day we spent time at Catechism or a biblical theme. Aside from Sunday and Holy Day Mass, we were often herded into church for various Novenas and other devotions like First Friday. On Saturdays, what would have been our one-day out of their clutches they dreamed up Confession, so the week was complete. As what usually happens with overkill, a number of students were completely turned off by religion. If all these prayers and services weren't bad enough, they pinned and draped things over us.

Sometimes we felt like a Christmas tree! I thought I was alone in all this until the start of each school year when all the boys had to strip to the waist for a pre-semester physical exam. I could see that I had a great deal of company. Depending on their ethnic background, most of them fared far worse than I did.

I had the usual Miraculous Medal and sometimes scapulars. These were cloth images of saints held by long ribbons around one's neck. Our Italian classmates raised the ante by wearing in addition to scapulars and the medal, a set of rosary beads, and just to cover all bets, strings of garlic and a small red horn to ward off evil spirits! I was amazed that they didn't choke to death while they were asleep.

In the belief that all work would make Jack (and Pat and Mike) a dull boy, movies were shown on Wednesday afternoons in the school auditorium. In addition to the main feature, which was usually a western, there were cartoons and short subjects. I never quite understood the rationale behind this unless they wanted to give the teachers a needed break. While that weekly movie was a rarity in most schools, St. Raymond's went a step further with a dancing class that was incorporated into the seventh grade schedule. Under the guidance of Miss Gearity, a slender, attractive brunette of about twenty, we were introduced into the mysteries of the waltz and fox-trot—no Lindy or Big Apple! I didn't appreciate the proximity of Miss Gearity's soft body in my arms, but some of my classmates were two years my senior, and this class became the highpoint of their week. Years later, whenever we meet and reminisce, Miss Gearity's image is forefront in our conversations. I could only curse the fact that her charms were all wasted on me.

It's incredible how many of my fellow sufferers I can remember from that class of 1935. And remarkably over sixty years later I'm still in contact with many of them (although recently the Grim Reaper has been taking his toll.). The class was large considering that the national birth rate for 1929 was among the lowest. But then, just about everyone else was a year or two my senior. The names also reveal that the Irish were in the majority.

I accepted most of the prayers and devotions as perfectly natural, but I chafed at the constant money raising. In the New Testament Christ threw the moneychangers out of the temple, but here they were, center stage at St. Raymond's every Sunday handling stacks of quarters, dimes and nickels in the vestibule. In addition to the main offering, there was a seat collection, usually ten cents, and often there was a special passing of the plate for whatever project was dear to the pastor and the bishop. All this occurred at a time when families, including my own, were at a financial breaking point because of monumental unemployment. Money never seemed to be going in the opposite direction, at least at St. Raymond's, and it significantly soured my outlook towards religion in general and Catholicism in particular. Collections weren't limited to the church—they even entered the classroom. Every student was given a small enclosure called a mite box. I'd never seen a mite, so I had no idea where the name originated. Our pennies and the rare nickel were supposed to be deposited in this box and then turned over to sister at the end of the month. This lucre ostensibly went to rescue Chinese babies who were being drowned because there was not enough food to go around. At least this is the story we were told. It seems that we were always trying to save Chinese babies—mostly female, but nothing was mentioned about the millions of needy children right here in the USA.

But the worst attack on Christian charity occurred at the end of the month when a special levy was laid on all of us. Compounding this shake-down was the publication of all the names and the amount of their donation. Aside from a very real violation of privacy, this practice achieved its intended result: the humiliation of hundreds of families struggling to survive in the worst economic disaster to ever befall the United States. I can still recall reading the list, the bottom of which included some unfortunates who gave five cents. That nickel was, no doubt, in many instances far more of a sacrifice than the ten or twenty dollars donated by some professional or self-employed parishioner. Along with most of my friends, my family was in the twenty to twenty-five cent category when it came to the monthly gouging. The rock bottom was usually filled with Italian names. All were recent immigrants with large families. Most of the fathers were in construction and there was precious little of that going on at the time. In spite of their many untapped skills they were looked down upon in a parish dominated by the Irish. My father told us that all of the exquisite marble work and the stunning frescos that graced the walls and ceilings of St. Raymond's were the direct efforts of Italian craftsmen imported by the first pastor during the church's construction. This quality extended to the rectory and the nuns residence, and the school. Every Sister of Charity who served there would refer to their St. Raymond's residence as the "palace." When the Catholic Church built something it was designed to last indefinitely.

Years later, reading a history of the Bronx, I discovered that the original parish boundary of St. Raymond's extended far into Westchester County. When the city residents moved out of Manhattan and the surrounding land became much more valuable, the pastor, Monsignor McKenna, sold off some tracts and used the money to erect what would be the showplace of the county. All this occurred in the first decade of the century.

The reigning pastor in my time was Thaddeus Tierney. My family used to call him, "The Bishop of the Bronx," and he certainly looked the part. Every winter, while most of his parishioners were barely surviving the Great Depression, Tierney would take six weeks in Palm Beach. My father in particular, hated his un-Christian attitude and left the Church early, never to return. It was an unwritten law that no one in the family ever discussed this or his reasons. I agreed with him that in other times and other places, men exhibiting Tierney's attitude would be shot.

One of the less desirable traits I inherited from my father's side of the family was stuttering. It afflicted my uncle George to a chronic degree and it caused me much embarrassment and pain. Children can be devilishly cruel and they gave me no mercy. As a result, I rarely volunteered in the classroom.

Fortunately, in the sixth grade, fate smiled on me in the guise of a school nurse who took pity and counseled my parents to enroll me in a free speech therapy class at Fordham University, about ten miles away. As a reward my father gave her free art lessons. (It later appeared that my father was always giving young women free art lessons.) Every Wednesday I made a regular two-trolley car trip to Bathgate Avenue. My therapists were two Dominican nuns, the first I'd ever seen. Their habits were very different from the nuns who had taught me at Saint Raymond's. Except for their hands and part of their faces, every part of their body was covered—including a white band across their forehead. Part of the therapy involved their placing their hands on my throat and diaphragm while I breathed deeply and recited passages from well-known poems. "Relax and breathe deeply, John. I can still feel the tension in your vocal chords. That's why you stutter. Repeat after me: 'A,E,I,O,U.'" I'd never been this close to a nun before and they had a distinctive scent—an odd blend of musk and soap. In about a year they had me well on the road to recovery. But under pressure, I'd often slip back into my old speech habits, and it wasn't until five years later in high school that a kindly priest finally cured me by the oddest of methods: enrolling me in the debating society! But even after that, the proximity of a pretty girl would resurrect the old torment, often at a most inopportune time.

Along with the oral problem came chronic blinking. That was something else I inherited, but this time from my mother's side of the family. I guess nature didn't want to play any favorites. For this there was no therapy, but happily the blinking disappeared in the seventh grade. Looking back, I was pretty much a nervous wreck at St. Raymond's.

My last years at that grammar school were not pleasant ones. I was fast approaching puberty and the school was absolutely no help in answering the scores of questions I had concerning all these strange feelings inside my body. From what we learned in school, one would have thought we really were delivered by the stork! Growing up in the city, I had no opportunity to watch animals mate, and as a result remained totally in the dark about sex.

Of course we all had theories, and as it turned out they were all wrong. I have to admit that at that time sex was not an over-riding consideration, perhaps because I was a full year younger than most of my classmates, and more important I had no older brother. My mother once mentioned at the dinner table that she could educate my sisters about the birds and bees, but not me. She looked to my father who just grunted. Since he rarely spoke to me, I'd figured that he'd be the last person I'd look to explore the mysteries of the female body. I could just see him, trying to explain the details of how babies are made. Fat chance.

Childhood is not as carefree as many people believe. I discovered that growing up is a very complex experience that involves learning societal norms and obeying parents and teachers, all the while trying to fathom your own existence. Not an easy feat!

About this time I started to have real doubts about all the religion we were spoon fed every day. I found it hard to imagine a God who would allow such evil and misery in the world: children dying, millions of people starving, and a clergy, at least in St. Raymond's that appeared totally unconcerned with the plight of it's flock. The hierarchy's paramount concern seemed to be focused on money over all else. For about a year I stopped going to mass and confession. I had real doubts. I thought I was alone, but later I discovered that what I was experiencing was fairly common among people in their teens and early twenties. Fortunately my next parish was far closer to the real teachings of Christ and what might have been an irreversible break was avoided.

Returning to the church, I embraced for the first time, the concept of a "personal God." I can't recall how I eased into this idea, but in essence, this notion of a God that I could communicate with filled a desperate need in my life. God filled my void of loneliness. It was as if I found the older brother I never had. Regardless of how disenchanted I became with the pronouncements of the Church, my personal God: friend, counselor, confident, confessor and psychologist, was always there.

CHAPTER TWENTY-ONE

WHO STOLE THE
SOUNDS OF SUMMER?

As each school year ended, we faced another New York summer. How I hated that season. We sweated and sweated, all through the thirties' and forties'. The sleepless nights, turning over and over, searching in vain for a cool part of the pillow. Removing the wet pajamas, but discovering it made little difference—sleeping in the buff, but still roasting in the unremitting heat and humidity.

The butter, quickly turning into the consistency of mayonnaise, the oven-like kitchen at suppertime—a fearful penance perhaps for all your unconfessed sins, a tired fan rustling the heavy air, but in the end just a waste of power, drops of perspiration making bookmarks on every page. Later, dancing with embarrassed young girls whose dresses clung to their backs. They'd reach back again and again to pull away the wet fabric, but it was all in vain. How you wanted desperately to go cheek to cheek, but in the heat one couldn't imagine anything worse than hot, clammy skin on hot, clammy skin.

During the day little moved. People sit under trees drinking lemonade. The Bungalow Bar Man does a brisk business. Some flavors already sold out. The streets smell of melted asphalt. Even the birds find it too hot to sing. Their chorus is taken over by armies of cicadas, chirping their high-pitched song. The air-conditioned movies are packed. No one seems to care what's playing.

The poor draft horses, dying in their harnesses when the mercury soared.

For the truly damned—the subway. Did the inventors of that dirty, screeching, jolting device ever imagine how brutal those interiors would be during a July heat-spell? A hell on wheels.

And yet, in my memory bank those childhood summers return, in some ways wrapped in the most endearing of cherished memories.

Our Bronx Lanai

While I was growing up in the thirties, we were exposed to a whole array of sounds and smells and experiences that are denied today's generation. In the days before most families could afford refrigerators, the ubiquitous ice truck was a familiar sight and sound on every street. And I remember the horse-drawn fruit and vegetable wagons that used to roam our streets, their hawkers crying out their produce in a musical jingle: "watermelons, fresh lettuce, just-picked corn." Bungalow Bar and Good Humor Ice Cream trucks were there too, jingling their familiar bells, and always mobbed by kids clutching their nickels. Finishing our chocolate-covered delights; we anxiously looked to see if we possessed a LUCKY STICK, which meant a free ice cream bar.

We always lived on the top floor of our apartment house at 1704 Seddon Street. I guess the rent was cheaper. Walking up those five flights on those warm summer evenings, I was privy to every dinner conversation. In the heat of the late afternoon, our neighbor's doors were left ajar to catch any errant breeze. I was often invited for a glass of lemonade or a taste of freshly cooked pasta. The kitchens must have been veritable Hades.

Climbing those stairs, I'd smell the corned beef from the Irish IRT motorman's first floor flat: Mr. Rooney. In ever-rising progression, there'd be roast pork and sauerkraut (Schneider), real Neapolitan spaghetti sauce (Gentile), and fish cakes (Loeffler). It was difficult to pass up those enticing aromas. By the time I reached number 57, our apartment, my mouth would be watering.

Along the way I'd also pick up all the local gossip—who was having a baby and who wasn't supposed to be having a baby. Who had just lost their job—a common occurrence, and a score of arguments, mostly about money. Fellow sufferers in St. Raymond's would call out—"Jackie, do you have the homework done yet" Can I copy it?"

In spite of the climb, being on the uppermost floor gave us an "in" when it came to staking out a good spot on our apartment house roof, which was always open. Everyone had those elaborate folding beach chairs that defied assembly, and most Saturdays and Sundays we'd repair to our "penthouses," –fore-runners of all the present day condominium lanais perhaps. The views were terrific. At night, we could see the Operating Room at Westchester Square Hospital; sort of a precursor to "ER." Completing our vision were St. Raymond's Church, and prior to 1939, the dreaded Protectory.

Living on the top floor also gave my mother another edge. When supper time approached and I was playing with my friends in one of the vacant lots a block away, she'd lean out the window and in her Ethel Merman voice call out to me: JACKEEE! I could have heard her in Yonkers!

At the time there was a great fear of infantile paralysis—the scourge of children and the dread of every parent during the first half of the century. No one knew how one caught it, but there was some belief that the local waters were not safe for swimming. On hot Saturdays, my sisters would often be lumbered with me, taking me to Castle Hill or Bronx Beach Pool, when they'd much rather be with their girlfriends trying to attract boys. One day, a terrific electrical storm suddenly came up and everyone retreated to the shelter of the locker rooms. I was hustled into the girls' section, but I was much too young to appreciate any sinful views I might have seen. At storms end—they put a bathing cap and a long towel on me, and passed me off as another girl! The pool was never as much fun as the real ocean, but no one wanted to risk polio.

But it was the summer evenings I recall the best. Dusk brought little relief as the brick walls, which had absorbed the sun's heat all day, radiated it at night. With the apartments effectively transformed into ovens, everyone moved outside. Folding chairs would appear, and neighbors would sit on the sidewalk, socializing, listening to baseball games or just rocking babies to sleep. Cold beer and iced tea made their appearance, and glasses were passed around.

With very few automobiles, the open street was our playground. Ring-a-lieveo, Tag, Take a Giant Step and sundry other games lost in the fog of time occupied our evenings from after supper until it got dark. On weekends, we might be allowed to stay up a bit longer. Sometimes we'd sit inside the abandoned cars left in the lots and imagine we'd be driving. Some of the older boys utilized the shades on the back windows to broaden their knowledge of the opposite sex, but we had little interest in girls. Our hormones were still dormant.

When it was too hot to run my friends and I would find some level ground and play marbles. Marbles came in a variety of sizes and colors: boulders, pee-wees, shooters, puries, aggies and cat's eyes. It took some practice, but in time I became quite adept at the game. Soon I had a huge jar filled to overflowing with my "winnings." When darkness came, we'd often just sit on the stoop and tell ghost stories or talk about what we'd like to do when we grew up. Adulthood seemed so far in the distance that few of us ever thought we'd make it, remaining forever trapped in those miserable short pants and knickers.

Sometimes we'd just sit quietly, surrounded by those endearing summer sounds all around us: cicadas, crickets, mosquitoes, the rustle of heavy leaves, and a fading siren. In the thick air, distant noises were as clear as if they were next door. Two blocks away, the Tremont Avenue trolley rolled by, its distinctive bell accompanying the humming sound of steel wheels on steel tracks. A little after ten, when the traffic finally died away, it was the chimes of St. Peter's Episcopal Church on Westchester Ave that rang every fifteen minutes. Keeping me company all night, there was reassurance in every measured tone.

At various times I could even hear the Pelham Bay subway, resonating in the quiet darkness. Although the elevated tracks were a good half-mile away, every time a train negotiated the sharp curve between Zerega and Castle Hill stations, it produced a sharp, raspy, screeching sound—much like chalk on a blackboard that never was forgotten.

When there was a breeze, we opted for the roof rather than the street. Again the chairs were out, along with iced-tea, sarsaparilla, and some Hostess Cup cakes—those marvelous chocolate- covered treats that were filled with cream. Some of the Irish families drank their "iced tea" with a head on it. On occasion I'd be pressed into service "rushing the growler" for our neighbors who rewarded me with a dime—big money for a kid in those days. (The "Growler" was a quart-sized pail that was filled by the local bartender.) They didn't want to climb all those stairs, especially after they'd downed a few. None of the bartenders appeared overly concerned about selling beer to a ten-year old.

As portable radios were in their infancy and usually came with a heavy battery, we'd bring our own table model from the apartment and power it with an extension cord snaked from our window just below the roof. Then we could enjoy the programs in the open air. Listening to the "Witches Tale" or "Suspense" carried a far more terrifying wallop in the darkness. Some nights after an exceptionally frightening program, I'd be afraid to descend to the first floor where my godfather lived, especially when one of the landing lights was out. I'd run as fast as I could down those darkened stairs and corridors, thinking every moment that some Frankenstein creature was about to grab me and carry me off. All those movies left an indelible imprint.

With every window open, I could often hear music or an entire radio program with little interruption as I made my way along the sidewalk. The network schedule had a rare universal appeal completely missing today. Everyone from seven to seventy enjoyed staples like the Lux Radio Theatre, or the Bing Crosby show. The same went for the popular songs of the day. My mother would sing along with the melodies that my sisters, Rita and Dorothy, brought home on those Blue Deccas or Brunswick records, every bit as much as they would. Sinatra was my sister's rage, but Bing still ruled in our house along with Kate Smith. (I often think my mother liked Kate because they both had weight problems.) I drew the line at the Major Bose Amateur Hour on Sunday mornings, where a bunch of drippy kids warbled in changing voices. The only thing worse was the Catholic Hour where one was forced to listen to the rosary repeated endlessly. My father always retreated from that one, thankfully adding, "Jack, how about a walk." For that I loved him.

Today, for most of us, all those mid-summer outdoor sounds, smells and adventures are gone: stolen by air-conditioning. Where once we knew all our neighbors, we're now shut in behind closed windows and doors. A prisoner of an advancing technology, the companionship of neighbors and friends is replaced by the ubiquitous tube. A poor trade-off. Today, when one walks along the humid lanes in the evening, the over-riding sound is the whir of compressors in place of the rustle of leaves, the joy of laughing children or the tolling of church bells. When I was fifteen, Cole Porter wrote a popular song that captured like nothing else the limitless freedom we all felt in those open-air days and nights. It was called, appropriately enough, DON'T FENCE ME IN. It could easily have been our motto.

"Oh give me land, lots of land under starry skies above. Don't fence me in."

Let me be by myself in the evening breeze, and listen to the murmur of the cottonwood trees,

Don't fence me in."

In spite of the heat and all those sleepless nights flipping our pillows, we enjoyed a special magic when we roamed the streets in those never-to-be-forgotten times. We were as free as the birds in the sky above.

The earth spins and the calendar changes, but something is missing. They may still call it summer, but for me it's not the same, and I fear the season I once knew has changed forever.

When it got to be New York Mid-Summer hot, sleep often became impossible. Sometimes I'd just sit by the window and watch the planes on their approach to LaGuardia Field and wonder about all those inviting names in our big atlas. But we never traveled any further than my grandparent's spartan bungalow on the Jersey shore, about forty miles from the Bronx.

CHAPTER TWENTY-TWO

WATER WITCH

SS Sandy Hook

From 1935 to 1942, when I was between the ages of six and thirteen, I spent all my summers in a big clapboard bungalow on the Jersey shore with my maternal grandparents: Charles and Ann Ludwig. Water Witch, a town on the Shrewsbury River (actually not a river, but an inlet separating Sandy Hook from the Jersey shore) claimed my time from June until Labor Day. "Water Witch"— what a magical name for a six-year old. It rolled off the tongue. How I impressed my playmates in the Bronx. They attached all sorts of imaginative descriptions to the title.

My mother's side of the family, the Ludwigs, had just as varied a background as my father's ancestors. Her maternal grandfather, John Charles Martin (for whom I was named) was born in Worms, Germany in 1842. When he was 21 he immigrated to New York to avoid military conscription. Under sail, the voyage took 67 days, arriving in Manhattan at Castle Garden on March 17th, 1859. He sired ten children and lived until his 96th year. His wife, Helena Ahrens Martin was born in Holland, raised in England, and came to New York as a young girl. Her maiden name was Van Decker. My mother's paternal grandmother, Margaret Forbach was born in Brooklyn and while very young married Charles Ludwig. They had fourteen children. Charles also fought in the Civil War, giving me two great grandparents who were part of the Grand Army of the Republic.

The journey to the bungalow became one of the summer's highlights. Considering that the entire distance from doorstep to doorstep was not more than fifty miles, it entailed preparations that would rival an African safari. First there were the two subway rides from the Bronx to Fulton Street in Manhattan. Coming above ground on Broadway in the financial district, we walked the few blocks west to the Hudson where we embarked in a New Jersey Central ferry to Jersey City. There we boarded a steam train for the two-hour ride to Atlantic Highlands. As exciting as the train was, it couldn't match the alternative route by sea. I always hoped for the latter.

That voyage took place in the venerable day-liner SANDY HOOK. We were transported from the Lower New York Bay to the New Jersey shore. This was long before I had an opportunity to ride the Staten Island Ferry, so all these fresh experiences were indelibly burned into my memory. Viewing the imposing skyline with some of the world's tallest buildings, Governor's Island, Ellis Island, the Statue of Liberty, and finally the Narrows with Forts Hamilton and Wadsworth acting as bookends to the harbor entrance, was a treat beyond belief.

My initial sailing was everything I'd expected from the books and stories I'd gleaned about the sea. SANDY HOOK was big enough to impress an apartment kid from the Bronx, with three decks, one of them open to the sky. The throbbing engine, the screaming gulls, and the long bubbling wake, all combined to make me want to see this journey never end. Steaming along at a steady 15 knots, we passed close by a variety of freighters, tankers, Coast Guard cutters, and the occasional ocean liner. I waved at every sailor manning the rails and they always waved back. If

I was traveling with my Aunt Irene, the open deck became an excuse for an al fresco lunch of tuna fish sandwiches, cupcakes, and iced tea.

One westbound trip afforded me a brief moment in the sun. We were at the halfway point when I saw a cabin cruiser drifting without power. As we approached, a man on deck furiously waved his shirt for attention, but no one onboard our ship seemed to be paying the slightest attention.

We steamed on. I brought this to the attention of an elderly man who was reading nearby. At first he seemed annoyed that I broke into his concentration, but then he saw what I was talking about. He got up and ran up to the bridge. The captain slowed and changed course to bring us alongside the disabled boat. The owner shouted, "My engine died. I need help or a tow." "I'll send a Coast Guard. boat out to you. Just sit tight," the captain replied. Sure enough, about twenty minutes later we spied a Coast Guard cruiser at anchor. SANDY HOOK'S captain sounded his whistle, but no one appeared on the cruiser's deck. Again and again he blew the resonant blast, but everyone appeared to be asleep on the Coast Guard boat. Finally, after more than ten minutes a sailor came on deck looking more than a little sheepish. He brought the boat close enough to receive our instructions and then off he went at full speed. Later the captain came down to our deck and congratulated me. "Young man, I'm glad you had sharp eyes. No one in my crew noticed the boat in distress. He could have been drifting all night." It was the first recognition I'd ever received. It made feel very grown up. My Aunt Irene must have told that story a dozen times that summer.

This world of seafront bungalow communities, and a very definite world it was, was to me, completely new; an entirely different life. It was the nearest thing to a Tom Sawyer existence, and the best of all possible worlds. Today, enclaves still exist along the Atlantic waterfronts, but now they're filled with trendy condominiums, must of which are gated. Water Witch was essentially a working class summer retreat. At a time when few wives were employed, it was common for the entire family to move in just after school ended in June, with the father commuting from New York by train. To a six-year old city boy, it was a dream come true. Dirt roads, no sidewalks, no electricity, no telephone, no street lights, kerosene lamps for interior lighting, and the clincher; a great steam train from the New Jersey Central that roared by only a block from our house. Rounding a curve about two miles up the track, I could hear the locomotive's distinctive whistle, just enough time for me to run up to the corner and wave to the engineer, who unfailingly returned my gesture. Except for trips into "town" and Sunday mass, every boy went barefoot. I was soon brown as a berry. In the mornings my grandfather tipped me off to follow the commuters up the street, looking for any loose change that might have fallen from their jackets as they ran to catch the train. It was a rare day I didn't pick up at least 15 to 20 cents—a real find.

Our bungalow was built recently enough to have an indoor toilet and town-piped water. What we drew from the faucet was rather taste-less however, so we took advantage of a delicious alternative source. At the foot of the Red Hill there was an ice-cold natural spring. It was always known as the Red Hill, because of the copper-colored soil. Every evening, just before supper, I'd accompany one of my sisters or an uncle on that half-mile walk up the road with two gallon jugs to fill. It was my most pleasant daily chore. No matter how hot the day, the little shady grotto with the eternal spring was always refreshingly cool. Sixty years later, I can instantly recall that taste: distinctive, robust, zestful, and above all, thirst-quenching. I could feel its welcome coolness as it descended down my gullet—the wine of the earth rather than the grape. The most satisfying drink ever created.

Like most of the other beach houses, my grandparent's bungalow was constructed from a simple design. Except for a small-screened area on either end, it was essentially one big room. Sandwiched between these open porches, its forty-five foot length included the toilet (on the back porch), kitchen-dining area, and room for four double beds. This cozy shorefront family house ballooned to fill the needs of a myriad of relatives. To say it was basic would be an understatement. It was bereft of landscaping, it had no sidewalk, it was plain, it was uninspiring—it was heaven!

The bungalow

The Ludwig Clan 1931

Supporting beams held up a peaked roof. No ceiling. Everything open. Lacking interior walls; the sleeping areas were separated by piano wire from which draw curtains were strung. It was informal in the truest sense. But for my grandparents, in their strapped financial condition, to have this wonderful hide-away, less than two hours by train from Manhattan was a Godsend. From what I recall they bought the lot in the late twenties' and erected the bungalow for a total cost of something in the neighborhood of $2,000. With six surviving aunts and uncles, countless cousins, and my two sisters, we never lacked for company. The characters seemed to change with the tide. It was a very closely-knit brood, easy to laugh, quick to cry, and blessed with the power to squeeze life out of every waking moment.

This family chemistry was often most apparent just after everyone had said their "goodnights" and the lights were extinguished. It would be so quiet for a minute or two that I could hear the waves breaking on the beach. Then the action would commence. "You should have seen this miserable kid on the train coming down. He screamed so much everyone was trying to figure out some way to drop him out the window." Some aunt would relate a happening on the subway with a pincher, and soon there would be a half dozen conversations erupting just as if everyone was sitting around the big oak dinner table. Jokes would be exchanged and then just as quickly as it began, it would stop. Silence. Then a stifled giggle would be heard, igniting another round of laughter.

The nearest I came to these sleeping arrangement was in the Navy where the rows of bunks were out in the open. In the bungalow there was of course the visual privacy afforded by the curtains, but all the various body sounds were right out there. Burps and on occasion more basic noises. Each one set off another volley of laughs and shouts.

To get a rise out of my sisters or a female cousin, I'd often pickup one of my socks that I'd worn for perhaps a week or more, stiff from sweat and emitting a mighty odor. Quietly, I'd creep next to the unsuspecting sibling's chamber and toss the socks over the top. "Grandma! Grandma!, you know what Jackie just did?" From the turmoil emanating from that corner, one would have thought I'd thrown a grenade! Finally my grand-father would say, "Ok, That's enough. Go to sleep." And we did.

These post bedtime sessions occurred about every ten days and were a hallmark of every summer. They became known as "the crazy hours."

When the mercury rose to a point where the asphalt on the city streets turned to the consistency of Jell-O, an entire echelon of aunts, uncles and cousins would descend on us. Every bed was occupied. Two uncles even bunked on gliders on the front porch. One weekend, my Uncle Johnny, the sailor, strung a hammock on the back porch and was fast asleep in a few minutes.

By six-thirty the next morning, my grandfather would be up and about, leaving the rest of his brood dreaming away. Soon I'd hear the big coffeepot gurgling away, followed by the strong scent of fresh Java.

An alarm bell couldn't have had a more telling effect. Except for my younger cousins and me, everyone would be up making their way to the bathroom where a queue had already formed.

Two or three others, to whom coffee was essential to their regaining a full state of consciousness, sat at the table eagerly draining their steaming cups. It was only after all these morning preliminaries had ceased that the conversations began. Barely pausing for breath, my Aunt Irene would lead off. Others might trigger parallel exchanges, but it never seemed to slow her down. My father used to say that Irene would have talked through the San Francisco earthquake!

But as voluble as my aunts were, their husbands were nearly mute. Perhaps they were so geared to working among other men that they had no small talk with mixed company. Like cats, they never completely relaxed. I don't know. After the breakfast dishes were cleared away, the women sat around the table nursing a second cup and continuing their non-stop chatter. In contrast, Charlie and Hughie (Flo's husband) would sit quietly on the porch and devour the Daily News that I'd been sent to fetch. Oddly, I never experienced any difficulty in conversing with them—in fact I was often the subject of their discussions. "Jackie, let's go fishing? How about a walk to refill the spring water bottles? How about a swim?"

My father's branch of the family couldn't have been more different. There, the men dominated the daily exchanges, while their wives remained in the background. This marked contrast even extended to personalities. In the Ludwig family the eccentrics and joke-tellers were my Aunts Irene and Flo, while among the Sauters, it was my father's brothers Joe and Harold who added the spice. I never could figure it out. It probably defied explanation.

Billy, my Aunt Evelyn's husband, became a brief exception to this pattern when he joined the baseball team, the House of David where all the players wore full beards! I shouldn't forget Uncle George, who while not in the same age group (he was my grandmother's brother-in-law), was nuttier than both families combined.

Oddly, the people I saw least were my mother and father. I think they used the bungalow and the good graces of my grandparents to warehouse me for the summer. With both my sisters old enough to be on their own, my parents enjoyed a rare freedom without having me underfoot.

Having a storybook grandfather who loved and guided me, I never missed them.

At the foot of our street, aptly named Ocean Avenue laid the beach and the river. Roxy's long fishing pier took up one side with a flotilla of powerboats. The remainder of the sandy shore was pristine—no lifeguards, no beach chairs, and except for one small beachcomber's shack, just the sea and me.

Matty was a real beachcomber—a recluse who lived all year long in his small shack. Constructed entirely of driftwood and whatever odd pieces of lumber he could scrounge, it could have been the subject of a Norman Rockwell painting. He fished for food, did odd jobs, and kept mostly to himself. Other than my grandfather, I never heard him utter a word to anyone. As Water Witch was a 'live and let live" society, Matty was left alone. My grandfather used to say that he had an ideal existence. "Mattie sees every sunrise and sunset, takes his nourishment from the sea, and never has to worry about taxes or bills or family. He might appear lonely to some, but this is his way. He's tuned his life to the rhythm of the sea." Blackened from the sun, with a battered Captain's cap on his head, he could have passed for the "Ancient Mariner." The nearest living image of a storybook character I'd ever seen, I thought he was wonderful.

In front of the bungalow 1935

When I wasn't with my grandfather, I lived on the beach. Fortunately, the sandy bottom remained quite shallow for some distance from shore. A family story relates that one Sunday, at age four, dressed in my best, I wandered into the river. Noticing my blonde hair floating on the surface, an alert young man jumped in and quickly plucked me from danger. The very next day my grandfather taught me how to float and swim.

Perhaps my best beach time was walking the shore when the tide was completely out. Little eddies, trapped by the receding water formed tiny ponds on the flat tidal sand. As I took each step, a "piss clam" would spurt up on the side of my leg. It never failed to fascinate me, this early communion with nature. Inhabiting the shallows, hundreds of small scrimp, crabs and mollusks vied for my attention.

Wading in the shallow water, one could walk out twenty yards or so before the water reached his chest. During the summer the river was always warm enough to swim or float in for hours. The warm air and the cooler water were delicious taken together just before dinner. Sometimes I'd enjoy just sitting on the sandy bluff watching the boats, the gulls and the rhythm of the waves. As the afternoon progressed, the sea's color changed from aqua to light blue to deep green, and billowy clouds created images in the sky that drew dark curtains on the surface. When the weather was right, the wind and waves would sing a duet. Its mesmerizing effect let my imagination run wild. Deep in silent thought I'd often forget the time until someone came down to fetch me. The only intrusion into this reverie was the occasional start-up of one of Roxy's powerboats. This paradise was but a few yards from our front door, and it locked me into a lifelong love of the sea.

On Independence Day we hung out a much worn and faded Old Glory. Every bungalow did likewise. In those days, patriotism was a religion. Bay Avenue, our one main street, would mount a modest parade sometimes featuring an ancient Civil War veteran along with their sole fire engine, but for the big events we had to wait until nightfall. At dusk, all the houses emptied and everyone moved to the beach. Carrying beach chairs, blankets, soda, beer, hot dogs and whatever was leftover from supper, scores of adults and a battalion of kids settled in. A long makeshift grill sizzled with franks and hamburger patties, and huge bonfires browned marshmallows and "mickees." By nine it was as dark as only a beach can be with no artificial light. Then the real fun began. A mandolin or an accordion would be broken out signaling the start of a songfest. Nearly everyone would join in, especially my mother, if she was down, and Irene and Flo. No bashful Nellies here! "Over There, "Till We Meet Again, Mary's A Grand Old Name, Give My Regards to Broadway" and "My Gal Sal," echoed across the water. Everyone in my family knew all the words. And after one summer, so did I.

One year there was a contest to see who could sing the oldest lyric. As I recall it was either my mother or my Aunt Irene who sang a rendition of "A Spanish Cavalier," dating from the 1860s. There was no lack of memory genes in my family.

For us kids, the best part of these affairs was our ability to remain up long past our usual bedtime. Primarily we were there to watch the fireworks display that commenced around ten o'clock. Suddenly, the blackness was punctuated with soaring rockets, Roman Candles, and brilliant showers of bursting red and gold streamers silhouetted against the night sky. It was a night we never wanted to end. With those glorious images ricocheting in our heads, the thought of sleep was impossible. Returning to the bungalow we broke out our flashlights. Except for Bay Avenue, Water Witch had no streetlights.

On warm evenings, we'd often just sit outside, talking, drinking iced-tea, or gazing at the stars. Without the distracting ambient light of the big city, Water Witch had its own copyrighted brand of enveloping darkness—total blackness. Never had I seen such a galaxy of stars and planets, and after awhile I could imagine myself floating in the Milky Way.

All those lazy summer days were enjoyed mostly in the company of my maternal grandfather, Charles Ludwig, beloved by everyone. I was the first grandson, and as such, received far more attention than anyone should have deserved. He taught me all the things that my father would have normally engaged in, had the times been ordinary. But the Great Depression was anything but ordinary, and my father, like most men, was scrounging for any work he could find.

Charlie, as everyone called my grandfather, had an incredible imagination. He knew how to entertain a six-year old boy on a rainy day without the benefit of any toys. Lining up four chairs, he'd make me believe that they weren't kitchen seats, but railroad cars. The tallest chair became the engine, and to it he attached a dinner bell. Other times he'd fashion a long wash line and tie tin cups and utensils to it. Pulling this the length of the bungalow— about fifty feet, I felt like an engineer. Some wealthy client had given him a set of ivory dominos and I spent many hours learning all the tricks of that ancient game.

He didn't smoke, but his snuffbox was never far from his hand. I can still vividly recall that sharp, tangy smell—strong but not repellent. In his early sixties he was essentially retired—not by choice, but simply because his skills had become redundant—a victim of changing tastes and bad times. A skilled decorative plasterer, he carved those intricate designs on ceilings and walls found in luxurious homes. He was also a master gilder, finishing brackets and sculptures in silver or gold. With the onset of the Depression, new construction, notably the lavish buildings he was called upon to enhance, became a memory. During my summers in Water Witch, he worked on and off for Harrison Brothers in Manhattan, and supplemented that with a small pension. His loss was my gain, and I have imperishable recollections of our precious time together.

Whether it was fishing from a pier or picking blackberries, it was a learning lesson, but always a pleasurable one. In between threading a fishing hook or batting a ball, he had a limitless supply of stories, usually humorous. He could make fun of the pompous, without being nasty. When I couldn't remember my evening prayers, he came up with one I've never forgotten.

"Now I lay me down to sleep.

I pray the Lord my soul to keep.
If I should die before I wake,
How do I know I'm dead?"

If you were ornery, he'd say, "If you don't be good, I'm going to make you eat five ice cream cones after supper!"
He could make up short verse seemingly on the spot.

"A peanut was sitting on the track.
His heart was all-aflutter.
Along came the 5:34
And now he's peanut butter!"

An inveterate baseball fan, every Sunday afternoon when the rest of the family was sleeping off their chicken dinner, he'd sit glued to his small radio, listening to Yankees, Giants or Dodgers. Since we were at the extreme range of the New York stations, one of my chores each spring when they opened the bungalow was to climb up to the top of the roof and secure a long aerial. Sometimes he'd take me to a night game at Atlantic Highlands, but most of the intricacies of the sport eluded my young mind.

Other hot days when the ubiquitous cicadas were deafening, he'd lead me up the "Pirate Steps," to the top of the Red Hill. Local legend had it that Captain Kidd buried his treasure nearby, and every summer there would be eager visitors digging for it. Another memorable attraction for this kid from the streets of the Bronx, were the Twin Lights, the only double lighthouse on the coast. My grandfather would ask the keeper if we could come in to see the giant revolving beacon, and he always agreed. Climbing the hundred steps to the top, we'd marvel in the view over Sandy Hook and the great Atlantic stretching to the far horizon. On sunny, bright days, the tall spires of the Manhattan skyline were clearly visible.

Sometimes we'd scour the hills for blackberries, always returning home with two buckets overflowing. The only drawback was the berry fields were infested with poison ivy, and I got it, but good. However, that annoyance was soon put behind me when I sat down to the marvelous berry cakes that my grandmother would whip up. With money in short supply, we "ate off the land," so to speak. To be totally accurate, I should say we ate off the sea. Most of the sport fishermen who went out in Roxy's big powerboats were only interested in posing for pictures with their catch. They were more than glad to give my grandfather a huge tuna or swordfish, from which he created many meals. On the beach, a child's pail and shovel were the only tools needed to dig up a bushel of clams. I was often happily enlisted in this task. And back in the kitchen, my grandfather had some special signature dishes that were memorable.

His clam chowder bore a close resemblance to the French "pot au feu," where a multitude of ingredients would be tossed in the pot to simmer for hours on the stove. Besides the clams, he added potatoes, peas, carrots, onions, celery, corn, and green peppers. All these preparations would be accompanied by an unending stream of patter—the spice of language seemingly just as essential as salt and pepper. As there was no phone and family members would often arrive unexpectedly, the simmering pot would be topped off with whatever was handy. The aroma was unforgettable. Another of his favorite recipes was called "frikadellen." I thought that he made the name up, but it turned out to be a German dish. These were patties made from fresh meat that he put through his own grinder. Besides the meat, he'd add eggs, onions, thyme, bread, garlic and seasoning. Fried with meatballs and mixed in a heaping plate of spaghetti, it became a favorite dinner. Both of these concoctions were relatively inexpensive and easy to prepare. That all the ingredients were grown nearby made all the difference.

Aside from what was on the stove, the over-riding aroma in the bungalow was kerosene. This oil by-product powered all the lamps, as well as the stove. Everyday at dusk, my grandfather would check the oil level at the base, remove the lamp chimneys, and light the wick. It was the stuff of Tom Sawyer. Two houses removed, I noticed a power line extending from a pole onto the roof. Electricity! The O'Brien's weren't wealthy. The father was streetcar conductor. We had gas and electric in our Bronx apartment, so it couldn't be considered an extravagance. But when you were seven and a guest in the house, you didn't ask those questions.

Back at the beach, one of my most enduring recollections was observing my grandfather floating immobile in the sea for an incredible length of time. Apparently he learned how to keep just enough air in his lungs to remain buoyant without moving. In a jovial mood, he once donned his derby while suspended in the water, and was photographed wearing it.

When the war broke out, the army moved in from their base just across the river in Sandy Hook. When I arrived in the summer of 42' barbed wire was strung across the beaches and anti-aircraft emplacements dotted the tops of the hills. Odd-looking antennas rotated from the Twin Lights—the hush-hush radar. That first winter and spring of the war were times of heightened tension. U-Boats were sinking tankers practically within sight of land. On the beaches of Long Island, only fifty or so miles to the east, a group of German saboteurs had landed from a submarine. They were quickly apprehended, but it proved just how vulnerable we were. So as not to silhouette our ships, all the advertising lights along the shore were extinguished or dimmed. After suffering terrible losses, our Navy finally followed the British system of convoying all our freighters and tankers. With wire strung across the beach, and armed soldiers patrolling the town, I imagined I was truly living in a "war zone." These happenings generated exciting stories to tell my playmates in Unionport. By July 4th, however, the army seeing the horde of beach invaders removed the wire.

Weekends at the "bungalow" were always special. Lacking a bathtub or shower never stood in the way of clean ears or shampooed hair. For those four and under it was a galvanized tub that made do, but for the rest of us it was the hose and a bar of soap. Fortunately, the pipes ran close to the surface so the water remained lukewarm. With neither gas nor electricity, there was no hot water heater. I'll never forget that intoxicating feeling of freshness after drying off. My skin actually tingled. Suitably groomed for Saturday night, we'd break out the flashlights and make our way up the five blocks of dirt road, always pot-holed and full of water every time it rained, to Bay Avenue (suitably named). This was the Broadway of Water Witch—all ten blocks of it. Sometimes we saw a movie: no concern over "R" or "PG" in those days, the Hays Office took care of that. My favorites included "Made for Each Other," with Carole Lombard and James Stewart, and the British classic "Four Feathers." But the real treat was a long anticipated visit to an original Carousel, located just before the bridge to Sandy Hook.

Built some thirty years before, this fantastically elaborate apparatus was mind-boggling to a ten-year old. Like the wheels of a locomotive, every piece seemed to be in constant motion. The grinding calliope music was no doubt original as well, and a perfect accompaniment to what in my eyes appeared to be an "infernal machine." Horses and seats were exquisitely crafted. Spinning round and round and up and down to those distinctive chords, I became giddier and dizzier with each revolution. In the middle of each sequence, a long bar would swing out from the side, holding a sleeve of rings. If one reached out as far as he could, he could just about snare one. The older boys were so proficient that by leaning way out from their horses; they could grab two—a sort of double-clutching. Every fifty or so rings contained one fashioned of brass—a ticket to a free ride!

Charlie and Ann Ludwig

Around the periphery of these extraordinary rising and falling horses were a profusion of games. My favorite was a glass box that held a crane with claws that one could try to position over a prize. Mostly, I came up with a piece of candy or empty. For the older patrons there was something resembling bingo or lotto. Since no one had much money, the cost of a game was usually ten cents.

When I had my limit of rides and my head was still whirling from the movement, the lights and the music, we'd step outside and prepare for what was always the final treat of the evening—a visit to the old corner drugstore with the long, marble soda fountain counter. Walking slowly back with my hand firmly inside my grandfather's, we could hear the pounding surf from the ocean just beyond the bridge. Sandy Hook was our breakwater, always keeping the Shrewsbury calm.

Inside the brightly-lit drug store, my grandfather would proudly lift me into one of those high leather covered stools that he'd first spin a few times for effect. Then we'd both sit down to a banana split. From the look on his face, I think he was having just as much fun as I was, if not more.

Sundays were serious business then, not only in the big city, but even in a beachfront community. It's astonishing when I recall how everyone dressed compared to today. Without a car, it was a thirty-five minute walk—almost all uphill, to the church in town. "Sunday clothes" was not just an expression. Everyone wore their best suits and dresses. The hottest days always seemed to come on Sundays, but it changed nothing. My grandfather would never venture forth without donning his black woolen suit with a vest, a starched white shirt and tie. Matching this handsome attire were gleaming black shoes and sharply creased trousers. Topping off his outfit with a derby, he looked so elegant I hardly recognized this man as my grandfather. This Sunday "uniform of the day," was shared by every adult male in town. My grandmother (not to be outdone) walked to mass encumbered with a long dress and several layers of underwear, including an uncomfortable corset. And never without a hat. Both my grandparents were drenched in sweat before they reached the church steps. To say they were devout would be a gross understatement. Returning home, there was always a stop at the bakery for rolls, crullers, and jelly doughnuts. No sooner had they reached the bungalow than preparation began for the main meal of the week—usually roast chicken. After dinner it was naptime in the heat of the day for the adults and the beach for me. The routine never varied.

Thinking back, when he was raising his eight children during the early years of the century in a railroad flat on the Upper East Side of Manhattan, my grandfather probably had few opportunities to lavish attention on any of his brood. The struggle to simply survive took all of his time. As the only grandson, I lucked out. It was only when I stopped going to Water Witch that I discovered how much I loved and missed him. That was in 1943, the same summer he died.

My grandfather explained many mysteries during those memorable summers, but there was one I had to return to the pavements of the Bronx to solve: girls.

CHAPTER TWENTY-THREE

FIRST KISS

Her name was Helen Quinn (you don't forget those things), and she was visiting from some fabled, exotic land—New London, Connecticut. We were the same age—eleven. One hot evening in June 1940, there were a half-dozen of us hanging around some house on St. Peter's Ave. (the street where I was born). The girls began to talk about the movie stars of the era—Clark Gable or Joan Crawford, and how they kissed. One of the girls asked me if I'd ever been kissed. "Sure," I said. "I've been kissed hundreds of times by my mother, my sisters, and my aunts." "No, no," she replied, "I mean REALLY kissed by a girl". I said, "No, but I don't think there's much difference."

We decided to see what the fuss was all about, but no one had the temerity to initiate an encounter. In the end we settled on "Spin the Bottle," a game that took the decision out of our hands and left it to fate.

I spun the bottle and it stopped in front of Helen. Secretly, I was over-joyed as she was the prettiest of the lot, but I had to act as if I couldn't care less. My accidental "partner" was about my height, clad in a white cotton dress that accentuated her red cheeks and hair. But what riveted my attention were her freckles. She had them everywhere.

The rule was you had to stand behind a parked truck in the driveway where it was dark. I was just as glad because I didn't have a clue about what I was doing and didn't want to look bad in front of my peers. Helen and I took up our positions, and fortunately for me she placed her hands on my shoulders, drawing me in. Our closed, wet lips met and the sensation was little different from all those past pecks from my female relatives. But we lingered, keeping our lips pressed together, figuring that's what Gable and Crawford did. My eyes were open, but

I saw that she'd closed hers. I closed mine, but it didn't seem to add anything to the experience. I enjoyed looking at her pretty face, so I saw no reason to blot that image out. Covering all bets, I settled for sort of half-opened eyes.

Neither of us wanted to be the first one to break away, so we probably held that kiss for about two minutes. By then it was getting a bit sloppy. I could feel her saliva running down my chin. We finally broke and returned to the group. I kissed two other girls that night, but somehow none of them had the lasting effect of Helen's embrace. There was nothing sensual about it. We were light years away from that. Locked in an embrace, breathing in her clean, unique scent, and the touch of her hair on my cheek, made this a special evening. That exquisite feeling of a very slender and bony body pressed against mine carried it a step higher.

Up until that moment, girls were a non-entity—kids that couldn't throw a ball very well or whom you teased by pulling their pigtails. In Catholic school we were separated by gender, so I had little contact with the opposite sex of my age, except for a cousin or two. Eleven years old or not, this creature was different than anything I'd ever felt before.

Helen was the first girl of my own age that I'd ever observed closely. Like a budding rose, she was teetering on the brink of young woman-hood. Unconsciously, she was also stirring something mysterious deep inside me—a sensation I couldn't begin to describe, but it was not unpleasant. She was probably my first signpost on the road to maturity, but I only became aware of this much later. If nothing else, I'd never look at girls the same way again.

Helen went home to Connecticut after that warm June night, more than sixty years ago, and didn't return to the Bronx. But I never forgot her. After Helen, the summer season would always be defined by that first kiss.

CHAPTER TWENTY-FOUR

UNIONPORT

In the late thirties, my neighborhood was an ideal place to spend one's childhood. Except for a few apartment houses, the streets of Union-port exuded a small town atmosphere. Empty lots dotted the landscape; bare weeded areas that provided us with an ideal platform to erect our huts and act out our fanciful adventures. One space, in particular, was situated between my apartment and the Westchester Square Hospital. Whatever I was doing, re-enacting some recent action film or roasting "mickees," my mother had a bird's eye view from our fifth floor apartment. When suppertime approached she called me with a stentorian voice that still rings in my ear.

1704 Seddon Street was cookie-cutter Bronx apartment house. A five-story walkup, with a center courtyard entrance, it was home to fifty-nine families. I spent my formative years here —1930 until 1942. Between the Great Depression and the Second World War, very few tenants moved. Everyone knew each other. Six of my classmates lived here, and the majority of the families were parishioners at St. Raymond's church. Friendships blossomed.

When cold weather precluded playing in the lots, we went ice-skating at one of the public parks. My father had been an outstanding skater, so our front closet had five pairs to choose from. He was so small that I could wear his skates when I was nine or ten.

My sister Rita was often employed as my chaperon. Five years my senior, she taught me how to ice skate, roller skate, ride a bicycle, dance, and just about everything except how to get around girls. That would long remain a baffling mystery. But with two sisters and a strong mother, I was taught to respect the opposite sex and was inculcated with the best set of manners in the East Bronx. I became every mother's favorite, but

it didn't help me with their daughters. That would be trial and error—
mostly error. At that stage in my life, the only girl I was in love with was
Rita. With looks like Deana Durbin, it wasn't difficult.

Rita and Dorothy 1939

By the time I went to St. Raymond's, my older sister, Dot, was already
in high school and shortly after, working to help the family survive. She
had a string of fascinating boyfriends who often brought me treasures
that they'd outgrown: comic books, models, picture cards, penknives,
and rubber balls. So, although I had no formal brothers, I had plenty of
surrogates.

Dot imagined herself a "glamour girl." Taking after my father, she
had a slender figure that looked inviting in any wardrobe. She used it
to great advantage. Being the oldest, and joining the labor force as a
teenager, gave her an emotional and "street-smart" maturity beyond her
years. Dot never lacked for boy friends.

Lana Turner was her model and she emulated her every style and
gesture. While not as close to me as my younger sister, Rita, Dot was
always generous with her time and never refused to give me a helping
hand. I was very fortunate to have two such affectionate and under-

standing siblings. If nothing else their actions enabled me to embrace a lifelong corollary: I LIKED GIRLS.

Having sisters brought some other advantages. Even a cursory observation revealed that these were very separate creatures from boys. I was barely on the cusp of puberty, but I enjoyed their close proximity for reasons that weren't apparent at the time. Their elaborate morning and evening routines made me thankful that I was born a boy rather than a girl. Spending long minutes in the bathroom—of which we had but one—plucking eyebrows, applying nail polish, combing their hair, straightening the seams in their stockings, applying face cream and seeing how they looked in this dress or that blouse. With two of them to contend with, they needed a great deal of "lead time" if my dad and I were going to leave on time for work and school. In contrast, my father and I could wash and dress and be on our way in ten minutes. We were an overture: they were a grand opera! There was no doubt that both of them looked and smelled infinitely better than we did— they always did. Beyond the makeup routine, the apartment reflected their woman's touch in every room.

My mother of course always tried to influence them. She was a great believer in marriage, which at that time was the only respectable career for a woman. Those who couldn't snare a man (no matter how bad a catch he might be) were considered lacking in some essential element of their gender. My mother's point was well taken. It's not that women need men, but that people need partners. You can't go it alone. It's too hard, and it's unnecessary. It's true that in marriage you have to give a little. You have to close your eyes to certain things. But it's a cold world, and everybody needs a home fire to come home to. Marriage is worth the compromises. From what I observed with my father, my mother certainly knew that. Her philosophy was unshakable. She believed every word of it. It was her faith.

One evening Rita and Dot were discussing the latest movie. Who was a better lover—Clark Gable or Lawrence Olivier? When they went out my mother began to iron. I sat at the kitchen table doing my homework. My mother had a far away look in her eyes as she sat down across from me. "Listen to them. Who is the better lover? What they don't know about love could fill a library." She turned off the iron and made a cup of tea for the two of us. I had the feeling that she wanted to tell me something, but didn't know quite how to start. "I'll tell you about love," she said all at once. I didn't know what to expect, wondering perhaps if I was going to hear the truth about the birds and the bees from this unlikely source.

"Love is a lot more than kisses and embraces, although they have their place. Love is many little things." She held up my father's clean, pressed shirt. "You see this? Pressing your father's shirt just the way he likes it is my way of showing my love. Having his dinner, hot on the plate when he comes home is another way. When I do these things for him it's like I'm pressing kisses into his collar or I'm embracing the meat and potatoes on his plate. This probably seems strange to you. That's not the way Clark Gable or Bette Davis do it in the RKO Castle Hill. I hope when you're ready to get married you'll find a woman who thinks like that. Those are the things that keep a marriage strong. Remember that."

I was surprised and more than a little relieved at her philosophy. It made a great deal of sense. My mother and father had been married for more than twenty-five years and still seemed very much attracted to each other. I was far too young to delve any deeper into her explanation, but it certainly was working for her. In school we were taught to offer up everything we did to God. I guess my mother was just taking a sliver of that belief and aiming it towards my father.

But being surrounded and influenced by females had its downside. With no older brother or father who took an active concern in my development, I was easily bested in street fights. Fortunately, I ran across few bullies in my neighborhood, and my sense of humor gave me a ready popularity. With my family background, I had an endless catalog of stories and jokes. In a pinch I could also run like the wind.

While in grammar school I engaged in few competitive sports. For example, I was seventeen before I learned to swing a baseball bat, and football remained a mystery long after that. As a result I was rarely, if ever, chosen to be on a team. I sat on the stoop and watched them. Even when they were short a player, I was passed up. They took it for granted that I'd be no good at stickball or football, and they were right. Short for my age, I lacked even the most basic coordination. I was just as glad that I wasn't asked to make a fool of myself.

At the time I didn't understand that there were other compensations for those not blessed with athletic ability, but it would take a move to a new neighborhood to introduce me into worlds undreamed of. I wasn't a complete outcast, however. Once the sun set, I came into my own.

On the warm summer nights when it was even too hot to play tag or ring-a-liveo, we sat on the apartment house stoop and told stories. I had no problem with coordination here—I reigned supreme. I had just entered my Edward Ellsberg phase of wonderful deep-sea diving tales and these adventures locked my friends in rapt attention for hours on end. This, of course, was a subject they knew nothing about. I was breaking new ground. Incredibly, as they hung on my every word, my stuttering disappeared. My father had a complete collection of Edgar Allen Poe's stories and they became the favorites of my recitation. For Poe, I'd break out a flashlight and have my listeners all move into a dark space in an alleyway, rendering Poe's frightening scripts a special cache. THE PIT AND THE PENDULEM and THE BLACK CAT were asked for again and again. Listening to a fearful mystery told in the dark is one of the most unnerving experiences imaginable. It also gave me a much-needed degree of anonymity to alleviate my insecurity. In truth, once I began a tale, I became totally absorbed in it and never gave what I was accomplishing a second thought. It was the first time I was better than anybody at something. In this endeavor I gained a self-respect, which I'd never had.

I enjoyed singular exercises—skating, rowing, swimming, running, climbing and walking. I found that competing with myself was far more gratifying than engaging in team sports. In truth, whenever I had free time, I was far more apt to have a book in my hand than a bat or a ball.

CHAPTER TWENTY-FIVE

CRISIS: THE SUMMER OF 1940

Brother Peter became our teacher at St. Raymond's when Germany invaded Poland in September 1939. Britain and France declared war on Germany a few days later, but their action had little effect on the fighting in Poland. In a month, it was all over. Having signed a non-aggression pact with Hitler in August, Russia entered the war in mid-September, and by agreement, occupied the eastern half of Poland. Britain sent an expeditionary force to France to help bolster the French Army which was holding a long front along the Belgian and German border, but they never engaged the Germans. France had the largest standing army in Western Europe, but their forces lacked mechanized divisions. More important, as it turned out, they also lacked good generals. Essentially they were preparing to fight World War I all over again. Unfortunately for the Poles, the only "offensive" action taken by the Allies against the Germans was the dropping of propaganda leaflets!

I was becoming very knowledgeable about these events simply because Brother Peter, in an assignment, made everyone in the class choose a stock from the NY Exchange and follow its progress through the school year. My father suggested AT&T. In a few months I became a lifelong reader of the NY TIMES. Its newsstand price was but two cents, so it didn't tax my personal finances. At first, I found the paper utterly dull, since unlike most of the all the other dailies, it contained no comics. (The NY Herald-Tribune was in the same boat.) But being a history buff, I soon began to read the detailed accounts of the Maginot Line and stories about life in the French and British armies. The Maginot Line was a series of French fortifications stretching from the Swiss border to Belgium.

Right after Poland fell, everything became "all quiet on the Western Front." The period from October 1939 until May 1940 became known as the "Phoney War." There were some exciting battles at sea with German pocket battleships, but for the most part there was little to report. I followed my stock, AT&T, with eager anticipation. My father complimented the brother on encouraging an interest in the stock market at such an early age. Aside from its detailed coverage of war news, the Times couldn't hold a candle to the News or the Journal. To make matters worse, the paper had very few photographs. But things were about to change with incredible speed and the results affected everyone in the world.

In April the Germans invaded Norway and AT&T became an afterthought. This was heady stuff—German paratroopers capturing airfields, Norwegian batteries sinking Nazi cruisers, and the landing of a British expeditionary force at Narvik. With absolute control of the sea, the Royal Navy destroyed most of the German naval forces, but the Germans ruled the skies. Pretty soon the tide of battle changed in their favor. Britain was forced to evacuate their troops from Norway. Brother Peter asked the class, "Can anyone tell me why Norway is important to the Germans?" I thought it gave them a long coastline with access to the Arctic and the Atlantic, nearly impossible to blockade. Brother Peter replied, "Very good, John, but there's another reason. Control of Norway is critical to the Germans because it protects their supply of iron ore from Sweden. And you were right, it also gives them hundreds of miles of seacoast—something they lacked in their homeland. It seemed that he was even more enamored of the campaign than I was. Everyday our blackboard was covered with maps of France and England. Most of the class was bored, but I was in my element.

While everyone's eyes were on Norway, the Germans hurled more than 70 divisions against the Belgian Army. The Germans had perfected the combined use of dive-bombers and tanks to smash through and demoralize the opposition. Blitzkrieg! The main British and French armies moved into Belgium to meet the attack.

On the French-Luxembourg border far to the east, there stood a rugged and heavily forested area called the Ardennes. It was thought to be impassable by tanks. Because of this, it was lightly defended by inferior troops. But the Germans had thoroughly reconnoitered the terrain and possessed the right equipment to open a path for armor. This they exploited with alacrity, utterly surprising and crushing the French Ninth Army. Within a week the Germans crossed the last natural barrier, the Meuse River, at Sedan.

Once on the other side of the Meuse, little stood in the way of their Panzers. They were inside the Maginot Line and racing for the channel.

The British Expeditionary Force and the French armies in the north desperately tried to disengage and move south to reform a new line, but the roads were choked with refugees who were continuously harried by Stuka dive-bombers. On May 20th, the Germans reached Abbeville on the English Channel effectively cutting off the entire First French Army and the BEF. The Germans had split the allied forces in two!

In the next week the allied troops formed a bridgehead around the seaport town of Dunkirk. On the evening of the 26th, the Royal Navy began to evacuate men from their encirclement. At first it was thought that only 45,000 men could be saved, but the Admiralty ordered every boat available on the coast of England to gather at Dover. Incredibly, 338,000 men, including many French troops were rescued. However, all their trucks, tanks and artillery remained on the continent. Britain, except for the RAF and her navy, was essentially naked to her enemies.

I followed all these momentous events with great interest in the pages of the Times. By now everyone else was watching the unfolding of this critical battle with a feeling of shock and dread. That the largest standing army in Europe could be defeated in a few weeks was nearly impossible to digest. For the first time, America looked vulnerable. Only England stood between Hitler and the Western Hemisphere. Now Congress began to act, authorizing huge expenditures for ships, arms, and planes. A peacetime draft was enacted, albeit for only a year. But armies are not trained in a day or squadrons of bombers built in weeks. Time was not on our side.

On the 23rd of June, France asked for an armistice.

In the spring of 1940 the US Army and Army Air Corps totaled 210,000 men. We ranked seventeenth in the world! We had almost no tanks and only a handful of bombers. Our Navy was in better shape, but soon it would have to defend two oceans with forces hardly capable of defending one. To make matters worse, the French Fleet was immobilized, but still within reach of the Nazis. If Britain faced defeat, it wasn't out of the realm of possibility that she would use her navy—the world's largest, as a pawn in the settlement. Then Hitler, along with his allies: Italy and Japan would have overwhelming dominance in every ocean.

The Battle of Britain commenced almost immediately. If the Germans could force a landing in England, there was little doubt about the outcome. During that fateful summer, while the Nazis prepared for their invasion, all America watched and prayed. Our choices were few. Who could imagine a worse scenario? Given the Nazis track record, everyone expected an invasion of England, followed by a quick German victory. To muddy the waters further, we were in the middle of a presidential election. F.D.R. ran for a third term, breaking with tradition. He seemed the logical choice to lead us at this time, just as Churchill was on the other side of the Atlantic.

Hitler's air chief, Herman Goering felt that he could bring England to her knees without a seaborne invasion, using air power alone. The RAF was a formidable foe, with excellent planes and well-trained pilots. But Goering knew as well as the British, that the ranks of their veteran airmen had been sharply depleted by the battles in France, especially the evacuation of Dunkirk. So it would be a war of attrition, grinding down the British air forces under the heel of the Lutwaffe's overwhelming strength. Meanwhile the Germans began massing hundreds of small vessels to carry their troops across the channel. But after facing mounting losses during the summer, Goering decided that he couldn't win the war by defeating the RAF. He switched tactics and concentrated on bombing London. He would destroy British morale and the people would sue for peace. A fatal mistake.

In the end, the British withstood the raids and they continued the fight. Hitler finally turned his eyes to Russia and attacked her in June 1941. The invasion was canceled.

I didn't mean to tax the reader with descriptions of bloody battles, but at the time every eye in the Bronx and America was focused on Europe. For the first time we felt threatened. The summer of 1940 brought more national apprehension than even those dark months after the attack on Hawaii, and the startling advances of the Japanese. We all knew that Hitler was the number one priority.

While the isolationists remained very strong, public opinion was shifting in support of aid to England. Some people in Washington felt that we should keep all our weapons for our own defense, weak as it was, but the administration rightly gave Britain all aid, short of war.

This debate fueled the presidential campaign, but fortunately, the Republican candidate, Wendell Wilkie, was, at heart, an internationalist. When he became privy to the state of our armed forces, he fully supported our arms shipments to Britain. In November, FDR was re-elected to an unprecedented third term.

It would be a little more than year before we were attacked at Pearl Harbor—December 1941. In retrospect, that breathing space allowed us the precious time to start to shape what would become an army of five million men and a navy second to none. In the global war that lay ahead, we would need all the trained soldiers, sailors and airmen that we could muster.

CHAPTER TWENTY-SIX

A NEW NEIGHBORHOOD

It was just after we became involved in World War II that both my maternal grandparents died. We just had a telephone installed—a sign of our new affluence, when we received our first call in the middle of the night. A pre-dawn ringing telephone has the same dramatic effect as having a telegram delivered to your door. Invariably, it's never good news.

My grandmother had been suffering from heart disease for as long as I could remember. Nitro pills were always in evidence. Her heart attacks were common, but her medication had always brought relief. That night however, in her New Jersey bungalow, she awakened after midnight with a special kind of pain—one she knew was fatal. Having no phone in the bungalow, my aunt Flo had to run up to the corner to a pay phone to summon help. Grandma Ludwig was gone before anyone arrived.

I was 12 then and she was the first dead person I'd ever seen. Of course, laid out in a casket, she looked as if she was sleeping. When I was brought in close (much against my wishes) I could see the gray color of her skin. As I knelt there saying the rosary, I was overcome with a desire to see what death did to someone, so I softly touched her hand. I pulled back quickly, but the feeling lingered—dreadful. She was like stone: cold and hard. That awful touch gave me nightmares for a long time.

My grandparents were very devoted to each other. Even in their sixties my grandfather could barely keep his hands off her. When she died, his internal life ended as well. It was as if a light went out inside of him. When her casket was being lowered, he leaned over and said, "You won't be alone long, Annie. I'll be right along." With that, he lost his will to live. Eighteen months later he was gone as well. I never realized just how much he meant to me until then. His death closed a whole chapter of my life.

In the fall of 1942, for reasons that still remain unclear, we moved a little over a mile to Gleason and Olmstead Avenues in Unionport. Again we were on the top floor, with five flights of stairs to negotiate. Our new quarters were larger, however, and after the long ordeal of the Depression, I think my mother just wanted to change her luck. I later discovered that my parents had lived in this same building just about twenty years earlier when they were first married. Oddly, the rent was about the same! Looking back, she got her wish. From that time on, the Sauter fortunes rose.

I was not happy with the move, however. For all the difference to me, it could have been another state. Not only did I have to change schools, but I had to absorb and acquaint myself with an entirely new neighborhood and array of friends.

Initially, I was shattered by the news. I'd been allied with this same group of schoolmates for close to eight years, and at that age, it's a lifetime. Suffering through a series of oddball teachers and principals, it was an experience that demanded closure. Spending years together, we were not only fellow students, but had shared confidences and established strong bonds of friendship, not easily duplicated. Several of my close friends were in the same marching band, so I pleaded with my mother to be allowed to roller skate to St. Raymond's and remain until graduation. After all, that goal was only seven months away. From our new apartment on Gleason Avenue, the distance was about a mile, all down hill on Castle Hill Avenue. I managed this easily enough all through September, October and most of November. I don't know what I planned to do when there was snow on the ground, but I never had a chance to find out. One day, gliding along with the wind at my back, I hit an indentation in the asphalt and fell face down in the street with some velocity. I was lucky. I wasn't scarred or permanently disabled, but I wasn't home free. My lower teeth went clean through my upper lip, but far worse, one of my front teeth was badly chipped. There was no money for an orthodontist even if we'd ever heard of one, which I strongly doubt. I lived with this distinguishing characteristic until I was thirty-five when I had a front bridge of capped teeth installed. That incident effectively sealed my farewell to St. Raymond's.

A new neighborhood is hard enough to absorb, but a new school and a whole set of new classmates made it doubly difficult. My teacher was a nun. Like the sisters at St. Raymond's, Sister Ann Veronica was Irish, and I immediately had two strikes against me. My name was German, and to make matters worse, I'd been inserted in the middle of the school semester-giving her extra work to bring me up to par. In our initial encounter, Sister Veronica glared at me, as if I was an annoying form of lower animal life. The dislike was instant and mutual.

My first hurdle was algebra, a subject this class had been studying for ten weeks. I took one look at the blackboard and cringed. $2X - Y = 15$. I thought I'd stumbled into a Greek class! Luckily, basic elementary algebra isn't too difficult to grasp, and a fellow student, Jenny McCoy, far more brilliant, and blessed with unlimited patience, took me in tow. I managed to pass, but just. A few years later I had an opportunity to repay her, but at the time I never would have imagined it. The rest of the curriculum was similar to my old class, and in some subjects I was more advanced. But the major change in study and a hostile teacher was more than offset by the biggest and most delightful difference between the schools—girls!

For the very first time in my life I had fifteen young females to observe up close; seven hours a day, five days a week. More than half of them were fourteen and had already reached that marvelous plateau: puberty. As it turned out—so had I! Observing their shapely bodies, none of them could be mistaken for boys—soft or otherwise.

Unlike many Catholic schools St. Helena's had no formal uniforms. The boys wore shirts and ties and the girls wore dark skirts and white blouses. And how some of them filled out those white blouses! Fortunately, all those bodies had their backs to me most of the time. I only went off track when one of them went up to the blackboard or had to give a recitation. I never heard a word. Because I was a new arrival, I was something of a celebrity for the first few months and got along famously with both sexes. As this was a brand new school, everyone was in the same boat. It was a bit like boot camp—nobody knew anybody else. So we were all experiencing the same pains of acclimation. My sole antagonist was Sister Ann Veronica.

St. Helena's church and school had just been completed before Pearl Harbor brought the wartime restrictions on steel and other vital materials. In contrast to St. Raymond's, it smelled brand new. I was to be in the first graduating class—June 1943.

My initial surprise came at Christmas—not from the school, but the pastor. Monsignor Scanlon was an unusual priest. He had just turned sixty-five and St. Helena's was his first church. By most odds he should have been thinking about retirement or a soft spot at some university, but he expressed a strong desire to finish his years in parish work, something denied him before, and his wish had been granted. He'd certainly paid his dues, spending his career teaching at St. Joseph's Seminary. In nearly every religious book we used, he was the censor. Scanlon held a doctoral degree in Sacred Theology, but a more human priest and one dedicated to practicing Christ's teaching never lived. It was this side of him that endeared him to his congregation.

The very first time I heard him speak from the pulpit I knew I was far removed from St. Raymond's. There were collection envelopes—this time weekly, but that's where the comparison ended. Scanlon said, "We have an envelope system. What you give is exclusively between God and you." The envelopes provided an essential ingredient lacking in the former parish—privacy. "If you don't have any money, put a button in the envelope. I use red ones", he told his parishioners, "my associates, black!"

For Christmas, instead of asking us to pressure our parents into contributing to a special collection, he gave every student in his school a gift: photo albums and wallets.

He had a magic touch. If he made a request for twenty men to help with the annual bazaar, fifty showed up. His bazaars were so successful that he paid off the close to a million-dollar debt for church and school in only seven years. At a time when the gambling laws in New York City were still very strictly enforced by La Guardia's reign, St. Helena's was running dollar-for-a-dime wheels in the schoolyard bazaar. The precinct officers were all weekly communicants!

Indoor roller-skating had long been a popular past time, but the war gave the sport a huge boost in popularity. Gas rationing severely restricted the pleasure use of automobiles, so young people looked for diversions closer to home. Never one to pass up an opportunity to engage his parishioners, Monsignor Scanlon utilized the school auditorium as a skating rink. As one of my previous birthday presents was a pair of indoor roller skates, along with the necessary carrying case, I was ready and eager to join in.

I took to indoor skating energetically, having been quite proficient on outdoor metal wheels. The sport also afforded teenagers an ideal excuse to visit all the local and not so local rinks. One was treated like to a world traveler, in that each rink awarded the visitor a colorful decal to adhere to the outside of his carrying case, just as these prestigious hotels used to identify their guest's suitcases. In a few months time I sported patches from FORDHAM, RIDGEWOOD (New Jersey), GAY BLADES (near Times Square), and MOUNT VERNON. More important, this sport attracted a multitude of attractive young girls who wore the briefest of costumes. I rapidly learned all the basic roller-skating dance steps: Circle Waltz, Collegiate, and Barn Dance. As St. Helena's School was but three blocks from my apartment, I spent many free hours practicing. It wasn't long before I became a part time guard, allowing me almost unlimited access to the auditorium.

One evening in May, I was doing the Circle Waltz with Catherine O'Brien, a neighborhood girl three years my senior. I was in heaven whirling this pretty young thing across the floor, when her skate struck a hardened piece of gum, pitching us backward. I tried to break my fall with my right arm, but only succeeded in breaking it. Catherine broke her collarbone. I would spend four weeks with my arm in a cast. Roller skates were really doing a job on me.

That December I celebrated my 13th birthday. While I was still the youngest in the 8th grade, I began to look upon my female classmates with more than a passing interest. One pretty Irish girl, Margaret McVey, soon had me gaga, only she never knew it. I thought about Margaret, dreamed about her, acted out a hundred fantasies, but never uttered a word to her. But my erotic daydreams seemed to elicit as much guilt as pleasure. All those Catholic teachings had made their mark. She lived about fifteen minutes away by trolley car, and many afternoons I'd ride the same car just to look at her. Love had me in its clutches. A sweet torture I was to experience again and again. It was painful, but I was addicted. I later discovered that I wasn't alone in this dilemma. A tough initiation to becoming a teen.

CHAPTER TWENTY-SEVEN

GLOCKENSPIEL

After the Christmas break it was back to the tough regimen as Sister Ann Veronica strove to get as many of her pupils into the best high schools. The largest diocesan high school for boys, Cardinal Hayes, had just opened in 1941. It was the crown jewel of Archbishop Spellman's tenure. While they accepted more than a thousand students every year, most of these were shuffled to annexes throughout the Bronx for their first year. An elite band of one-hundred pupils were accepted at the Main Building on the Grand Concourse. Most of these "geniuses" belonged in places like Regis, but their parents couldn't pay the tab. Hayes was essentially free, heavily subsidized by the diocese.

That March, I went down to this enormous white building to take the entrance exam. If I didn't make the cut, it would be a public high school for me. Nothing wrong with that—most were excellent, but my mother had her heart set on a Catholic education for her only son. I had never taken a multiple-choice exam before. By the time I figured out how it worked, I'd used up half my time. I was sure I'd failed.

Just prior to the exam, there was an announcement over their public address system— something else totally new to me—directing anyone who could play a musical instrument to the auditorium later in the afternoon. I was numb anyway, so I joined a small mob heading towards this cavernous space that if nothing else, strongly resembled a smaller Radio City Music Hall. Once inside there was a series of quick auditions. Quick wasn't the word. You had maybe ten seconds to show Father Zeimack, the music director, that you had the right stuff.

Strongly influenced by the popular instrumentalists of the day, there was a multitude of "Harry James'" playing the trumpet and "Gene Krupas'" on the drums. I'd been playing what was called the "bells" in a marching band since I was ten, and had memorized most of the popular marches and the hit songs of the day. I had accomplished this by what is commonly called "playing by ear." When I approached the imposing Father Ziemack, he asked me what instrument I played. "The bells, Father, "I stuttered out, and pointed to one of two sets standing on the stage. He answered sarcastically, "They're not bells, stupid, they're called glockenspiels. Take some music and play a few bars." "I don't need any music, "I replied, and that brought an even more caustic reply. "Play something, damn it!" I picked up two mallets and proceeded to play the Stars and Stripes Forever. After a few bars Ziemack smiled and said, "You're in. You're my glockenspiel player." I had no idea how rare I was.

Playing the glockenspiel in the American Bluejacket Band 1944

I returned to St. Helena's and the school year inexorably drew to a close. Letters of acceptance came in to Ann Veronica from St. Barnabas, Cathedral, Power Memorial, Fordham Prep, one from Regis to the class Einstein, and seven from Cardinal Hayes—all to a local annex. I had nothing. I was resigned to my fate.

Then one morning in late May I was summoned to the principal's office. There stood Ann Veronica with the biggest smile I ever saw on a nun standing next to the "boss," Sister Prissima. (Where did they get those names?) "John," the principal said, "We're very proud of you. I must say you surprised us. You've been chosen to go to the Main Building at Cardinal Hayes." Ann Veronica almost fell over herself congratulating

me. I think if Prissima wasn't there, she'd have hugged me. I was mysti-
fied. I'd completely forgotten about the musical audition.

If entering high school wasn't a big enough hurdle, an even greater
one loomed— my first job.

CHAPTER TWENTY-EIGHT

THIRTEENTH SUMMER

There was a lot going on in the world on that last Sunday in June 1943, besides my graduation from grammar school.

In the Mediterranean, British and American forces were about to invade Sicily, after having recaptured all of North Africa from the Axis. On the other side of the world in two climates that couldn't be more contrasting, Attu, in the Aleutian Islands had just been secured from the Japanese, and thousands of miles to the south, we were slowly slogging our way up the Solomon chain, island by bloody island. World War II was nearly four years old and our involvement had lasted a bitter 18months.

In New York City, we were settling into a wartime routine. While no bombs fell, there were occasional air raid drills and blackouts, meat and gasoline rationing, and scrap metal drives where many a favorite aluminum pot disappeared when our mothers had their backs turned. The Great White Way became a memory as lights were dimmed to prevent the U-Boats from silhouetting our ships off the coast. In every movie theater, the heroic image of our war-weary President drew instant applause.

A few months earlier, a rather unusual musical opened on Broadway. Unlike anything previously seen, all the pretty young girls wore dresses down to their ankles and never appeared in a chorus line. The plot concentrated wholly on cowboys and farmers, sure death for a New York show. And yet, coming on the scene in the second winter of a dreary war with precious little good news, "Oklahoma" was just what the doctor ordered. When it closed five years later, it had broken all existing records for the longest-running musical on Broadway.

In my own family, our fortunes had recently improved. My father had finally found permanent employment with the Empire Trust Bank as a stock analyst, a position he would hold until he retired in 1964. In the grip of the Great Depression, he'd been out of steady work since 1932. This sea change was also evident in a noticeable upsurge in his painting activity. He was now turning out brilliant watercolors, one more exquisite than the next. With his employment secure, he could now concentrate on his first love—painting. This monetary improvement was also reflected in our spacious new apartment, just outside of a huge complex called Parkchester.

My mother spent her days as a bookkeeper at the Unique Balance Company on Alexander Ave. in the South Bronx. My older sisters, Dorothy and Rita, held secretarial positions with AT&T and The Great American Insurance Co. respectively. My sisters and my dad all worked within a few blocks of each other in the financial district of lower Manhattan. As my mother belonged to that school of parents who believed that "an idle mind is the devil's workshop," I would soon join my sisters and father in that morning subway ride on the IRT.

Graduating from St. Helena's grammar school on a Sunday afternoon, I was hustled off early the next morning into the heart of the city—my dreams of a lazy summer with friends at Orchard Beach, remaining just that: a dream.

I didn't know it at the time, but that decision of my mother would put my life on "fast forward," and catapult me into adolescence with a capital "A." These next few months were going to be the most tumultuous in my entire life. First job, first time in a school that wasn't within walking distance to my home, settling into a new neighborhood, and discovering the joy and fascination of girls. My body was also undergoing changes that for the most part were a total and puzzling mystery to me.

I was perched in that never-never land where I was neither child nor man. Similar to a ship on the ways, where for a testing moment, the vessel teeters precariously between land and sea I was ready to try the waters of maturity. But the job was first hurdle. The other challenges would be met down the road, so there was little sense in worrying about them.

I'd been on the subway many times before, usually to visit my mother's parents on East 96ᵗʰ St. On other occasions, my father would take me on a Sunday outing into the depths of Manhattan, painting vivid pictures of what the city was like during the Revolution when Indians roamed the land. He was well versed in the city's past, and we'd walk the narrow alleys of the financial district for hours. I learned how he felt in his first job as a runner and messenger, and how he read everything about the history and background of what was then collectively called "Wall Street."

On that Monday morning, I accompanied my dad and sisters to the Castle Hill Avenue station of the Pelham Bay Line of the IRT. Rita, my closest sister in age (five years my senior) worked as a legal secretary for the Great American Insurance Co. on One Liberty St. It was she who was instrumental in getting me this summer job. I just about made the grade as I was barely 13, and most of my associates were much older. But the war had snared most of the young men, and having a relative in the company worked wonders.

Nobody spoke much in that long ride into lower Manhattan. Squeezed into a subway car that was stifling hot and deafening, just breathing was a major accomplishment. The subway had a unique smell that once experienced, was never forgotten. The sum of many parts, it drew its "perfume" from among the following: warm transformers, lubricating oil, and decaying food from sandwiches past. Add to this mix, the odor of a hundred bodies, mostly unwashed. A weak fan barely rustled the heavy air, and the only real breeze, albeit heavy with heat, humidity and grit came from the open windows. After the train passed the high bridge over the Bronx River, at Whitlock Ave., we quickly descended into a gaping black tunnel just before arriving at Hunts Point station. That would be the last daylight I'd enjoy for nearly an hour until we exited at Fulton Street. Underground it was a roaring and putrid ride that lasted interminably.

Coming up the steps into the blinding sunshine, my father and older sister Dorothy, went their separate ways, and left me with Rita. Sensing my trepidation she cautioned, "Don't be nervous, the job will be fun." But inwardly I was terrified. It's more than a little tough to enter the adult world at thirteen, but the die was cast. We walked down Liberty Street from Broadway, and in a short while we were next to a huge castle-like structure, built of massive granite blocks. This was the Federal Reserve, the place where all the money originated in New York. Armed guards stood outside and armored trucks rumbled in and out of an underground garage.

One of the first things I noticed was the manhole covers leaking steam. I'd seen similar pressure escapes before in films about volcanic eruptions—namely Vesuvius. I had no idea what manner of geological disturbance lay beneath my feet, but I didn't tarry that morning. I wondered perhaps if this had something to do with the security of the Federal Reserve. I would solve that mystery later.

Great American Insurance Co.

Before I could fully absorb this new image, I became aware of another sensory shock. My nostrils were assailed by a pungent odor that for a moment defied identity. All at once, it came to me: the strong smell of burnt coffee. Rita explained that most of the ships from Central America disgorged their coffee cargo only a few blocks away, and the beans were roasted nearby. This distinctive aroma hung like a cloak over the entire area, and remained for all the years I spent there.

Across the street from the Federal Reserve stood an odd-shaped structure; one that closely resembled the famous Flatiron building on 23rd St and Fifth Ave. Only 18 feet shorter than its famous look-alike, it was a beautifully corniced, white-brick, slender pie-wedge structure set down at the confluence of Liberty and Maiden Lane. I didn't know it then, but this would be my primary working home until I enlisted in the Navy seven years later. Sadly, it was demolished in the mid-seventies just to widen the street for more cars.

Built in 1907, it was originally called The German-American Insurance Co. With the coming of the First World War, anything named "German" was quickly changed. Since all the corporate logos were "GA," someone came up the name GREAT American Insurance Co., and it stuck. By 1943, only a few old timers had any recollection of the original designation.

While forty years is not considered "old" for a steel and brick commercial building, the rapid strides in high-rise construction had left this narrow slab decidedly dated. A modest façade broken by a flight of front steps led to an elaborate entrance. Once inside, it was all marble balustrades and fancy brass and ironwork. Four banks of hydraulically run elevators took up most of the lobby. The entire first level was open with only an occasional glass wall separating the private offices. But before I could absorb every detail, I was whisked up to the 10th floor to meet the people I'd be working with.

As soon as I stepped out of the elevator I realized just how small and narrow this place was. Thirty-five paces would bring one to the end, or front of the building. If nothing else it resembled a ship with the bow facing the East River and Brooklyn. For obvious reasons, all the executive offices were located here.

I was taken to Mr.Gieser, the Assistant Comptroller. He gave me a strange look, wondering perhaps how someone so young could have gotten working papers. He rose from his desk and put out his hand. "Welcome to the Great American Insurance Company. I won't tell you anything about your job. It's very simple. Just follow the instructions of Mr. Arntz. He's in charge of your department." "Department" I discovered, was a rather inflated description of our operation, as I was the only employee besides Arntz. He had a first name, which some time later I learned was Henry, but no one ever called him anything but Mr.Arntz.

Dickens would have loved him. A short, compact man, he carried himself well. Like a character from another age, he still wore separate-collared shirts, usually striped, adorned with a fancy tie clip and gold cufflinks. One could have cut bread with his sharp trouser crease, and his highly polished shoes would make some Marines envious. Like other men his age, Arntz wore those calf-high shoes—a style I didn't see again until I was issued a pair in boot camp. His age was a mystery—I was a long way from being able to judge that aspect of a man or woman, but I'd guess that he was over seventy. He gave the impression of someone who'd once owned his own business, but he never spoke of his past. At my age it wasn't a subject that was broached. He exuded a genteel affluence. Arntz could have passed for one of the bosses, except for the fact that he was a nervous wreck. For whatever reason, he acted as if his job was the most important thing in the world, and maybe it was.

From the very first day we got along fine. I was a very neat dresser and he told me that he admired that in a man. "John, I see you're wearing a white shirt and tie. That's good. I'd like everyone in my department to dress like you. Did you just get a shoeshine, or did you do that yourself? "Mr.Arntz, I don't have money to waste on shoeshine blacks. I always shine my own shoes." He smiled. One of the habits I acquired in the American Bluejackets was polishing my shoes every morning. I took great pride in having the best shine in the building. I was flattered by his remarks, since it was the first time that anyone had ever referred to me as a "man." "Your duties are simple," he explained. A long table that ringed our "office" contained a dozen open boxes—one for each floor that we serviced. These receptacles held the letters and parcels that the mail department would fill in the morning, and periodically during the day. Later, inter-office messages would compete for space in these cubicles. "Your primary task is to keep those baskets empty by carrying these letters and parcels to offices on the various floors. Sometimes you'll have to deliver packages to other banks and insurance companies, throughout the city, but mostly in lower Manhattan."

I wasn't "on the job" an hour when I had my "baptism of fire." "Here's your first delivery, John. Take this package of checks to the Chief Cashier at the First National City Bank on Wall St." I was directed to walk west on William St. for three blocks. I couldn't miss it. I'd heard of the "canyons" of New York, but until I strode alone among them, I never appreciated how intimidating they could be. Reaching Wall St., I was faced with an array of imposing granite facades—all suitably dressed with soaring columns. Not having a street number, I finally turned to a huge Irish cop standing on the corner. He was so tall I had to strain my neck to see his face. "Excuse me," I said in my most polite manner. "Could you please tell me where the First National City Bank is?" He glared at me with the hard look of someone being made a fool of. In a thick brogue he said, "How long have ye been workin' here, lad? " I said about an hour. Breaking into a wide smile, he muttered, "If it had a mouth, it'd bite ye." With that, he turned and pointed just behind him. There in letters six feet tall was a title cut into the gray chiseled granite: FIRST NATIONAL CITY BANK OF NEW YORK.

It was a good lesson. If you were polite, the police and just about anyone else would give you good directions.

Delivering these letters and packages was the best part of the job. Within reason, my time was my own, and I had ample opportunity to fully absorb what to my 13 year-old mind was a truly exhilarating experience. Nothing I'd seen in the Bronx could match the sights on nearly every block.

On my initial lunch hour, I headed for the river, only three blocks away. The cobblestones were still glistening from a recent shower as the first storefront brought me up short. There, sitting in full view sat five middle-aged men in shirtsleeves, all rolling cigars. I must have looked shocked as the one nearest to the open door invited me in. I don't think he spoke English, but he took some tobacco leaves from a stack behind him and demonstrated how he fashioned a cigar. The aroma was sweet in a strange way, and although I'd never smoked anything, I could see the allure. I'd often been pressed into service fetching cigars for my father from the corner candy store, but I had no idea where they came from or how they were made. It was a revelation.

The river was a beehive of activity. Another odor, far more powerful than the tobacco, and much more familiar, hit me like a fist. Fish! I was standing right next to the famous Fulton Fish Market. Not much was going on now, mostly workers loading the last few trucks and hosing down the street. Chatting with these burly men wearing long rubber aprons and boots, I learned that all the action here took place while I was still in dreamland in the Bronx—between 5 and 6 A.M. At that time, scores of fishing boats unloaded their catch from the Atlantic, and the food stores and restaurants bid for their produce. A few weeks later I made up a good story to leave the apartment at 5 A.M. so I could view the operations I'd heard` so much about.

The subway was nearly deserted at that hour, something I never experienced again.

Fulton Street announced itself with bright lights and the only open business for blocks around. The open sheds resounded with the shouting of sellers and buyers and the slamming of hundreds of fish-laden boxes into waiting trucks. Hand-trucks clattered by, groaning under the weight of more fish than I'd ever seen. Watching the mountains of boxes grow higher and higher, I was nearly run down by an electric cart scooting among the chaotic commerce. Fascinated by this strange, but enthralling parade of characters, I completely forgot the overpowering odor of seafood.

The East River

Unfortunately, the close proximity of all that fish left me with a lingering souvenir of my visit. I don't notice it at first, but when I stopped in a local coffee shop for some breakfast the counterman noticed my white shirt and tie and he inquired about my job. He smiled and said, "Young man, you're not going to be long in the insurance business with that stink surrounding you. Come around back in the kitchen and take off your shirt and trousers. Meantime, put on this apron." He took my shirt and trousers and deodorized them by the steam table. I discovered that being a kid has its advantages. Everyone goes out of their way to be nice to me.

It was a memorable dawn, but I decided not to share it with my family. My mother would certainly frown on my excursion.

But it was the river traffic that most fascinated me. Fulton Street was only a few blocks from the imposing Brooklyn Bridge, and just under that soaring structure stood a place of my dreams: the New York, or as it was more popularly known, the Brooklyn Navy Yard. What more could a history buff ask for? In these yards some of the greatest ships that ever sailed under the Stars and Stripes were built: the Civil War ironclad, MONITOR, and the battleship ARIZONA, sunk at Pearl Harbor. Here, great ships were constructed, and repaired. On that day I can see the outlines of the nearly completed battleship MISSOURI. The complex is closed for security reasons, but I later discovered that by taking a subway to Brooklyn, the train traverses the Manhattan Bridge directly over the yard. This afforded me a full and unimpeded view of everything from battleships and carriers, to cruisers and destroyers. I was only 13, but I'd been a Navy buff for three years and I couldn't find enough books for me to devour on the subject. But now, instead of just photos (which were all pre-war and woefully out if date), I have a chance to see the real thing. How different these warships look from the old pictures in my books— anti-aircraft guns on every open space, and those odd bedspring-like devices that grew from every mast. It would be sometime before I would learn that they were the hush-hush radar antennas that were always deleted from all the newspaper and magazine images. Later I would save up and purchase a small telescope.

From that time I would spend part of my lunch hour with my sister Rita on the 19th floor in her legal department. There I could read the small numbers on the bow and identify the name of the cruiser or destroyer as she sailed in and out of the facility. Earlier, I had made up a ringed notebook listing every ship in the U.S. Navy. No birdwatcher ever searched more diligently. Mr.Whealen, one of the attorneys Rita worked for, looked at my basic telescope and said, barely suppressing a smile, "Now I know that all the Sauters are Nazi spies!"

The view from the 19ᵗʰ Floor

Since the great Brooklyn Bridge dominated the entire area, it was just a matter of time before riding the subway across on its sister (Manhattan Bridge) would not totally satisfy my aspirations. As we worked only a half-day on Saturday, I told my mother that I was going to spend a couple of hours downtown with a friend, and then I navigated the entire span both ways. There's no way to do justice to the elation I felt perched high above the river, watching the fantastic procession of tugs, barges, tankers and warships all vying for space in the narrow river. How they avoided collisions, I'll never know. There were two other spans in close proximity: the Manhattan and the Williamsburg bridges, but somehow I was never drawn to walk them as I was to the Brooklyn Bridge.

As June eased into July, I gradually became acclimated to the area and my job. Our mail deliveries encompassed ten floors; the lower ten belonging to the Great American Indemnity Co.; a corporate difference I could never quite fathom. Since the majority of the employees were women, I was something of a minor celebrity in that I was much younger than anyone else in the building. And I didn't even look my age.

At this embarrassing stage of my life I was still known as "short legs Sauter." I would suddenly and inexplicably grow six inches during the fall and winter, but at this point, that didn't do much for my esteem. But my shortness of stature and what was to many a "baby face" made me immediately recognizable on any floor. The most common remark was, "Doesn't your mother know she's breaking the Child Labor Law." More than anything else my appearance forgave a lot of misdelivered mail, and soon I was every department's mascot. It wasn't long before I was pressed into service running little errands for the women and the few male employees who were not permitted to leave the building except during their lunch break. I'd bring them coffee and cigarettes and was always rewarded with a dime, or on payday, perhaps a quarter. This was big money for me.

BobLipeles with Harold Czubaruk in front of his parent's stationery store.

Generated by the war shortages, most staples were rationed. As a result, long lines of people seem to populate every street. Cigarettes were a big draw, along with nylon stockings. But purchasing cigarettes wasn't all that easy. Receiving only a small allotment of the popular brands like Chesterfields, Camels and Lucky Strikes, the canny distributors made the storekeepers buy another supply of some inferior company. As a result, Kools, Virginia Rounds and Fatimas were foisted on the public. Most of them tasted so bad that my customers just threw them away. But these "windows of opportunity" were short and not preceded by any warning. One had to be "Johnny on the spot!" As I had the run of the street, about a dozen male and female employees had me on sort of a "retainer." Every time I saw a line, I got on it without question. I was always carrying about five dollars of their money, and had a little address book to keep track of my purchases. Their tips helped me enhance my purchase of books and records.

The variety of accents, eating habits and the photos displayed on every woman's desk propelled me into a world I'd scarcely imagined. Their talk was of distant locales in mysterious boroughs I'd only seen on a map. Queens, Kings and Richmond were their formal titles, but not one in a hundred employees knew that Brooklyn was Kings, and Staten Island was Richmond. My neighborhood in the Bronx was equally baffling to them. The only familiar landmark was the home of the hated Yankees—Yankee Stadium.

Many of the younger girls pasted pictures of actors on the walls and pillars adjoining their workspaces. Alan Ladd, Loretta Young, Rita Hayworth and Van Johnson were big favorites. More than half the desks also boasted the smiling image of a soldier, sailor or marine—boyfriends, husbands, brothers or sons.

My daily allowance was a dollar. From that I had to pay my subway fare (roundtrip 10 cents) and buy my lunch. Often the office girls, especially the buxom Italians, would invite me to share a meal that they had carried from such strange-sounding places as Gowanus or Bensonhurst. Their lunch—usually a cold chicken cacciatore, or lasagna, was always large enough to feed a family. Every desk drawer it seemed held a box of chocolates. When that happened, I could skip lunch and bank the difference, using the money to buy a book or a classical album. Records were very expensive at that time—usually a dollar for each 12" disk, so I limited myself to one album of records every bi-monthly payday. Beyond these tips, I received an allowance of $5.00. This I received once a month, after turning my paycheck over to my mother. She was the family "banker," and everyone else followed suit.

In those days, a symphony album would usually comprise four or five records, all very fragile. No mother ever carried her baby more securely than the way I cradled that parcel on the subway. At this point I had amassed five classical albums, and much to the consternation of my sisters who were Artie Shaw and Frank Sinatra fans, I was wearing the records out. One album in particular: Siegfried's Funeral Music from Wagner's Gotterdammerung drove my sisters nuts. "Why would you want to sit indoors on a sunny day and listen to funeral music?" they'd ask. But the Toscanini recording was one of the most exciting pieces of music I'd ever heard.

My love affair with the classics had begun the year before in the darkened recesses of the RKO Castle Hill movie theater. There, in the middle of some forgotten movie, the strains of Wagner's Liebestodt from TRISTAN und ISOLDE lifted me right out of my seat and made me an instant convert.

What was the allure of classical music to a 12-year old? It's hard to put into words. Just about all the albums I listened to, symphonies, concerti, overtures and suites, had no program. It was pure music. But the themes had a pattern of development, and the melodic line often gave me an emotional "high" I'd never before experienced. Listening to the slow movement of Brahms Second Symphony, for example, I'd be shaken to my toes. I don't think this is something that can be taught. One can be exposed to it and if it takes, fine. I've never had similar feelings with other works of art. .

A few weeks after my movie experience I met Bob Lipeles, the son of the owner of the stationary store in my apartment building. It didn't take long to discover that Bob was a musician par excellence and extremely knowledgeable about everything I needed to know about this new art form. We became close friends—just the one I desperately needed in this new neighborhood. A new path had opened just when I needed one.

The dollar wasn't strong—it was prodigious! A man could think seriously of marriage on a dollar an hour. Small homes sold for five to six thousand, and used cars in the low hundreds. I'd often see signs in parked Chevrolets: "$50.00, as is!" It had been more than a year since a new car appeared in a dealer's showroom. We wouldn't see any new models until 1946.

Even pennies acquired premier status. There were penny post cards (postage on these was a HALF CENT!), two-cent newspapers, five-cent subways and streetcar fares, as well as nickel soda, beer and hot dogs. That copper (soon to be steel) penny, also bought gum, chocolate candy, and told your weight and fortune. Although the packs were sold for 15 cents, many candy stores offered single cigarettes for a penny. My sisters, Rita and Dot were regularly taken to Broadway by boyfriends, for dinner and a show. The cost for both: the incredible sum of five dollars! Restaurant chains such as Child's and the Automat, regularly served 45 cent lunches, and Chinese locations routinely undercut them. Jack Dempsey's Steak House on Times Square advertised a full dinner for $1.35! If this seems like a dream world, one must remember that these dollars were hard to come by. My pay for an eight-hour day—five and a half-day week, was $55.00 a MONTH! Granted, I was at the bottom of the totem pole, but even the Chairman of the Board took home only $25,000 a year.

Ad for Jack Dempsey's Restaurant on Times Square

In the Great American, the average salary for a male employee was about $1,800 a year.

During my office conversations with the women, I was astonished to learn just how provincial their attitudes were when it came to Manhattan. Raised in neighborhoods as contained and clannish as any Mid-western town, they looked upon the big city with deep suspicion. Crossing the East River, whether above or below ground, was a journey filled with trepidation—a trip to the unknown. In many respects they resembled the sailors of old who thought the earth was flat, and if one traveled too far he would fall off the edge. As a result they could never relate to my stories of all the remarkable discoveries I'd made on my daily rounds. None of them it seemed ever deviated from a well-charted path. Leaving the subway, they always walked the same path to 1 Liberty St. When they left the building to lunch or shop it was always on the same few blocks of Nassau Street, one avenue from us. Some of them had been working at that location for ten years and had yet to venture up to Broadway, City Hall or the Battery. Many had never walked the three blocks to Wall Street. It was as if they were modern Hansels and Gretels, dropping bread to mark their trail.

Perhaps once a year, at Christmas or Easter, their parents would venture to Times Square or Radio City, but this was hardly universal. I had to admit that most of my own family wasn't much different. My father, it seemed, was the only one with any interest in the history and background of the city.

Leaving the building for lunch brought another revelation. From noon until two, the area was so packed with humanity that nearly everyone walked in the street. With the war, there was little automotive traffic except for the occasional delivery truck. To make walking even more difficult it always seemed that the adjoining streets and sidewalks were being dug up. Under those manholes lay a myriad of pipes, cables and telephone lines, the ganglia of a 20th century city, and always in need of repair or addition. In a fashion unique to this section of the city, all the buildings were heated by a central source: New York Steam. Occupying an entire square block only a few hundred yards away, this huge generating plant supplied power by a network of steam pipes running just beneath the street surface. That's where all that escaping steam from under the streets originated on my first day on the job. This underground system eliminated the ubiquitous coal truck, a common sight just about everywhere else in the city.

The lanes of lower New York had been laid out by the Dutch when the town was called New Amsterdam, and hadn't been enlarged much since. Towering skyscrapers shoulder to shoulder, only made the feeling of confinement more intense. I soon learned that after the Empire State and Chrysler Buildings, the section below City Hall, or "Old New York," contained the next five tallest structures in the world. Sixty Wall Tower, The Bank of the Manhattan Company and the Woolworth Building were just some of the giants soaring into the sky. When the clock struck twelve, thousands of workers poured out into the crowded streets, making every noontime a veritable New Year's Eve at Times Square.

Restaurants abounded. One of the most unusual and one I never saw duplicated, was the E&B cafeteria (commonly known as Eat Em' and Beat Em"). Everything was on display and marked with the price. You were expected to remember what you ate and you told the cashier on the way out. She then calculated your tab. They had a spotter to make sure that nobody took advantage, but I never saw anyone being questioned.

Close by there was an Automat. A few years earlier I'd been introduced to this "children's paradise" of an eatery, and my fascination hadn't been reduced one iota by the passage of time. Upon entry, one immediately faced a middle-aged woman sitting in a booth like a sentry. Here she changed your large coins or bills into nickels. Watching her grasp a handful of silver coins and dispense the exact amount with a flip of her wrist became one of my favorite pastimes that summer. She never missed! Except for a hot plate section, which was beyond my budget, all the sandwiches and deserts were displayed behind little glass doors. One inserted the required number of coins and voila, the door would snap open. As many times as I went there, it never failed to astonish me. Their meals and sandwiches were always of high quality, and without a doubt, this was the best buy in New York.

Automat

Later that summer I stumbled upon the Quality Luncheonette, right next door, where I discovered their heavenly tuna-on-toast sandwiches. Accompanied by a Cherry Coke, the tab was 35 cents. From that day on, I ate exactly the same lunch until the job ended just after Labor Day! When I told one of my sister's bosses, he said, "Jack, you'd better be careful or you'll start growing gills!"

The Brooklyn Bridge was the highpoint of my "discoveries" until one day I had to make a delivery to the U.S. Custom House, located at the very foot of Broadway. This imposing structure was the most elegant architectural gem below City Hall, and perhaps in the city. The central hall contained a rotunda, ringed with imposing murals of maritime Manhattan. These were world-class paintings, but I discovered years later that at the height of the Depression the works had been commissioned by the WPA, and the artist was paid by the hour in typical 1930 wages! Another great artist, Daniel Chester French, sculpted the four huge statues that anchored this monument. He had also created the Lincoln Memorial and the Minuteman statue at Concord. Just below that impressive building lay the Battery and the Upper Bay; another intriguing body of water to rival the East River. Walking through Battery

Park, which contained the ruins of Fort Clinton and the Aquarium, I came upon a group of ferry slips and the entrance to the Staten Island Ferry. For only five cents I could sail round-trip across the entire upper Bay of New York harbor. In the distance I could make out the Statue of Liberty and Ellis Island. And on a clear day, even Staten Island was visible from the Battery. This was another borough I'd heard about in passing, but had never set foot on. My goal that summer was to at least visit Brooklyn and this mysterious island that was incredibly part of New York City. I was beginning to feel like Admiral Byrd or Vasco de Gama.

In past summers, I'd made the voyage across the harbor onboard the venerable SANDY HOOK and MANDALAY: the popular day-liners on the way to my grandparent's summer bungalow on the New Jersey shore. But now on my initial sailing I could take the time to really explore the shoreline and the various islands. Positioning myself as far forward as possible on the upper deck, I reveled in that constant warm breeze generated by the ship's speed. Governor's Island was immediately upon me and filled my vision. In 1943 it was an active Army command headquarters. Our ferry didn't stop there. They had their own boat and no civilians were allowed without a special pass.

On most Saturdays I'd make this round trip after work. How I envied those commuters on Staten Island, having the stimulation of a sea voyage every morning and evening in the open air, and privy to those magnificent vistas of the Manhattan skyline, while I in turn was condemned to traveling underground on the miserable IRT. I was astonished to learn that most them ignored the passing vista and couldn't care less!

Boasting the busiest harbor in the country, the waters were filled with ships of every description. Freighters and tankers vied for my attention with the occasional troop transport or warship. Often we'd pass close enough to wave at the seamen at the rails. We both secretly wished to change places, but I didn't know it at the time. Like most thirteen-year olds, I longed for adventure. In spite of the allure of all these foreign-flag ships, the vessels that most fascinated me were the long, low barges that carried railway cars from New Jersey to New York. New Jersey was the terminus of most of the eastbound rail lines, and the freight cars were piggybacked across the Hudson to be re-hooked in Manhattan. It never failed to stir my imagination: a freight train floating on the waters' surface! Nearly every out-of-town visitor was amazed at this sight.

Lady Liberty was a big favorite. Looking back, I find it strange that I never took the sightseeing boat out to Bedloe's Island and explored the interior. Perhaps I wanted to retain the enchanting aura of mystery that only a distant view could impart. Once the ferry reached the end of her run, I'd usually just remain onboard and walk to the opposite end in order to be at the best possible location for viewing the skyline. Returning to Manhattan, the skyline appeared to be rising above the water as if floating on air. Unforgettable. But one day I decided to spend the extra nickel just to say I'd once walked in another borough. Once past the terminal Staten Island was as bucolic as an upstate small town. Regardless, it seemed like an ideal place to live, especially in close proximity to the Big City.

All these initial explorations occurred within the first few weeks of my employment. Later I would learn that I'd only scratched the surface of Peter Stuyvesant's New Amsterdam. And right under my nose there was a whole new world within the confines of One Liberty Street.

CHAPTER TWENTY-NINE

INSIDE THE OFFICE

Aside from my sister's haunt on the 19th floor, most of my time was spent in the confines of our little messenger's office on the tenth level. Mr. Casey, our cashier, always had checks to be signed by the executives one floor below. Often there would be a bundle of fifteen to twenty drafts awaiting signature. Since the dispensing of cash was always a priority, Casey told me that I could break into any meeting by just appearing with his instruments. In a very short while I became acquainted with everyone of any importance in the company. I discovered that many long-term employees had never spoken a word to anyone higher than their immediate superiors. In 1943 there was an unbroken caste system far more stringent than anything in the military.

Again, my very youthful looks gave me a unique access to this inner circle denied to many. Most of them knew my sister and often asked about my family. The fact that Rita bore a striking resemblance to a Hollywood starlet didn't hurt. I soon felt far more relaxed in their presence than I did with Mr.Arntz. The Chairman of the Board, Mr. Phillips, took a particular interest in me, remarking at how resourceful I was to seek employment at so early an age. (If he only knew!) "John, I understand that you're only thirteen. I went to work on a farm when I was ten, but my grandchildren had everything handed to them. I wish they were as ambitious as you are." I didn't know it then, but in the years to come, I'd get to know him very well.

As pleasant as the top bosses were, it was their secretaries who treated me like the sons they never had. To these forty-something women, the Great American Insurance Company encompassed their entire world. Most of them lived with their parents, a common practice at the time. Unless some miracle occurred, they would spend their lives at One

Liberty Street. Any possibility that they might have met a young man in the company was sharply diminished by the war. But one former stenographer gave them hope. Jesse Phillip's wife had died just a few years before and he'd married his secretary. But those instances were rare.

At the other end of the hierarchy were the elevator operators, the only blacks employed by the company. I was always gave them a cheery "good morning," and quickly learned their first names. It was an unwritten law that no one ever addressed them by anything but their first name. At that time operating an elevator for a bank or an insurance company was a prized position for them, because it was usually a lifetime job with health and retirement benefits. Being nearly a constant passenger, I often traded jokes or discussed the war with them. All their other conversations were usually comprised of "Good Morning" or "Good Evening."

Like most other New Yorkers, I was raised in a racist household. Words such as "Sheenie, Coon, Wop, Mick and Spic" were common occurrences at the dinner table. (I never did discover, what, if anything, they called us German-Americans—'square-heads', perhaps.) But there was a difference. My father's art interest cut across many racial lines, and much to the consternation of my mother, we often had Negro artists (as the blacks were then called) for dinner and conversation later in the evening. This upset my mother no end, not so much because she didn't like these people (deep down she was a very tolerant and compassionate person who had struggled through the Great Depression), but simply because we lived on the top floor. Every time a Negro came to visit it was common knowledge on every floor in the apartment house. None of my parent's immediate family or their friends shared their viewpoint. I wasn't aware of it at the time, but this exposure to the inner life of these people, gave me a rare insight denied everyone I knew.

If I ran across one of the elevator operators in a luncheonette, I'd ask him if I could join him. A few eyebrows were raised, but I never gave it a second thought. I figured that if their company was good enough for my father, it was good enough for me. This put me in good stead with all of them. More often that not, they'd make room for me in a crowded elevator if they knew I was in a hurry to get home. I'd often wondered what their private lives were like, but that was an insurmountable gap in 1943.

My messenger duties continued to take me far afield, with new discoveries daily. Trinity Churchyard became a favorite hangout. Among the gravesites were Alexander Hamilton, Robert Fulton, and the Navy's heroic Captain Lawrence, most recalled for his dying words during the War of 1812, "Don't Give Up the Ship!" More solemn advice concerning the brevity of life and how we should address our mortality appeared on other ancient stones, now nearly worn away from time and weathering. It was always an oasis of tranquility in one of the nosiest and most congested parts of the city. In good weather, many office workers lunched there.

A few doors down Broadway loomed one of my prime places to visit—over and over: the Cunard Building. While the QUEENS and their smaller sisters were engaged in carrying troops, for the duration, the line was still very much in the freight business, albeit in convoys. Aside from a brilliant mosaic-tiled ceiling, the highlights for me were the large scale and extremely detailed models of their great ships; past and present: QUEEN MARY, BERENGARIA, MAURETANIA, and ACQUITANIA. These renderings were awesome—eight to ten feet long! I'd never seen any of these behemoths in the flesh, but my friend Bob Lipeles had recently introduced me into the fascinating world of ocean liners, and I was hooked. Many a Saturday afternoon I'd be stretched out on his living room floor, studying the deck plans and the gorgeously illustrated travel folders of such beauties as NORMANDIE, ILE DE FRANCE, EUROPA, BREMEN, AMERICA, REX and all the Cunarders. I didn't know it then, but many of them would never grace New York harbor again.

Further up Broadway stood the most elegant skyscraper of them all: the Woolworth Building. A gorgeous wedding cake towering above New York! My father had filled my head with hundreds of statistics, not the least of which was the fact that the Woolworth Building had been for some years the world's tallest. More intriguing was the fact that Mr. Woolworth had paid for the entire structure with one check: Fifteen Million Dollars! And all that from a five and ten cent business!

Next door was a lesser-known church: St.Paul's. It also held a secret. Hardly anyone was aware that George Washington had given his Second Inaugural Address from these steps. If another friend were unfortunate enough to be in my presence near these sites, I'd literally drive them away with all this extraneous knowledge. The location of his initial acceptance speech was easier to find. A huge likeness of the general dominated the front of the Sub-Treasury on Wall Street. Diagonally across was Broad St. where my father had clued me in to the free tour offered by the New York Stock Exchange. In time this became a great asset when I was pressed into service showing the visiting broker's wives the many jewels of historic New York while their husbands were at meetings.

New York summers were infamous, and 1943 was no exception. Air-conditioning was strictly reserved for a few top theaters: Radio City, The Roxy and the Capital. Warm weather fabrics were years away, and a "summer suit" was composed of light wool! Hats were de rigueur; the straw version remaining very popular.

Most men wore three-piece suits with white shirts and starched collars. Those who looked for comfort bought seersucker garments. While they were no doubt a lot cooler, the wearer looked as if he had spent the night sleeping on a park bench. The material defied pressing. It was one big wrinkle! I wore "hand-me-down" heavy woolen trousers and the itch drove me crazy. Because of my age, I could dispense with a jacket, but I was never without a tie. Regardless of what you wore, that hour on the superheated subway gave you and all your companions a frazzled look. (In later years, when I'd schedule a date in Manhattan on a Friday evening, I'd carry a fresh white shirt and change of underwear with me to work. Shortly before quitting time I'd strip down in the Men's Room and give myself a quick ablution. This routine was practiced by scores of young men, whose dates no doubt wondered how they remained so fresh.)

The poor women had it worse. Every girl over the age of twelve was expected to wear a hat and gloves, as well as long stockings. Having sisters, I knew that no self-respecting woman would go out without a full slip and garter belt to hold up those stockings. Unless you were built like a movie starlet, an uncomfortable girdle and brassiere was added to their torture. Knights in full armor had it easier. How they maintained their decorum after an hour in the inferno of the subway, was always a mystery.

Inside the office there was little relief. The sole concession to the heat of summer was a few fans whose sole purpose seemed to be blowing all the papers from your desk. One's arms were so clammy in the sweat and humidity that desk papers regularly stuck to your skin every time you moved. And yet we endured it simply because we had no choice. How I looked forward to the autumn and winter. Heat was never a problem in those seasons. It could never get too cold for me.

Sometimes when the August temperature reached record proportions, the family changed their commute to the Third Avenue El. It meant getting up a little earlier, and a trolley car ride over to Third

Avenue—a trip of about twenty minutes. But at least the entire journey was above ground; a major improvement. Riding high over the street, it also afforded us an enlightening view into the inner life of the city apartments. With Manhattan a Hades, privacy took second place to comfort. Besides, those who lived next to the El were so used to its proximity that they scarcely gave it a second thought. We had an unobstructed vista of hundreds of kitchens and bedrooms, their occupants sitting in their underwear and all engaged in eating breakfast or digesting the Daily News. Many tenants slept on their fire escapes—their bedding still visible as our commuting train rumbled by. Ancient wooden cars were the hallmark of the el, but regardless, it was a mighty leap over the steaming tunnel.

Towards the middle of July, the job improved radically with the addition of Ed Barron, a sixteen-year-old boy from Bayridge, Brooklyn. Ed was everything I wasn't: tall, good-looking, suntanned, self-assured, and blessed with an engaging personality. He quickly became a surrogate older brother.

Ed Barron

Ed had two main interests in life: girls and the Brooklyn Dodgers. Baseball was subject to the weather, but Ed was tuned to girls all four seasons. In his case, he was the magnet and the office girls were metal filings. It was that easy. It only took him about ten minutes to have three lovelies hovering over him. Of course Mr.Arntz wasn't amused and told the girls to get back to work. I'd had females fussing about me, but they were usually old enough to be my mother. Every time Ed would deliver mail to a floor, I'd have to go and fetch him.

The Comptroller, his assistant, and the Accounting Manager were on our floor and had buzzers with direct communication to our office.

When they sent a signal, we were expected to be at their door within seconds, if not sooner. If both of us were away, Arntz would be on edge until one of us returned. The last thing he wanted to do was be confronted by any of the bosses. In Arntz's eyes, the most frightening person on the floor was O.H. Robertson, the Comptroller. None of us knew what a "comptroller" did, but whatever it was, he was no one to trifle with. Wearing a perpetual scowl, he always walked as if he were in a foot race. We could see him rise from his desk through the glass partitions, and the cry would go out; "Robertson is coming!" Arntz would put down his Between the Acts miniature cigar and quickly grab all the loose mail in our boxes and shove it in his desk. He wanted to make sure that Robertson couldn't complain about undelivered mail. As Arntz chain-smoked these tiny "stogies," the edge of our desk was a succession of cigar burns. It looked as if some erstwhile prisoner was charting his days on the wall of his cell!

Sometimes Ed would shout, "Robertson is coming," even if he wasn't just to drive poor Mr.Arntz crazy. With this new face on the scene, it was never dull.

As someone always had to be around to answer the phone or the buzzer, Ed and I never had the same lunch hour. But I so enjoyed his company that we spent a number of Saturdays after work exploring lower Manhattan. It didn't take long for him to come up with an interesting theory. "Listen to me, Jack. If you're looking for the best girls let the street names direct you. For example, here we are located right at the foot of MAIDEN LANE. What better clue! Then there's ANN, PEARL, CATHERINE and HESTER STREETS. Let's not forget BROAD STREET!" Of course with thousands of young women crowding the narrow lanes, how could he miss? Beyond that there were all the SLIPS—OLD and CONTIES, for example. I tried to explain that these were wharves before the land was filled in, but Ed said "Don't get too technical, just go with the flow. Wait a minute there's another name: Flo! (w)." I couldn't resist telling him one of my grandfather's favorite jokes. "What's the hottest street in New York?" he'd ask. When no one answered, he'd reply, "Fulton Street, because it lies between John and Ann!"

At this point I only had the vaguest idea of how the female anatomy functioned—least of all my relationship to it. With a mother and two sisters always underfoot, I had a pretty good clue that they weren't "soft boys," as one of my friends called them. But except for a couple of photos of naked women, my knowledge of their physiology was practically zero. In my circle of friends, everyone was as dense as I was.

Ed decided to broaden my 'education" He didn't know the real names for all the parts, and his grasp of what "disabled" these poor creatures once a month; every month, was sketchy to say the least. However, this stuff rarely came up in mixed conversations. I had a sneaking suspicion that many men went into marriage with not much more savvy than we had.

It had become fairly obvious to everyone in my family that I had passed into puberty. I overheard veiled conversations between my parents. My mother would announce at the dinner table, "I can tell the girls what they need to know, John, but I can't tell Jackie. That's your job." He just grunted and the subject was dropped. I could see the tension in my mother, and then one day as off-handed as I could, I said, "You don't have to worry about the birds and bees anymore. Bob (an older neighbor) explained everything." She looked relieved, but not nearly as much as I did.

Where Ed excelled was in reading all the female signals. He seemed to know what the girls were thinking almost before they did. It was a game, he said, and one had to learn all the rules or be left in the dust. For example, when it came to attracting girls, logic was thrown out the window. I always thought that to make a girl like you, you had to play up to her, flatter her and do her small favors. "All wrong," Ed revealed. One had to employ what he called "reverse psychology. "If you really want to meet a girl, don't pay her any compliments—just ignore her. Play up to her girlfriend instead." I thought he was crazy, but it worked every time.

So between us, we split the distaff complement of the Great American. One might think I was hopelessly saddled with matrons, but many of them had followed my sister's routine and brought their daughters into summer employment. As most of the routine office jobs in an insurance company were simple and numbingly repetitive, they could step into their roles in a few minutes. I had my eye on a number of 15 and 16 year-olds, but I never screwed up the courage to ask any of them for any companionship. Ed tried his hand successfully, but I was just too young to be in the running. I was just as happy to be left out. Confronting any female under twenty usually left me tongue-tied.

At the ripe age of thirteen, I'd never been exposed to many girls who weren't related to me. Only in the final months of my last grammar school were there any females in my classroom. Both religion and sex segregated my first seven years. While I rarely got up the nerve to engage any of these daughters in the usual office banter, that didn't mean that I wasn't deeply attracted to some. But it was strictly an "admiration society" from afar. I was content to observe all the incredible feminine gestures, movements and body language that held the promise of glorious mysteries to be revealed later, when I was finally admitted into the portals of maturity.

Sometimes on a quiet afternoon, I'd sit at my desk and focus on Shirley, a young brunette of 16, sitting not ten feet away. She had only to push back an errant curl or adjust one of her shoulder straps to lock my attention. Observing her apply lipstick was a special treat. First, she'd carefully coat her upper lip. With her mouth open she'd admire her handiwork, and then satisfied, she'd bring the two lips together pressing them firmly several times. Relaxing, she'd slowly rub her tongue ever so lightly across each coated surface, leaving them glistening. A simple routine, perhaps. But it left me mesmerized for some moments, deliriously imagining what it would be like to be kissed by those two lips. There seemed to be no end to the secret knowledge these creatures possessed. I figured they must have started practicing when they were six!

I imagined myself impressing Shirley on a walk into all the historic streets; she hanging on my every word. Incredibly, we met years later in this same building after I'd returned from Korea and was already married. She was engaged to someone in the Air Force. One day, in the employees lounge over coffee, she revealed that she'd had a crush on me back when we both began working, but was waiting for me to make the first move. I'm glad she didn't wait —she could be collecting Social Security!

My two big passions were music and the Navy.

CHAPTER THIRTY

AN EARFUL OF MUSIC

By now, my friendship with Bob Lipeles had blossomed. He'd recently graduated from Music and Art High School and was an accomplished pianist. At this time my radio listening was dominated by classical music. I considered myself incredibly fortunate to meet someone who could answer all my questions, as well as educate me on other levels. This was the kind of information one doesn't learn in a classroom. We could have been siblings. Bob took me under his wing, and although there was a five-year difference in age, we became inseparable. I reveled in listening to his vast record collection, and over those two summers became the recipient of a first-class musical education. Many Saturdays found us in the city, taking advantage of a multitude of free concert tickets to which Bob, who played the bassoon in the Brooklyn College Orchestra, had easy access.

The rise of fascism and the war had caused most of Europe's great musicians to flee to our shores. Never in our history had so much talent been concentrated in one small place at one time. As a result, conductors and instrumentalists who normally would be commanding top billing now had to be content with secondary roles. Everyone competed for a place in the musical life of the city, which had never been richer. We heard the NY Philharmonic conducted by the likes of George Szell, Artur Rodzinski and Bruno Walter; violinists the caliber of Jasha Heifetz, the acknowledged leader, along with Stern, Milstein and Elmann. Among the pianists were the great Vladimir Horowitz, Artur Rubenstein, Claudio Arrau, and Robert Cassadessus. If you didn't mind climbing to the upper reaches of Carnegie Hall, tickets were usually less than a dollar. In the warm weather though, the hall could take on all the earmarks of a sauna.

One day, Bob asked me, "Jack, how would you like to hear good music in the open air?" Would I! That's how I was introduced to Lewisohn Stadium, on the grounds of City College.

The stadium

This was the summer home of the New York Philharmonic for just about as long as anyone could recall. General admission was thirty-five cents. We sat on rows of concrete benches, and the more knowledgeable carried their own cushions. The chance to hear great music under the stars at those prices brought crowds upwards of 25,000. For Bob and me it was a two trolley-car ride across the Bronx and into the upper reaches of Manhattan. No air-conditioning, but in those simpler days the trolley side panels and windows were removed in the summer, replaced by open wire enclosures. The journey took an hour, and in the course, my musical background was enhanced. Just about everyone in the audience had strong opinions about the program and the artists, and very often, heated discussions punctuated the intermissions. Mayor La Guardia always opened the season conducting the National Anthem or the Stars and Stripes Forever, invariably bringing the house down. Along with Roosevelt, he was the most popular politician in New York.

Indoors, music was everywhere. Besides the major houses, nearly every high school and college offered concerts and recitals. While I was growing up, the city's population was heavily Jewish and German, two ethnic groups steeped in classical music. All the performances were well attended.

I would have loved to study the piano, but in our family's tight financial condition that was out of the question. So, as I mentioned earlier, I settled for a key place in the American Bluejacket marching band. The American Bluejackets was a junior naval organization that operated out of the public school buildings in the Bronx. My parents were very active—my mother collecting dues and my father providing the art layout for their military reviews. Only ten years old when I joined, I soon gravitated to the band. Later, in Cardinal Hayes High School, I performed in both their band and orchestra.

Marching and making music can be an addictive pleasure. Beating drums was my initial lesson in rhythm, and I soon acquired an innate sense of musical timing—a great advantage when I later played in a band or orchestra. Parades of prodigious lengths were common then; St. Patrick's Day carried the marchers from the mid-forties to 116th St. But distance meant nothing when I was happily marching along to a good beat and utilizing my entire repertoire of marches.

Reinforcing my ever-increasing musical knowledge was the radio, and endless source of good listening. WQXR even had its own program guide where I charted every hour and underlined the symphonies and concerti I wanted to hear. It cost but a dollar a year! So with Bob as my mentor, I increased my storehouse of knowledge in leaps and bounds. Cataloging the "greats;" all the symphonies and concerti of Beethoven, Brahms, Schubert, Schumann, Sibelius, Haydn and Mozart became as familiar to me as the melodies of Rodgers and Porter were to my sisters and friends. However, I wasn't a complete "long hair." I loved and was constantly exposed to the popular music of the day that was without question, very good.

Unrealized by most of the people at that time, we were living in a golden age of American standards. Richard Rodgers, with his new collaborator, Oscar Hammerstein, was just embarking on an incredible streak of musical productions with OKLAHOMA. Cole Porter, Jerome Kern and Irving Berlin were all in their creative prime and churning out new hits every year. Sammy Cahn, Hoagy Carmichael, Meredith Wilson, Frank Loesser and Jimmy Van Heusen chimed in with "Hit Parade" level songs. And we were blessed with some of the best interpreters ever to grace the stages and airways—Bing Crosby, Connie Boswell, Judy Garland, Dinah Shore, and Perry Como. A skinny newcomer sang with Tommy Dorsey's Orchestra at the Paramount. His name was Frank Sinatra. Top orchestras backed all of them. The movies competed with radio for the most lavish musical numbers.

In spite of the burning desire to hear everything just like in the concert hall, my listening was achieved with a cheap table-model General Electric radio with an exposed turntable on top. Of course I didn't know any better. High-Fidelity was years away and only the very wealthy could afford the few high level radios like Stromberg Carlson.

Back at my workplace, every desk held a copy of the Daily News. Only the bosses ever carried one of the other morning journals such as the NY Times, the Herald-Tribune or the Wall St. Journal. The Daily Mirror was the other "people's paper," but except for different comics and columnists, it was a carbon copy of the ubiquitous News. The afternoon and evening papers were different, with New York City boasting of nearly a score of "late" journals. Among the favorites were the Journal-American, the World-Telegram, the Sun, and a wartime entry called PM. All contained voluminous sports coverage, especially baseball. Since most of the games were played in the sunlight, everyone read an evening paper to see the results. In the summer of 43,' the only New York team in contention was the Yankees. But my interest in baseball, or any other sport for that matter, lay years in the future.

Unlike the New York Times or Herald-Tribune, the Daily News was compact enough for a subway rider to handle without disturbing his fellow passengers. I loved to observe the ingenious methods employed by all the strap-hangers to continue their reading, unimpeded by the fact that each passenger had about ten inches of usable space to hold his paper. The News could be folded and folded again to be held in one hand. The war news was not nearly as voluminous as the Times or Tribune, which actually printed all the casualties and communiqués from the various fronts, including those from Germany and Russia, but it gave one the essentials. That took three pages. By page four the content was juicier and flirted with being censored in those far more innocent years. In the early forties, the off-screen adventures of Errol Flynn gave the News a quantum leap in circulation that not even D-Day could match. Seemingly, every newspaper on the morning subway was opened to "page four."

Errol Flynn's sexual adventures held no great interest for me—that would be many moons down the road. I was far more enthralled by the adventures of Dick Tracy and "Flattop," "Smilin' Jack", "Gasoline Alley" and "Terry and the Pirates." Jimmy Jemail's "Inquiring Photographer" was another popular feature I read everyday.

Besides the major dailies, there were local papers that highlighted neighborhood happenings. We had the Bronx-Home News and for those on the other side of the river the Brooklyn Eagle filled the bill.

For many riders newspapers fell short of fulfilling the inner man. While some passengers carried hard cover novels, the most common companion was the new "Pocket Book." These cost only 25 cents and were compact enough to fit in a pocket—hence the name. This creation literally caused a revolution in reading habits. The very first title was Dale Carnegie's "How to Win Friends and Influence People." It was an instant best seller, but I never saw anyone on my subway or at the Great American reading it. More apt to be found on a desk was "Rebecca," "See Here, Private Hargrove," or "A Tree Grows in Brooklyn."

These softbound volumes soon had me under their spell.

My reading at home ran to naval adventure stories like C.S. Forrester's Hornblower series or "Mutiny on the Bounty". I also enjoyed non-fiction accounts of the war, and the output of Edward Ellsberg, whose submarine stories like "Men under the Sea," often kept me up late at night. Other volumes that graced my shelves were "Northwest Passage," "Thirty Seconds over Tokyo," and Ernie Pyle's "Brave Men."

LIFE was by far the most popular magazine. Bringing photojournalism to heights undreamed of before the war, their dramatic photographs and well-crafted prose broke new ground. LOOK was its major competitor, and for those who held reading to a higher priority, THE SATURDAY EVENING POST and COLLIERS were a good choice. .

But elbowing out all the books and magazines in the popular culture were the movies. Just about everyone saw two films a week, and actors like Clark Gable and Irene Dunn became as familiar as the members of our family. In the early 40s the big hits were "Mrs. Miniver, Yankee Doodle Dandy and Casablanca." In the days before television, the movie theatre also provided a unique opportunity to see live pictures of events taking place overseas. Sandwiched in between the ever-popular cartoons and short subjects, the newsreels always engaged the audience. A preview of television, but at the time we didn't know it. Twelve cents could bring one an entire evening's entertainment.

While the magazines and books filled the reading needs of most people, for the younger set it was the comic book that held center stage. Just prior to the war, the first of the "super-heroes appeared, appropriately named SUPERMAN. At first the publishers rejected his character as too unbelievable to grab the interest of young readers, but they totally underestimated our unlimited capacity for fantasy. SUPERMAN became an instant hit, vaulting Action Comics to the top rung. The famous phrase, "Look, Up in the sky—It's a bird, it's a plane, it's SUPERMAN!"

became part of the language of the day. It later spawned a popular radio show and movie serial. Expressions like, "Who do you think you are, Clark Kent?" were heard everywhere.

This "man of steel" was closely followed by BATMAN and ROBIN, (the first character to have a young assistant. Imitations followed: SUBMA-RINER, THE TORCH, CAPTAIN AMERICA, and scores of others, but SUPERMAN and BATMAN captured the imagination of the majority of America's kids. Pretty soon nearly every boy had a rolled up comic book sticking out of his back pocket. Years later, when I was in the Navy comic books were still the major source of reading material for thousands of men in their late teens and twenties. The story lines were simple, the artwork riveting, and the action flowed—endlessly. In a very real sense comic books were pocket movies. Best of all they only cost a dime. And of course they were endlessly recycled. With the coming of World War II the super-heroes had a built-in supply of villains in Nazis and Japs. In a throwback to an earlier age, nearly every character wore a cape. Pretty soon, the garment manufactures couldn't keep pace with the demand for capes of every style. Many a mother's shawl disappeared to fill a desperate need.

Sometimes, the reality of war struck home with far more vividness than any magazine or newsreel. On occasion, one of these servicemen whose pictures graced the desktops would be the subject of a War Department telegram. It happened twice that summer. One, a sailor, was "missing in action;" in the other case a Marine was wounded. The sailor was in a submarine, so his chances of being found were very slim. It was a grim reminder that all those headlines weren't relating something abstract, but involved the very sons and husbands and fathers of all those women who worked at the three hundred desks at 1 Liberty Street. One gold-star mother, Mrs. Maher, wore black for the entire war. She'd often stop me on my rounds and look me in the eye. "Jack, I pray to God this terrible war will be over before you're old enough to be called up." I always thanked her and assured her that it would be over soon, but secretly, my friends and I were hoping for just the opposite. Every eager teenager, filled with the excitement of all those war films, desperately wanted to get into the service before it all ended.

In the summer of 43' there were no indications that the end was even remotely in sight. While the Russians continued to bear the brunt of the German war machine, as they had since June 1941, it was pretty certain Hitler would have to be finally defeated by an American army on the continent. At that stage of the war one could barely imagine that happening. In the vast Pacific, we were just beginning to capture the outlying outposts of the Japanese Empire. The Japanese were a tenacious and resourceful enemy; far more cunning than our early propaganda would have us believe.

Other times, poor Mrs. Maher would grab me as I stopped to deliver her inter-office mail. She'd be staring at her son's picture with tears in her eyes. The more intensely she looked the tighter her grasp. Then she'd gaze up at me and repeat the same sentiments. "Jack, you raise a boy from the womb; nurture him, watch over him, protect him from disease and bad companions, and what happens? Just when he's about to go into the world and make his way as a man, a war comes along and he's taken from you forever." I never knew what to say in those circumstances, except, "I'm sorry." There wasn't much more that anyone could say. I guess the poor woman had to talk to someone, and unfortunately I reminded her of her Jimmy. It made me think twice about all those heroic war films. Hollywood rarely showed you the other side the story. What happened to all those mothers left behind with only photographs to show for a life's work?

On Sunday, my one day off, my friends would tease me with stories of their carefree days at Orchard Beach, swimming, playing ball, and for those a bit older, the pursuit of girls. Sunday was a tough day to try and catch up. By the time I returned from Mass and finished Sunday dinner, which was always at noon, the day was well worn. We had no car, so a trip to the beach entailed a trolley and a bus. And none of my crowd had the slightest interest in my job or lower Manhattan.

I always had hopes that my father would take me into Manhattan for a day on the town, but my last big night was my birthday in December 1941. On that day, after Sunday dinner, we'd visited the Museum of Natural History where I got a crash course in Darwin's Theory of Evolution. It made perfect sense the way my dad explained it, but I ran into a brick wall when I later wrote a composition about this for my sixth grade Catholic school English class. My father asked me to pick a restaurant, and I blurted out the only one I'd heard of –The Brass Rail. It was a meal to remember—shrimp cocktail, veal cutlets, corn and mashed potatoes, all topped off with apple pie. Then it was on to the Strand for Jimmy Cagney in "Yankee Doodle Dandy." When we came out on Broadway, the Times Building electric news display revealed that Wake Island was still holding out in the face of renewed Japanese attacks. For a number of years that evening would be the benchmark of my relationship with my father. It helped dispel a terrible doubt that I was an unwanted son.

In those days Sundays belonged to the people, not the stores. It was truly a day of rest. It gave the country a much-needed pause in the mad rush for money. Most businesses closed, and sometimes even finding a restaurant was a real challenge. It was day for families to visit museums, walk in the park or the zoo, or just lay around the house devouring the monumental Sunday papers. The streets of Manhattan were empty and for the most part silent. Most of the buses and trolleys shut down. With the majority of companies working at least a half-day on Saturday, this break was very welcome. Unfortunately, that respite disappeared in the sixties when the "blue laws" were successfully challenged. One only has to visit most of the European countries to see how the quality of American life has suffered.

CHAPTER THIRTY-ONE

SETTLING IN

Right after Pearl Harbor our situation in the Pacific went from bad to worse. In less than three months the Japanese juggernaught had accomplished the following: the sinking or disabling of our Pacific battle line at Pearl Harbor, the capture of Guam and Wake Islands, Hong Kong, the entire Dutch East Indies, Malaya, the great British naval base at Singapore, 90% of the Philippines, the Gilbert Islands, and French Indo-China. In the course of this advance, they sank or disabled seven battleships, an aircraft carrier, a dozen cruisers, and scores of destroyers and other vessels. In the Philippines, a few thousand American and native troops held on to a narrow peninsula called Bataan, and a tiny island: Corregidor. Except for a few submarines, the islands were completely cut off. All the Japanese objectives had been met. They accomplished this incredible feat at a cost of one light cruiser, a destroyer, and a few submarines.

MacArthur had escaped to Australia, but his command scarcely comprised a few thousand men. Most of the Aussies were fighting Rommel's Afrika Corps in Libya with the British Army. The Japanese could seemingly move at will, and were planning to take Samoa and New Guinea. This would effectively sever MacArthur's supply line.

Sadly, we believed our own propaganda about the inferiority of the Japanese for far too long. The reality was like a bucket of ice water in the face. We learned the hard way that their ships were well constructed, and the officers and men who manned them were rigorously trained and disciplined. Their night gunnery was unsurpassed; their Zero, the most maneuverable fighter in the sky, and their torpedoes were far superior in explosive power and range than those in any other navy.

And they NEVER surrendered! It was going to be a long and costly war in the Pacific.

Between the war and my long-term interest in the Navy, it was only logical that I was drawn to the American Bluejackets, the largest sea cadet groups in the city. The Captain's son, Billy Kaiser had been the reining bell-player in their band, but in the summer of 43' he enlisted in the regular Navy, leaving his spot open for me. My enjoyment of playing in a marching band was further enhanced when a group of my school-mates joined our ranks. Larry McBride, Al Nicolas and Dick Ryan had all been in my classes at St. Raymond's. They remained in my company for the next seven years, until the next war took us away. Later, another boy joined us—Ed Menninger. He began as a drummer, but quickly became our drum major. Our friendship would blossom in high school where he excelled in everything.

We drilled once a week at PS 12 near Westchester Square, and marched in every parade. In those days, before the unification of the armed forces, there were parades for both Army and Navy Days, in addition to all the national holidays—not to forget St. Patrick's Day. During the war those patriotic events would include the Corps of Cadets from the Military Academy at West Point as well as scores of high school bands and ROTC contingents. The 75,000 participants would be cheered on by over a million New Yorkers.

My parents were drawn to the Bluejackets mostly because of a strong friendship with Bill Kaiser, its founder and head. He was always known as 'Captain Kaiser', and though he never wore a real uniform, he looked every inch the part. In the real world he drove a hook and ladder for the New York City Fire Department.

Every year the organization held a military review in a local state armory. Initially it just involved a parade with music, but in 1944 my dad became close to the regimental commander of the State Guard of the West Farms Armory and he decided to broaden the program. Colonel Farrell was a factory inspector for the state safety board, and as such had access to just the kind of building materials my father needed. In short order my father had lumber, muslin, chicken wire, and more important, a crew of carpenters to do his bidding.

The first year my dad built the full size bow and bridge of a Navy destroyer. I was pressed into service to play the part of the Captain on the bridge. I needed binoculars, so the prop department fashioned a pair from two Coke bottles taped together. Unfortunately, they employed shoe polish for a realistic effect, and after I came down my eyes looked as though I'd gone a few rounds with Joe Louis! On the far side of the armory floor his crew constructed a Japanese island village with palm trees, bamboo huts and a group of machine gun emplacements. "Landing craft" with wheels carried the "invading Americans" who engaged in "combat" with the enemy. All this action took place under the cloak of darkness, rendering a high degree of realism to what was really a stage show. The good Colonel supplied enough noisy charges and pyrotechnics to scare the living daylights out of everyone in the audience. The patrons loved it!

Photo #42 Marianne

Colonel Farrell kept my dad staging these events for the next two years. The Bluejackets raised enough money for the regiment to buy a fully equipped ambulance. There was no money in this for my father, but I think he gained something far greater in his book— recognition. All those years suffering through the Depression, erratic employment, my mother supporting the family, all the time painting literally in the dark; and now he had an audience who appreciated and respected his ability. Neither the Colonel nor anyone in that cavernous hall had ever seen anything like it.

It was about this time that the Bluejackets decided to add a girl's band to the ranks of their distaff cadets. A 12-year old girl of German parentage was one of the applicants. She took an immediate dislike to me—deciding that I was the most conceited boy she'd ever seen. She formed that opinion by observing that I always held my head up—or as she put it, "my nose in the air," while marching. She was unaware that this had nothing to do with a superior attitude—I had little to be superior about in any event, but the fact that I had to assume that pose to play my instrument properly. In return, I made fun of her braces—an unforgivable sin. Like most 13 year-olds, my behavior was boorish.

Her brothers later joined the band and since my mother collected the weekly dues, our families became good friends. In the ensuing years their sister dated just about every one of my friends, and while I was a frequent guest at house parties, the two of us never went out alone. But to coin a baseball phrase, I became "the player to be named later." As exquisite proof that no one knows what life has in store, Marianne Hockemeyer and I fell in love nine years later while I was in the Navy during the Korean War. I proposed by mail from the carrier MIDWAY and she accepted. That was more than a half-century ago.

When it came to the opposite sex we truly lived in an age of innocence. While my close proximity to a whole new array of young girls stirred my imagination, there wasn't much else I could do with them in that second summer of the war. The rare times I held a girl in my arms on a dance floor was usually under the stern eyes of a Sister of Charity or a Christian Brother. Probably, neither my partner nor I were particularly keen on developing a romantic relationship with each other. If we entertained any fantasies, it was with the likes of Loretta Young or Van Johnson.

By mid-August I was firmly entrenched at 1Liberty Street. I'd lost the fear of being sent out on a message and becoming lost in the wilds of all those "name streets" below Union Square. Unconsciously, observing the differing architectural styles that formed the patterns of lower Manhattan I was enriching my knowledge of the city. I didn't appreciate it at the time, but I was experiencing something extremely rare in the history of New York—an unchanging cityscape.

There's an old joke that says, "New York City will be wonderful place—when they get it finished!" But the metropolis I was absorbing was frozen in time—something that had never occurred before, and would probably never happen again. The one-two punch of the Great Depression and World War II effectively shut down all new construction for close to two decades—an eternity in Manhattan. The city streets I walked down were little different than they looked the year I was born— 1929. Adding to this time warp, the accumulated grime from a thousand coal-fired boilers and the normal dirt and debris of a teeming metropolis took its toll on the facades of every structure. Strangely, it imparted a weathered-look of centuries to buildings scarcely twenty years old. More than anything, this stage-set effect made one half expected to see Mark Twain or Teddy Roosevelt walking down Broadway.

Certain sections didn't need any aging. The early experiments in steel high-rise construction were graphically expressed in the flying buttresses of the old World Building on Park Row and even in the exposed interior girders of One Liberty Street. It appeared as if the engineers weren't absolutely sure of their calculations and added some additional supports for safety's sake. Warming the heart of a history buff, large areas from the early 19th century and even the late 18th century were left untouched. Some of the best examples were found around the streets adjoining the Fulton Fish Market. With a sharp eye, one could easily pick out a few sail maker's lofts and tackle shops. In later years this was transformed into the South Street Seaport Museum. The reproductions in the calendars of the Seaman's Bank clearly showed the bowsprits of huge clipper ships extending out over South Street. And there were a number of people still around who recalled seeing these beautiful sailing vessels crowding the piers of the harbor.

In the office On occasion I had to deliver a parcel up to West Houston Street, a few miles north of City Hall. Completing my assignment I was astonished to discover another small town right in the heart of the city. Flowering trees shaded two and three story brownstones, and here and there sat frame houses more reminiscent to my neighborhood in the Bronx. With music pouring from open windows, and knots of people sitting outside on folding chairs, it seemed to be a continent away from lower Broadway. Corner markets sold fresh fruits and vegetables right next to open-air restaurants. Delightful cooking smells invited entry. I didn't have time to explore this little village, which I later discovered was called just that—Greenwich Village, but I vowed to return. New York appeared to have no end of surprises.

Back at One Liberty Street more recent inventions intrigued me. One of our chores included the picking up and dropping off of "Ediphones." This early form of a dictating machine employed wax cylinders not much removed from the type used by Thomas Edison in his early sound experiments—hence the name. The person dictating would speak into a tube, which in turn would record the information on a wax cylinder. Later, in an adjoining building, office girls would listen to the message and type the letters. One of the problems was the fragility of these cylinders. If you were unfortunate enough to drop one, it shattered and you had to go hat-in-hand and apologize to the underwriter who composed the letter. Obviously, you didn't want to do that too often. On one occasion, Ed Marron, ever the cut-up, recorded his own message and acted as if one of the bosses wanted a date with the typist. The poor girl was half way through the letter before she realized it was a joke.

Sometimes we'd be employed in the filthy job of moving some dead records stored in long rows of file cabinets in the basement. Resembling a scene from a science-fiction movie, all this 19th century generating machinery reminded me of the photos I'd seen of some early ocean liner engine room—hot water boilers, huge hydraulic wells for the elevators, an ancient electrical panel and the original gaslight apparatus. Yes, the building was originally designed for gas illumination!

The three maintenance men who occupied this space lived in a world of their own. No bosses hanging over them, no clocks to punch; their time was theirs to plan and execute the repair and upkeep of this aging twenty-story pie-wedge set down on a postage-stamp site. They had a coffeepot perking and invited us into that special circle of real men doing real work. No paper shuffling here. "Take off your shirts and undershirts—otherwise you'll look like a couple of coal miners. When you're finished you can use our sink and soap and you'll be ready for a coupla' of hot dates." I had yet to be on any kind of a date, hot or otherwise, but it was something to think about. The proximity of all those young girls was giving my hormones a boost. I'd just turned that corner into that new and delightful world of puberty, but as yet, I wasn't completely aware of it.

Jack at the office

Beneath that façade of office routine— ringing telephones, papers read, filed, delivered and mailed, there was another drama unfolding: the inevitable interaction of male and female. It was only natural that working together for eight hours a day, five and a half days a week would lure people into a social as well as a business relationship. Gradually I began to notice a vast network of romantic intrigue in the midst of all that routine. Much like a petri dish reproducing bacteria, the Great American Insurance Company was a perfect culture for bringing people together. Since personnel directors tend to hire pliant workers, the makeup of the employees was more than a little homogeneous. Platoons of recent Catholic high school graduates populated the rows of desks in Bonding, Compensation and the Liability departments. It was common knowledge that the nuns instilled a firm dose of discipline and obedience—the skills most desirable in a young employee. As a result the majority of the office clerks were Italian and Irish. The executives were, with few exceptions, Protestant. I don't recall ever seeing anyone else. So the bulk of the permanent office staff was subtly set up to mix and mingle. Possessing the same ethnic and religious background eliminated a lot of hurdles, and set the stage for nature to take its course.

During my initial summer three couples got married. I wasn't clued in at the time, but one of the primary motivations was the military draft, which was in full swing. Married men had a higher classification, and those with children were even more insulated from Uncle Sam's grasp. Hardly a week passed without some desk being decorated with white ribbons and stacked high with engagement gifts. In most cases, One Liberty Street was more of a home than their own address, and their fellow employees were closer than many a family member. These girls rode the subway together, worked together, ate lunch together and shopped together. Bonds were forged that would last a lifetime.

Sticking out like the cherries on the top of a sundae, there were probably only a dozen men under 35 in the entire building. With an office staff of better than 400 women, most of them under 21, nearly every young man stood out. As the youngest of the young, so did I!

CHAPTER THIRTY-ONE

AN ODD COUPLE

While the over-whelming amount of desk space was allocated to the insurance company, there were a few private offices within the building. Up on the sixteenth floor, tucked away in a hidden alcove was a door inscribed with the names "Goff and Griswald, Attorneys at Law." As a courtesy, we always delivered and picked up their mail. This added to our workload, but unlike the other departments, these men would regularly tip us. But there was a downside to their generosity. They desperately wanted someone to talk to!

Like Mr. Arntz, their dress was unique, as if they'd just stepped out from another century, which of course they had. What I noticed first, were the spats they both wore. Spats, for the uninitiated, were fabric ankle coverings secured with buttons. Up until that time, I'd only seen them on actors portraying gangsters or wealthy men in the movies.

Their opening remarks were a quiz. What was my name; where did I live; what did my father do for a living; how many siblings did I have? That out of the way, I tried to exit gracefully, but no chance. They wanted to tell me their stories. I never realized just how lonely older people were, but it was obvious from their mail that most of their clients had died. Apparently, so had their spouses. I was trapped. I did however ask them to call Mr. Arntz, not that he thought I'd fallen down some elevator shaft!

Each in turn then proceeded to spin out the most fantastic tales of serving with Roosevelt's "Rough Riders" and later working on General MacArthur's staff during the First World War. At one point, either Goff or Griswald (I could never tell them apart and was too embarrassed to ask) reached down and raised his trouser. I thought he wanted to show me his spats, but he revealed a long scar from his knee to his ankle.

"Shrapnel from a Spanish shell near Santiago." To my 14-year-old mind, the Spanish-American War seemed as distant as the Crusades, but his war wound made a profound impression. I started to like these two old guys.

They had practiced their estate law with a declining clientele while the world around them roared past—the catastrophic Crash, strikes, the New Deal and the Second World War. From their conversation, all these events appeared to have had little or no effect. Apparently they'd both come from money. They'd met at Columbia Law School and been together ever since. Their walls were crowded with fading photographs of military units in France and subsequent reunions, as well as images of Teddy Roosevelt and Warren Harding. In their niche at 1 Liberty Street, time had stood still. The building itself was cut from the same mould, reflecting the technology of a simpler time before the First World War. Using the inside staircase, the very trapped air reeked of antiquity.

The only way I could break away was to tell them that I could lose my job if I didn't return to my desk—that other people were waiting for their mail to be delivered. But Goff and Griswald had a great deal of pull in the higher circles, so they put my fears at rest. In time, we became good friends. When it rained, I'd often pick up their lunch for them, lingering to hear another tale of life in the trenches. One day, after delivering their coffee and sandwiches, they handed me a package. They said don't open it until you return to your desk. Upon reaching the 10th floor, I was astonished to discover a three-volume set of the complete works of O.Henry. Sharp-eyed, they'd noticed a small volume peeking out of my back pocket. This experience was an object lesson: one never knew what lay behind a closed door.

A much more exciting event took place later that month right on my own floor: the return of Miss Blakely.

CHAPTER THIRTY-TWO

GLAMOUR GIRL

I'd never heard of Miss Blakely, but I soon discovered that I was probably the only male inside the confines of 1 Liberty Street who hadn't. Her regular job had been as a secretary to Mr. Everett, the Chief Accountant, who occupied one of the executive offices on our floor, but she'd been temporarily transferred to one of our other buildings nearby to cover for a girl who was ill. Word had gotten out through the grapevine that she was returning, and Gwen (she was the first "Gwen" I'd ever seen) was the talk of the entire company. I didn't understand what the fuss was all about, until she made her first appearance. She hit the Great American like a bombshell.

Gwen, as she asked everyone to call her, was simply a dream. Tall, willowy, with shoulder-length black hair, she filled out her clothes as if they'd been sewn on her. Real nylons covered the most perfectly shaped legs I'd ever seen, and her high heels, unlike many other office girls, appeared to be an appendage rather than an uncomfortable enclosure. (I never asked her where she acquired her nylons—rare as new cars in 1943, but if anybody could get real nylons, Gwen could). Her tight, cotton skirt was knee-length, and as she made her way from the elevator past our location her movements were pure legato. She didn't walk— she flowed! She was the kind of woman whose first glimpse brought everything to a halt. Ed and I both agreed that Gwen held the signal distinction of being the prettiest girl we'd ever seen in the flesh.

Passing our desk she beamed an incandescent smile at Ed and me that buckled our knees and left us with a feeling not unlike being punched in the stomach. A breathless silence followed her passage to her desk in the far reaches of the corner. It was as if someone had slowly turned down the volume on a radio. Even after she passed, Ed and I thought we could still inhale the lingering scent of her perfume. As I recall, the remainder of our day was spent trying to determine when Gwen would make another transit. She had a rapturous effect on us. I estimated her age to be about the same as my sister Rita, or perhaps a little older. She had certainly reached full maturity, both physically and emotionally. Gwen was in complete command of every encounter, and she knew it.

Secretly, I prayed that she'd never speak to me. For as long as I could recall, I'd suffered from a chronic stuttering problem, inherited from my father's branch of the family. Two years of speech therapy with the Dominican nuns at Fordham University had helped, but I was a long way from being cured. My affliction would be instantly triggered by agitation, stress or the proximity of a pretty girl. Gwen would bring on all three! (Years later, when I related this problem to a close friend, he laughed and remarked, "Now I know why you proposed to Marianne by mail.")

Ed and I were way too young for any romantic interest on her part, but perhaps that's why she spent some time with us. We figured she might be giving us a small preview of life's pleasures. To say that we were grateful for her attention would be the understatement of the century.

But some of her actions had embarrassing consequences.

She had a habit of stopping by my desk with some Manila envelope to be delivered, and leaning forward as she spoke to me. "Jack, be a dear and find out how much postage I'll need to mail this." I would have gladly gone to Washington on foot if need be. Gwen favored what was popularly known at that time as "peasant blouses." (Ed remarked that he never saw any peasants who looked like her!) Placing her palms flat down on my desk, she leaned forward, locking me in her gaze and revealing the voluptuous swelling of a marvelous bosom. That her fabulous suntan ended at this juncture only accentuated those uplifted curves. I tried to look elsewhere, but some greater power held my eyes riveted to that neckline. Her aimless small talk only reinforced the feeling that she was engaged in this posture for a definite purpose. And that purpose was being fulfilled in spades! At this point I was in some physical pain, but there was no way on earth that I could shift my position. I prayed silently that Mr. Robertson wouldn't buzz me. I had no Plan "B." Of course she gave Ed the same treatment.

When she walked away, Ed turned to me with a big grin. "Are you religious, Jack?" he inquired. "I guess so," I said, surprised at his question. "I've spent all my life in Catholic schools, and I go to Mass every

Sunday." "That's good. Because whether you realize it or not, you've just seen the Promised Land!" Then I asked him what he'd do if Robertson buzzed. Ed just rolled his eyes and said, "Screw Robertson!"

Gwen dominated our conversations for the remainder of the summer, which was now dwindling down like the lyrics to "September Song." I'm sure that her image lingered in far more recesses than idle talk. She became the leading lady in a hundred dreams and fantasies—mine included. If there was any doubt that I'd crossed the threshold into puberty, Gwen put those thoughts to rest. At least temporarily, she edged out both the Navy and music in my commanding interests.

One of the other secretaries planted a rumor that she'd passed a Vice-President's office where Gwen was taking dictation and that she'd observed her lifting her skirt to adjust her garter, never missing a word. Ed and I wondered how long it would be before one of these ancient executives would be carried out on a stretcher!

After she returned, I'd be regularly quizzed by the older executive secretaries as to what I thought of her. I'd always reply as innocuously as possible. If they were looking for dirt, they'd have to find it somewhere else. I guess Ed and I would have lied for her on a stack of Bibles.

Ed continued to meet all the new young girls on every floor. Never at a loss for words, one of his best lines to any number of winsome lasses was, "Let's go up to the Bonding Department and bond!" It was one of the few offices where no one after worked beyond 5 P.M.

CHAPTER THIRTY-THREE

WINDING DOWN

Labor Day came and went, and while the subway still ranked with one of Dante's rings of hell, there was no doubt that the summer was trickling away. The early scent of burning leaves was apparent, even way up on the 5ᵗʰ floor of our apartment. Even stronger, the crisp morning air carried the welcome hint of autumn. My Manhattan merry-go round slowed a bit and I got ready to jump off. My ten weeks in the adult world was rapidly coming to a close.

Settling in to this new and often exciting office routine quickly erased any disappointment over missing out on a summer at the beach. Being accepted into the responsibilities and rewards of this fascinating world eclipsed even the monetary enhancements. That July and August, I added three more classical albums to my growing collection. When I unwrapped my "treasures," my sisters moaned.

I began to make my farewells on each floor that I serviced. Much to my surprise nearly every department had taken up a small collection for their summer office boys, which was, at least to me, very touching. I thought I was very grown up, but I nearly broke down a few times as I said goodbye. Most of the girls that we'd befriended and all the older department heads gave us a quick goodbye kiss. Miss Blakely didn't have any tangible gifts, but she gave both Ed and me a big hug and a full kiss on the lips. I'm not sure about Ed, but that was definitely a ground-breaking jolt for me. I don't think we washed our faces for the rest of the day!

But I guess my biggest surprise came from Mr.Kean in the Mail Department. "How would you like to work in my department after school? But make sure it won't interfere with your school schedule." The Great American Insurance Co. wasn't quite through with me. I couldn't begin to imagine that I'd be employed there after I was married and that the experience would eventually shape my life-long career in this field.

The move into high school returned me to my own generation and a more disciplined environment. More than anything else, I missed the freedom I'd enjoyed and being accepted as an adult. At Cardinal Hayes High School, the priests and brothers treated us as immature teenagers and kept us on a short leash. There were a few female office workers and a nurse, but none of them looked anything like Gwen.

My prowess with the glockenspiel garnered me a place in the school marching band and orchestra. A few months later I was sitting on the 50-yard line at Yankee Stadium watching one of the great football games of the century: Army-Notre Dame. Perfectly matched with undefeated seasons in their final meeting, Army, with Blanchard and Davis, and Notre Dame, with their great quarterback, Johnny Lujack, played to a 0-0 tie. Wartime travel restrictions had prevented the Notre Dame band from accompanying their team and we were pressed into service. But it was all wasted on me. I hadn't the slightest interest in football. Perhaps if I could have made a pass at Gwen it might have been different, but football, like most sports would have to wait a few more years to grab my interest.

That same month afforded another musical experience, this one far more rewarding. The Hayes Band played at a huge War Bond rally in the Bronx Winter Garden. Paul Whiteman, who had conducted the world premiere of Gershwin's "Rhapsody in Blue," and Mayor La Guardia, led us from the podium. Among the items auctioned to raise money was one of Toscanini's batons. It went for ten thousand dollars—a huge sum in 1943.

By Christmas, my demanding high school curriculum was pushing my summer recollections further and further back in my mind. But some refused to die. All those extraordinary sights and sounds and smells, not to mention a cast of characters I'd scarcely imagined, would remain in my memory bank for years to come.

Elsewhere, the world war ground on. Along with the British, our troops had just landed in Italy, our first venture on the European continent. In the east, the Red Army had turned the tide and had the Nazi legions in retreat. Closer to home, we were at last winning the Battle of the Atlantic. In the Pacific we'd captured the first of the Gilbert and Marshall Islands. Guadalcanal with its bloody naval struggles was behind us, and the death of Admiral Yamamoto promised better days ahead. But the war was far from over. A profusion of newer and larger cruisers, carriers and destroyers frequented the Brooklyn Navy Yard, and servicemen of all branches soon outnumbered the civilians, especially in railroad terminals and places like Broadway and Times Square. My sister, Dot, was engaged to a soldier, and she recently returned from visiting him alone in Joplin, Missouri. This conduct would have been unheard of before the war. The very fabric of American life was changing, and in most cases, for the better.

In the world's scheme of things, the following summer would be much more tumultuous. In June we'd cross the English Channel in the greatest invasion in history. In the Far East we'd secure airbases to bomb Japan. The end would be at last in sight.

But in spite of all those historic events, for me, nothing would ever displace the summer of 43'. Looking back on that wondrous time, I never discovered if the idle mind was indeed the "devil's workshop," but secretly I thanked my mother for giving me the best season of my life.

CHAPTER THIRTY-FOUR

HIGH SCHOOL

Cardinal Hayes High School

That first day of high school was like no other. The previous April I'd been to Cardinal Hayes High School to take the entrance exam, but this was different. For one thing there was little doubt that I looked far younger than all the other teenagers heading for the main entrance. My father accompanied me to within a few blocks of the school, but once he realized that I knew where I was going, he said I'd feel more comfortable on my own. That was certainly true. I couldn't imagine a worse humiliation than being taken to high school by one of your parents. Inscribed over the entrance of the school was its motto, "For God and

Country." I guess they were covering all bases. I soon discovered that God was heavily favored in the makeup of our day.

Hayes was situated at the very end of the Grand Concourse, the rather shabby end, I might add. Nearby, the main Bronx Post Office was spanking new, but that was a solitary island in a sea of rundown commercial warehouses and factories. This was the path we took to school from the trolley or subway on 149th Street, but a few blocks in the other direction, the neighborhood took a distinct turn upward.

Within walking distance stood the most elegant hotel in the Bronx: the Concourse Plaza. Just off 161st St. stood the imposing county court-house, where some of the most notorious criminals of the era were tried. A little further along we saw a much happier edifice: Yankee Stadium. Being thirteen was bad enough, but I was also extremely short for my age. I felt as if every eye was locked on me, wondering how anyone so tender would be let inside. I could see that some of my companions had already begun to shave! By September 1943, many in the senior class had already left Hayes to enlist in the Navy or Marine Corps.

The loudspeakers were issuing directions left and right (another revelation), and I followed a surging crowd into the cavernous audi-torium. Nature had played a cruel trick on Father Krug, the priest who makes the announcements. He has a terrible lisp. THHISS ISS Father Krug, SSPEAKING! He has major problems pronouncing the words "Students" and "Conflicts," words he has to employ time and time again that first day. I look forward to hearing him. He helps break the tension in my gut.

I was one of a very few freshmen—roughly a hundred out of a student body of 2,500. (The bulk of the freshmen were assigned to three annexes throughout the city.) No wonder some of the older students and the priests and brothers were staring at me.

Teenagers change rapidly over a four-year span. I was at the lowest rung. I soon found myself assigned to a class—1C. Here we were inter-viewed by counselors and asked to choose one or two elective subjects. Essentially, this boiled down to choosing between an academic or busi-ness course, and if it was academic, a choice of language. Latin, I soon discovered was mandatory. I floated on a stream. My syllabus card read: English, History, Latin, Religion, Elementary Algebra and French. I looked at that card and whispered, "Wow!"The first thing I liked best about Hayes was the anonymity. In St. Raymond's or St. Helena's, I was but one boy out of 20 or 30—locked in to one teacher. Here we changed classes and joined a different instructor and mix of students six times a day. For the most part I faded into the background. Unless you were a budding genius, the teacher didn't notice you. My class had a few budding geniuses, but I certainly wasn't one of them.

There were no formal classes that first day. Our time was spent in indoctrination sessions. This enabled us to become acquainted with the physical layout of this sprawling four-story building, and the time frames that controlled every minute of our lives inside. In addition to our studies, there would be a myriad of religious services to attend, from morning mass to later afternoon benediction. Every class opened with a prayer, and after that first hour I knew I was going to need all the divine guidance they were dispensing.

My mother had pushed me into grammar school a year earlier than the rest of my friends. In the rather open ciricculum of those basic classes, I soon fit in, but this was the big league and my shortcomings were soon apparent. But I went with the flow. I had no other choice.

Marketing was not a formal course, but we were all exposed to the tender mercies of capitalism as we joined a throng in the courtyard buying and selling textbooks. Because there were so few former freshman in the school, my task took longer. I guess my friends in the three annexes had no choice but to purchase new books. I got mine at half price or less, simply because the sellers market was so small. I soon discovered one of the unadvertised assets of buying used books—all the notes scribbled in the margins to help the student highlight the important sections. It saved me many hours of study.

Aside from assigning classes and subjects, we were also directed to a lunchroom hidden away from the rest of the school. It was almost as if they were ashamed that the students had to eat. Located in the basement at the end of a long curving windowless passageway, it was spacious enough to accommodate most of the student body. Peace and quiet was not one of its attributes. Perhaps the harshest shock of all was discovering that we had but TWENTY-FIVE minutes to eat. And this included getting there and returning to our next class! Hot food was served cafeteria-style at very reasonable prices. For the first time, I was exposed to dishes like ox-tail and bread pudding and found that I liked them.

Just about everyone in this student body was one small step above the poverty line and those in power knew it. Our monthly tuition was $5.00. I later discovered that many parents couldn't afford even that. It was clear that Cardinal Hayes High School was heavily subsidized by the diocese.

Harboring strong doubts about my ability to swim with this crowd, I wondered how long I'd survive. Latin was my first stumbling block. Instinctively, I had an innate aversion to any subject for which I could see no possible value, now or in the future. This, of course, worked against me. In all the excitement of becoming part of this regimen, I completely overlooked the real reason I was chosen for the Main Building. Nothing in my letter of admission mentioned the band, so I assumed that I was brought here for some other purpose. I didn't have to wait long for my answer.

A week into the fall semester, I was sitting in Father Nolan's Latin class wondering just how long I could hide my ineptitude. Latin One and Jack Sauter were totally incompatible. A few years before, I couldn't even master enough of the simple prayers in Latin to join most of the altar boys serving mass. I was shunted into service at weddings, funerals and Novenas. This day my Guardian Angel made a much-needed appearance.

I was half dozing in the middle of a warm September afternoon, listening to Father Nolan droning away about Cicero or some such Roman, when suddenly I was snapped back to reality by the flinging open of the door to the corridor. Framed by the entrance, stood the most unlikely priest I'd ever laid eyes on. John Ziemak could have been Charles Laughton in a pair of shiny black trousers. Obese, unshaven, red-eyed, clad in a in a soiled undershirt with a lit cigarette dangling from the corner of his mouth, he leaned against the wall and looked with disgust on everyone in the class. "Say, Joe, you got a SAUTER in this class?" he asked. I perked up when I heard my name. Nolan looked in his register and said yes. I stood up and Ziemak motioned me out into the hall. "What are you doing here?"he asked incredulously. I mumbled something about being assigned, but he paid no attention. The door was still open. "You're supposed to be my glockenspiel player, don't you remember?" Then I recalled that session after the entrance exam.

He pointed to the blackboard. "Well John, it's your choice, me or Latin One?" I looked at those incomprehensible words and said, "I'm with you father." He broke into a big smile and placed a meaty arm on my shoulder. He had an expression of pure delight. His search for a glockenspiel player was over. Happily, I traded Caesar for Sousa.

Before entering high school, my studies were conducted only a few short blocks from my apartment. Now I had to navigate two subways or trolley cars. That first year I traveled pretty much alone. All of my former classmates from St. Raymond's and St. Helena's who were going to Hayes had been slotted into annexes.

Sometimes, especially in warm weather, I'd take the two trolley cars from home to school. Along Boston Road, we'd pass the Bronx High School of Science. At the time I wasn't aware of it, but that school was among the finest in the country. The kids who went there resembled no one I'd ever seen in my neighborhood. They were predominantly Jewish and always carried massive briefcases. But their most distinguishing characteristic was the large eyeglasses they wore. The lenses were so thick it made their eyes appear to bulge, like a frog. Most of my friends made fun of these "old before their time" teenagers, but in a few years these students would go on to be the nuclear scientists and the computer engineers who planned the lunar space missions.

Hayes was spanking new. Opened just before Pearl Harbor, it carried the strong scent of floor wax and wood polish. Fine craftsmanship was evident in every detail—it was the most modern building I'd ever been in. St. Helena's Grammar School was the same age, but it could have been tucked into a corner of 650 Grand Concourse. Architecturally, it was a groundbreaker for a diocesan building. Constructed of white granite, its' uniquely curved façade and two supporting arms extended back, forming an elongated "U." It drew admiring looks from nearly every driver and was rightly called Archbishop Spellman's pride and joy. Hayes had the distinctive look and feel and smell of an ecclesiastical building. It shouted "institution." Every Catholic structure, whether a rectory, a nuns residence or the church itself, had this signature identity. A blind man could walk through the entrance and instantly recognize it.

The sole decorations in these stark white classrooms was a crucifix and a 48-star American flag—God and Country. Polished to a high gloss, the passage linoleum resembled a Hollywood sound stage awaiting Fred Astaire and Ginger Rogers. The whole building radiated order, purpose and tradition. What impressed me most was the great arc of the structure that faced Grand Concourse. I'd never seen walls that curved. On the first floor, just off the impressive entrance, hung a portrait of Cardinal Hayes, the bishop for whom our school was named. He looked saintly—the soft contours of his face gave him an almost womanly appearance. He

234   Jack Sauter

didn't look like someone who'd belt you, but I didn't think I'd want face him in the confessional.

Swiftly immersed into the freshman class I had little time to admire the architecture of my home away from home. Something new, however, caught my eye. Row upon row of lockers, each one the sole property of every student. I had to supply my own lock, but everything else was gratis. In my entire life this was the first time I had a secure space to call my own. Some might consider a locker of small consequence, but it gave me, at 13, a real sense of growing up.

One class followed another in a jumble of diverse subjects. I was still mulling over some math problem when I was called upon to read some French dictation. Every teacher I had wore a black cassock except Mr. Frank, Father Ziemak's music assistant.

Poor Mr. Frank. More than his non-descript suit set him apart. He was a nervous wreck, especially in the presence of "Big John," as Ziemak soon became known. Catholic schools were notorious poor payers, so the lay teachers were at the economic bottoms of the barrel. He was supposed to familiarize us with the great composers, but he couldn't even pronounce their names!

What he did add was a degree of levity, sorely needed in that atmosphere. Every time he became excited his upper denture would slip out, breaking up the entire class!

Years later, at a formal dance at the Commodore Hotel, I met Mr. Frank. It turned out that he was a first-rate jazz pianist, and according to the other instrumentalists, could jam with the best. In 1943 he was down on his luck and took any job he could get. He even remembered me. I guess glockenspiel players are hard to forget.

Ziemak was something else entirely. No nonsense here. He knew his music in spades, and was knowledgeable about every instrument in the band and orchestra. Every year he could take a raw group of teenagers and mould them into a decent musical ensemble. We not only played Sousa Marches, but tackled some Wagner, Mozart and Verdi as well. Some students brought their own instruments, mainly violins and trumpets, but the rest were provided by the school.

As an indication of the level of musical excellence Father Ziemak achieved, Cardinal Hayes was only one of two high schools in the city receiving a full Regents credit for music—the other being the prestigious High School of Music and Art.

Advanced Band was my first course in the morning and it woke me up in a hurry. Sixty musicians blasting away in a confined space rapidly removed any cobwebs from the night before. If some one was inattentive and missed one of Big John's cues, he would think nothing of leaving the podium and plowing through the entire woodwind section to throttle the culprit.

Advanced Band was never dull!

Occasionally, when I went to the Boy's Room, I was always struck by the remarkable quiet in the corridors. But when the bell sounded the end of the class, doors crashed, feet shuffled, and a foot race ensued for more than a thousand young men. The only comparison I can recall is General Quarters on board ship in the Navy. Rights-of-way were strictly enforced, especially on the staircases. There were elevators, but they were reserved solely for faculty and honor students.

Members of the Student Council, a sort of teenage police, enforced these rules. Regardless of

how far your next class might be, you had but two minutes to get to your next assigned room. While Ziemak was the most colorful of my First Year instructors, each priest or brother brought with him a steadfast dedication unmatched in the city. It was obvious that they were handpicked for this job.

Hayes was a plum assignment.

Father Dan Brady was my history teacher and he made an indelible impression on me. Brady had been deeply involved in the Catholic Labor Movement; a group organized to thwart the recent communist influence in unions. He gave us an in-depth course in the history of the American labor movements with all its struggles and bloodshed. He always came to class with a bundle of newspaper clippings and books, rendering his arguments unassailable. Many of the students' fathers were union members, and they learned for the first time how difficult a path the workers had to endure in order to achieve collective bargaining. Father Brady opened our eyes to the terrible abuses in the coal mines and steel mills. A recent coal strike had recently gripped the country, and with the war, most Americans were solidly against the miners and their colorful leader, John L. Lewis. After Brady's class all of us would have gladly joined their picket line!

Other teachers were equally demonstrative and had little difficulty keeping our attention. Brother Theodore, my French teacher, brought in a French newspaper: POUR LA VICTOIRE. Wesometimes used this for translation rather than the prescribed text. Much of it was beyond me, but once into a war story I was inspired to break out our French-English dictionary when I got home.

Theodore's first language was obviously German, and he still retained a heavy Teutonic accent. His French sounded odd, to be sure, but if nothing else, it made "dictation" easier. Brother Ignatius, my Geometry teacher, would take off his cincture, using it to demonstrate the converging lines in a plane. Father Grace, our English teacher, eased us into early Anglo-Saxon literature, not exactly a sure-fire path to enlist new readers, but we plodded on. Beowulf, unfortunately for us, couldn't hold a candle to The Canterbury Tales, which I had found in my father's library and loved.

Our Dean of Discipline was Father Buckley, a short, tightly built priest, bursting with energy. I don't think anyone every forgot him standing in front of the main entrance, watch in hand as hundreds of students rushed past in those final minutes before the class bell sounded. Once that bell rang, all the remaining boys were shuttled into an office where they received a "detention slip." The words, "You're late, son," remained locked in our memory. Detention meant spending an extra hour after school under the sharp eyes of another clergyman. And you couldn't do your homework!

The brothers' and priests' subject matter was clearly delineated. With few exceptions the priests taught Latin, English, History, and Religion, while Math, the sciences, modern languages, and business courses were the brother's realm. We didn't realize it at the time, but the separation was a forerunner of college: Liberal Arts and Sciences. There were other differences. After school one often found some of the younger brothers working out on the parallel bars or playing handball. They were all in terrific shape.

At this time, totally immersed in our own milieu, we didn't think much about the lives of these priests who were entrusted with our welfare. For one thing they were a great deal older than the brothers we had in St. Raymond's. We also knew that this was a life vocation, not just a few years. On the other hand, a number of the brothers had taken limited vows, essentially to receive an education. After five or six years, many returned to the non-religious life. More often than not, they got married. While I was in senior year I ran across Brother Peter who had terrorized our 7th grade class, pushing a baby carriage near Westchester Square.

Thinking back, part of our good fortune was being raised at a time when Catholic schools, especially ours, were blessed with an abundance of devoted priests, brothers and lay teachers. Whether it was physics or history, math or music, all our mentors knew their subjects in spades. In what was truly a labor of love, our faculty not only excelled in their profession, but they came to class with a singular purpose that had few parallels in the outside world. For many of us these teachers became the father we rarely saw, the older brother we never had. Our character banks were filled with precious assets we would draw upon again and again for the rest of our lives. Qualities like faith and love, guts and fortitude, compassion and charity; all these and more were put there by our men of the cloth.

That first year was pretty much a blur. I struggled mightily, but there was some question if I'd even survive. Hayes graded its students every two months and I managed to fail a different subject for each of the first three periods: algebra, history, and French—not an easy task. At least I didn't show any favorites.

Upon receiving my report card, I had to take it home and have it signed by one of my parents. This requirement led to an embarrassing incident for one of my close friends. On the reverse side of the card there was four printed lines on which the parent had to sign—one for each marking period.. One day, shortly after the cards were returned, John Curran was called down to the Dean of Discipline's Office.

"John," the Dean said, "I want you to think very carefully about your answer to this question. If you tell me the truth I'll go easy on you. If you lie, it'll mean instant dismissal." John told us he couldn't imagine what he'd done to warrant such a severe penalty. "Ask me the question, Father."

Father Buckley replied, "Did your mother sign your report card?" Without hesitation, John said yes.

"You're absolutely sure? " Yes, he answered again. "If I told you that I'm going to send for your mother, would your answer still be the same?" Again, John said yes. "Ok. You've made your decision. I'm going to get in touch with your mother and have her come in here."

John's mother, like most of our mothers, worked, but she took time off, thinking that her son must have done something horrendous to have her lose time from her job. The following Tuesday she appeared at Buckley's office. Mrs. Curran was an Irish immigrant, so she wasn't intimidated by the "men of the cloth," as they were called in Ireland. "What's this all about, father?" she inquired.

Buckley took the card very carefully from his desk. He handled it as if he was revealing some secret plans, or as John's mother later told her neighbor, perhaps there were some pictures of naked women, or worse. She was quite relieved when she recognized the report card. "Is this your signature?"

Buckley asked. "Yes," she replied scarcely glancing at it. John looked at the card in his mother's hand, and for the first time realized that the first name: Deirdre, was misspelled. She had signed on the previous two lines, so it was clear that the writing didn't match. She had left out the first "r."

All at once it dawned on Mrs. Curran why she was called down. At first she was embarrassed, but then her embarrassment turned to anger. "You mean you made me lose a half a day's pay for THIS? Yes, I misspelled my name. I was in the middle something when John handed me this card.

You know it's not easy taking care of a house, a husband, four children and working full time. I hope you all have a good laugh over this. Don't you people have anything better to do than try to have people make fools of themselves? Come by my house and I'll find plenty for you to do."

Apologies flowed profusely. The Dean went to the cashier and drew out $20.00 to reimburse Mrs. Curran for her lost wages and carfare. Actually it was nearly twice the amount she'd lost, but she didn't say a word. A few days later, she received a formal letter of apology from the Principal, Monsignor Furlong.

Fortunately for me, my father just gave me a lecture and told me to do better. Thinking back, I wonder if Father Ziemak might have had some influence on their retaining me. I was his sole glockenspiel player. In any event, I made it through, but just barely. Part of the problem stemmed from my obsession with World War II. I used to devour the NY Times and Life Magazine, closely following every battle and campaign. My ongoing interest in the Navy fueled further reading. None of this helped my schoolwork since the current struggle wasn't on the Hayes agenda.

In November, without any warning, I began to grow—and grow! In three months time I gained six inches, bringing me up to an even six feet. I was overjoyed. If nothing else, I'd certainly beaten the odds. I was long convinced that being shorter than most was my place in life.

My father, his father, and all of his brothers were five foot six or less. My mother's side was just as bad; her two brothers and her father being in the same category. But unknowingly I had an ace in the hole; two uncles (my mother's brothers –Joe and Charlie who died in their early twenties before I was born.). Photos from the family album showed them both at six feet, towering over everyone else. Besides growing out of all of my clothes, my voice deepened so much that I was enlisted to sing bass in the school chorus. Then body hair started to appear where it had never been before. Just about all of it was blond and uneven. One would need a magnifying glass to find anything on my chest or face. I didn't have to shave more than once a week until I went into the Navy at twenty. I toyed with the idea of growing a mustache, but to no avail. My father's mustache was an indelible part of his character since his mid-twenties. Except in old photographs, I never saw him without it. Subconsciously I may have been trying to imitate him.

While I still had a stuttering problem, I made up for it with a clear complexion, unlike most of my friends who were cursed with acne. My fear of not being able to get the words out placed me well into the background, however, rarely if ever, volunteering an answer. I was glad to see June roll around. The end of my first year coincided with the invasion of Normandy, which dominated my attention. At last I could finally concentrate on the war without trying to memorize irregular verbs and mathematical formulas.

That June I returned once again to the Great American Insurance Company. My education was continuing, but on a different and much more pleasing plane.

I soon discovered that being fourteen and a great deal taller was infinitely better than thirteen, and now I could benefit from a whole previous summer of experience. After nine months of an all-male environment at Hayes, it was a joy to once again be the company of a multitude of young girls, many of whom were my age. I'd yet to venture into the world of dating, but I spent nearly every waking hour watching and dreaming of the opposite sex. Socialization was far easier in the confines of 1 Liberty Street, where I was happily immersed in a corporate world of anonymity. I continued my exploration of Manhattan and even ventured into Brooklyn once or twice to attend a birthday party for a fellow employee. The city held endless fascinations and I was gradually being introduced to them. Ed Marron returned as my associate messenger and our friendship blossomed. It was just too bad that he lived in Brooklyn, too far for us to meet after working hours.

Concurrently, my body was still undergoing radical changes, often leaving me moody and depressed. I had a lot of company. Fortunately, there was so much going on that I had little time to worry about myself. If I thought that New York harbor was a caldron of intense activity the previous summer, it was nothing compared to the ceaseless efforts being put forth to supply the greatest invasion in history. Convoys were formed in the lower bay and huge liners carrying thousands of GIs silently made their way down the Hudson. Everywhere in New York, their uniforms now outnumbered civilian garb. Adding to the mix, WACS and WAVES were commonplace.

Nearly all the clerical duties in the local military and naval offices were performed by women. My sister Rita tried to join the WAVES, but my mother killed the idea. No one ever won an argument with Mom.

In New York all eyes were focused on Normandy. For awhile it appeared as if the invasion was permanently bogged down, but six weeks into the campaign we launched a devastating attack by land and air to blast a hole in the German lines at St.Lo. Patton's tanks poured through and quickly liberated most of France.

There was little doubt that I was one of the few students who were concerned with the battle in France. My classmates were far more interested with the problems of the New York Yankees, Giants and Dodgers. I'd heard of a few of the players—DiMaggio was one: he had a popular song named after him, but I could more easily identify the various army and navy generals and admirals.

With a fierce and bloody struggle taking place, one that would shape our future and that of the world as well, sports seemed like a distraction at best. Probably my feeling was generated by my lack of any aptitude for team athletics. What physical activity I engaged in continued to be solitary: swimming, walking, and skating.

That summer my passion for music was further enhanced by returning to the outdoor concerts at Lewisohn Stadium at City College, with my mentor, Bob Lipeles. While the admission price was a mere 35 cents, sometimes Brahms had to compete with an airliner or a bus. But sitting under the stars somehow placed the music in another sphere. My "education" was continuing apace with the learning of a new symphony or concerto nearly every couple of weeks. One night Jascha Heifetz, the great violinist, was performing the Beethoven Violin Concerto when it began to rain. Inside the stadium, the orchestra and soloist were under a shell, but the audience was in the open air. With the first drops the concert stopped and the musicians began to close up their instruments. In spite of the rain, which was now falling quite heavily, no one in the 24-thousand member audience moved. After conferring with the conductor, Heifetz turned to the gathering and said, "If you can take it. I guess I can!" Resuming the concerto, he was met with a huge outburst of applause.

Soon I was building a memory bank of themes and motifs. By the end of the year I could whistle whole chunks of Beethoven and Brahms symphonies and concerti. Doors were opening into a world I scarcely knew existed. Whatever spare money I had from my meager earnings at 1 Liberty Street was spent on records. None of my neighborhood friends or classmates shared my interest however, so except for Bob, I spent many solitary hours listening to WQXR, WNYC or enjoying my 78 RPM record collection. I often thought of how satisfying it would be to fall in love with a girl who would have similar feelings. When I mentioned this to Bob's mother, she made a wry comment. "Jack, it's not important that your wife enjoy your music, only that she'll tolerate it." At this point in my life, my fourteenth summer, I had no girls, musical or otherwise.

My Sundays were spent at Orchard Beach or one of the local pools. On rare occasions the head of the American Bluejackets, Bill Kaiser, would drive us to Jones Beach for a real taste of the ocean. Mr. Kaiser took a liking to me. Billy, his only child, had been the chief glockenspiel player in the marching band before he went into the Navy. A glockenspiel is similar to the Xylophone, except that it's comprised of twenty-five tuned metal bars and carried vertically. When I was eleven he let me take the instrument home with me one summer, and I promptly memorized all the marches and most of the popular songs of the day. I experienced the surprise, discovery and joy of making music.

In some mysterious way I had solved the riddle of using the instrument to bring forth a continuous stream of right notes. I couldn't read music, but I had a good ear. I could pick out a melody—polish it a few times, and it was mine. Sometimes on a rainy day I'd play for six or eight hours. I loved every minute. Without realizing it, I'd acquired a life-long avocation. Within two years, I became the chief bell player and it enabled me to lose myself and forget all the pains of puberty and high school. At the time I was unaware of just how important that skill would be in shaping my future.

I marched in all the major parades with the Bluejackets, except for St. Patrick's Day when the Hayes band required my attendance. The glockenspiel was a rather unwieldy instrument, weighing more than twenty pounds. It was carried in a sturdy steel harness that rested on my shoulders.

I was learning to read music, but I couldn't sight-read fast enough to play an unfamiliar piece. My friend Bob gave me the orchestral scores of Brahms First and Beethoven's Ninth Symphonies, which went a long way to help me understand all the various instruments, along with basic counterpoint. I devoured them.

August 25th came, and with it the liberation of Paris. I was delivering a parcel to an office near Rockefeller Center on that day, and an American opera singer, Lucy Munroe, sang an impromptu MARSEILLAISE, right next to the esplanade. The crowd went wild. I felt as if I'd just been a witness to history.

That was also the summer that Bob introduced me into the marvels of ocean liners. Up until that point, all my energy was directed towards warships. The only liner I knew was the NORMANDIE, recently lying on her side in the mud of her pier after the disastrous fire that had swept her in February 1942, while being fitted out as a troop ship. Bob had a fabulous collection of deck plans, exquisite color brochures and photos of just about all the pre-war giants. QUEEN MARY, MAURE-TANIA, REX, NORMANDIE, AMERICA, BREMEN, EUROPA, were just some of the multitude of floating palaces. His passion was sparked by his French teacher who, before the war, had a friend in the French Line and arranged for a tour and lunch onboard one of their liners.

With the onset of the war, there was no way to visit any of these marvels. I looked forward to the day when steamship travel would return to normal. Sadly, neither Bob nor me realized that most of the foreign flag giants would be sunk or burned before peace came.

In January of 1944 my oldest sister, Dorothy, was married to Johnny McDonald. The wedding photos reveal me as a gangling youth rapidly growing out of all of his clothes. Johnny was in the Army Signal Corps and was about to be shipped out to England to prepare for the invasion. We all thought he would land in Normandy, but his army was destined to take part in the invasion of Southern France the following August.

Dorothy spent nearly every evening writing letters, joining most of the rest of the population. My mother bought a star to hang in the window, specifying that this household had someone serving in the military.

Now the war took first place in the newspapers and the radio. My father listened to a number of in-depth programs, and I reveled in the skill and scope of the announcers. Ed Murrow, Eric Severied and Elmer Davis were just a few of the top radio reporters we tuned in every night.

With my father's enhanced income we now had a telephone in the apartment. It was a big step. I don't know if my Aunt Irene felt left out, no longer being enlisted as the intermediary between my sisters and half the eligible young men of the East Bronx, but I'm sure the neighbors enjoyed the tranquility that came our having our own phone. Our number was TAlmage 2-4021. Unlike today's sterile numbers, all the exchanges contained historic titles or names denoting wealth or position. It didn't take an Einstein to figure out where you lived from your telephone ID. Some exchanges like PLaza and BUtterfield held envious cachets that some people would almost die for. In our neck of the Bronx, we didn't have anything quite as luminous as a PLaza, but in our own way a pecking order evolved. HAvermeyer, WEstchester, TAlmage, TYrone (an Irish influence perhaps) MOtthaven and UNderhill became popular call signs. Since the population remained relatively stable, and there were no cell phones, computers or faxes, you and that exchange remained locked in a lifelong marriage. Address books lasted forever.

CHAPTER THIRTY-FIVE

SECOND YEAR

Sophomore year was an improvement, but not much. One plus was a change in my program. I dropped ADVANCED BAND and ORCHESTRA and signed on for General Science and Biology instead. Ziemak never checked me out. He probably assumed that I'd flunked out. A pretty fair guess. By now he'd enlisted another glockenspiel player. Having no intention of making a career of music, I wanted to broaden my studies.

Biology was an eye-opener. I finally learned something about the inner workings of my body—all except the parts that I desperately needed to know about. We dissected frogs that reeked of formaldehyde, but what I really yearned to know was what lay under all those skirts and blouses! I had a strong suspicion that girls were a bit more complicated than frogs. For a science project I prepared some drawings of the human digestive system. My dad was pressed into service—quite willingly I might add, and I won first prize. I was enthralled by science. Having just read THE MICROBE HUNTERS by Paul De Kruif, I found it a subject of endless fascination.

My English teacher was a major improvement over my first year. I was still too insecure to volunteer in class, but when Father Sheehan assigned some topics for essays and I chose, "Judging People by the Music They Listen To," it opened a path to a relationship that changed my life. The subject was right up my alley and I spent a few hours editing it. Joe Sheehan gave me an "A." He asked me to come up to his room after class. (The priests lived on the top floor.). Heavy-set, with a pallid complexion and thinning gray hair, he was a rather forbidding-looking character. He never broke a smile in class. This wasn't a meeting I was looking forward to, but I was pleasantly surprised. "John, I'm more than satisfied with your writing," he said. "You obviously enjoy good music and it shows. What I can't understand is why you never volunteer in class." I told him that I didn't want to invite ridicule with my stuttering. "I think I know a way to solve your speech problem. I'm going to enroll you in the debating society!" His method was an ice-cold bucket of water in the face, but it worked. I became so involved in my arguments and those of my opponents, I completely forgot my insecurity. Self-confidence is what I desperately needed, and that's what I got. I became a fairly efficient debater and our team made it to the finals. Our subjects were Mandatory Universal Military Training and Government Sponsored Health Care for all. (Things haven't changed much, have they?)

Joe Sheehan was my first real friend in the clergy and became for all practical purposes, a surrogate father. At that stage of my life, he was just the steadying influence I needed. He remained a close friend and confidant for the next decade until he died at the age of 48. More than any other person, he helped melt away the strangeness that comes with any new surrounding.

But it wasn't all work. Sometimes humor was injected where we least expected it. Early in the semester everyone in English 2 had to tell the class the most interesting film he'd seen that summer and why he liked it. Joe Roe, a hulking fifteen year-old who played first string football, got up and uttered the following immortal words: "Well Fodder, My favorite pitcha' last summer was HENRY DA VEE, with Lawrence OLIVER!" Sheehan, normally in complete control, nearly fell off his chair laughing. After we became good friends, he revealed that he had another gem that he couldn't share with the rest of the class. On a Religion quiz, the question was, "Why did the Catholic Church put women on a pedestal. One young rogue answered, "To make it easier to look up their skirts!" Joe Sheehan encouraged my writing, engaging me in a number of subjects. I had a small talent for humorous verse that he asked me to enlarge. I wrote a rhythmic parody of some of the faculty. He thought it was priceless (his words), but kept it under wraps.

My biggest jolt, and one that was shared by most of the world, had nothing to do with school. One April afternoon in 1945, I was sitting home listening to the Symphonic Matinee, one of my favorite afternoon programs. The phone rang (it had just been installed) and I picked it up. It was my Aunt Irene. Her voice sounded unusually tremulous. She said, "Did you hear the terrible news, Jackie?" I said no. She said, "President

Roosevelt just died." I felt as if I'd taken a body blow. For most of my friends and me, the words "President" and "Roosevelt" were synonymous. Many people thought "President" was his first name. I couldn't imagine the country and the world without him. There was great a foreboding about the unknown new President: Harry Truman.

Now, for the first time I felt fully immersed in the essence of Cardinal Hayes. The school had so much to offer—even after school, if only one took the time to jump in.

Subtly, yet surely, each of us was absorbing those myriad bits of an American Catholic culture that Cardinal Hayes High School espoused. This agenda was cleverly fashioned to affect how we would vote, how we would view authority: political, corporate and religious, and finally, how we could change the status quo to reflect our beliefs. Our motto was FOR GOD AND COUNTRY, but even a cursory study of our history would reveal a wide gulf existing between these two ideologies on many issues. Of all the priests I had in class, only one taught us to question these "truths." All the rest accepted them as holy writ. More than anyone else, it was my father who nurtured this secular approach. He was a true disciple of the Age Of Reason. "Be your own man," "question everything," and "accept nothing on face value." were his bywords. It wouldn't be easy.

CHAPTER THIRTY-SIX

FIRST MOVES

The three of us

By 1945, Rita and Dorothy were not just siblings, but fully formed mature young women. They joined forces with me and tried to help me bridge the gap between my early teens and. budding manhood—a very difficult time in everyone's life.

A boy is lucky to have sisters, especially older ones. I was blessed with two. A mother's love is unique, but a sister's love can have greater influence because of their closeness in age. The right sister will try to mould your character in such a way as to keep the best and remove the imperfections. It was a bit like editing a story. Observing Rita and Dorothy I could see that girls were totally different emotionally from boys. Indirectly some of their qualities rubbed off on me. They radiated sensitivity, warmth, tenderness, compassion and an innate romanticism. I found some of these same feelings in music, only on a different plane. When I reached sixteen Rita gave me some good advice. "We all can't look like Tyrone Power or Lana Turner, so use what qualities you have. You're tall, you have a good complexion, and you've been blessed with a marvelous sense of humor. Learn to compliment every girl—even the homely ones. Lie a little bit.

Tell them how nice their hair looks, and what a pretty smile they have. Everyone looks good when they smile, so you're on safe ground there."

One Sunday Rita accompanied me to a football game and brought forth a shower of comments from my classmates: "Where did you find that doll, Jack? " I was so embarrassed that I blurted out that she was my sister. Rita was taken aback, obviously relishing her role as a fifteen-year old. Having a girl along was a major advantage, however. At least I knew that I was expected to have one, just like everyone else. Living with two older sisters imparted the kind of knowledge I couldn't find in any books. It had little to do with sex, but rather with the evasive and exclusive language spoken by the opposite gender—the essentials of what made girls different. Double meanings were the norm. In certain circumstances "No" meant "Yes" or even "Maybe." Facial expressions often revealed far more than the spoken words. This was the kind of "inside stuff" denied most of my friends. Even a cursory examination would reveal that there were no quick answers to these mysteries. It would be a challenging and life-long study.

On a more physical level I'd received the usual "street knowledge" about sex –most of it totally wrong. Fortunately, my music mentor, Bob, had taken college biology so he gave me an in depth clinical explanation denied to just about all of my friends. For one thing, looking at a woman's body from a scientific perspective certainly put a damper on romance. It also made me glad I was a man. All those veiled conversations at the dinner table suddenly had meaning, and I began to plumb the mysteries of the opposite sex. There was a great deal to learn.

Sophomore year brought another advantage. All my childhood friends from St. Raymond's, who had attended annexes, now came to the Main Building at Hayes. I had the invaluable advantage over my friends of having a year's experience of this enigmatic experience called "high school." Several of them were also members of the Bluejacket Band.

Larry McBride and Ed Menninger joined me at 650 Grand Concourse. This return of familiar faces brought into sharp focus my inseparable friendship with Larry McBride.

(Photo of Larry and me) Larry and I had been classmates in the First Grade at St. Raymond's in 1935. In those initial years he suffered so much from chronic asthma that we were often asked to pray for him. He missed so many classes it's a miracle that he wasn't left behind. But his health seemed to improve with age. Like everyone else in my class, he was older than I was. During high school, he always seemed to snare the prettiest lass, and since girls rarely traveled alone, I usually ended up with her girlfriend. That wasn't always a disadvantage. I was rapidly learning that there was far more to a female than mere looks.

Larry towered six feet, three, and he was all legs. With a winning smile, a shock of black, wavy hair and complexion inherited from his Peruvian mother, this "black Irishman" could have been a leading man. Tall, dark and handsome! His piercing dark eyes literally sparkled—a trump card when meeting a girl for the first time. Unlike a number of "ladies men," he was immensely popular with men. Twice he was elected class president. His innate and spontaneous sense of humor carried him over every obstacle. Larry was always in demand.

One shared pleasure was walking. On brisk fall evenings I'd walk across Castle Hill Avenue to Larry's house on Tremont near St. Raymond's church. Then we'd walk down Tremont to the Square, across Westchester Creek and up the hill into Throggs Neck—a distance of more than five miles. Throggs Neck drew us like some hidden magnet. Some nights we'd stop by to see Harold Czubaruk, who lived next to my fraternal grandmother on Wellman Avenue, but mostly we'd continue all the way to the end of Tremont. Like most streets in New York City, this one ended in a river. Then we'd amble over to Pennyfield Avenue to play some miniature golf and try to find some girls. If the weather was warm, we'd often continue inside Fort Schuyler and go right to the end of the neck.

Just before Fort Schuyler there was a path along the water's edge that was so bucolic there was little doubt that it had been created in the previous century. Cut into a cliff rising above the Long Island Sound shoreline, it meandered its way past a group of modest beach houses that possessed one of the most panoramic views of the city skyline. It was called Indian Trail. This became a favorite place to take young girls, especially at night when the city lights looked as if they were inspired by a Hollywood set director. The Whitestone Bridge dominated the foreground. Resembling a sparkling necklace, twinkling lights punctuated the long and graceful suspension cables that supported a roadway holding few cars. It was quiet, it was safe, it was dark and it was private. What could be better? It was probably the most romantic place in the Bronx. Larry and I frequented this site so often we knew exactly how many lights graced the structure and probably garnered a kiss for each one.

On more than one occasion Larry and I walked home from Cardinal Hayes, a jaunt of about ten miles. Both of us having been raised without benefit of a family car, and used to the incredible convenience of New York City's public transportation, these distances were considered routine. The girls we dated were also expected to cover what in today's world would be considered vast treks. If nothing else, walking developed beautiful legs, and helped to keep their weight down. Best of all, motion always seemed to generate good, solid conversation, attaining a level not often reached while standing or sitting. Nearing a turning point in our lives, we explored all the available options open to us. Neither Larry nor I had any firm ideas about our future, but somehow just discussing it brought us some degree of consolation.

I don't know what his father did for a living, but he always seemed to be home when I stopped by. If anything, their economic situation was more precarious than my family's, and it didn't improve after the war began as it did for most others. In those days none of us ever wondered about those things. We just accepted them.

Musically, he was a natural. His ability as a master drummer in our Bluejacket Band was matched by his prowess with the harmonica. Larry never had a lesson. It was just part of him. We performed together in the bugle and drum corps as well as in the Hayes band and orchestra. When the local American Legion Post had a function requiring martial music, our talents would often be tapped. We'd be enriched with a dinner and a five-spot each for our evenings' work. Born with an engaging stage presence, he displayed an incredible memory for verse, stories and jokes. He was the "life" of every party. He possessed a rare quality that made people feel good just being in his presence. Larry and I remained close all through school until the war separated us. When I was married, he was my Best Man.

December brought not only the infamous Battle of the Bulge, but also my 15th birthday. It was a huge step. No longer could I wear my father's shoes, shirts, and trousers. (Unfortunately, hand-me-downs from a 50 year-old family friend replaced his clothes, and I began to resemble a 15 year-old bank executive!) My shoe size grew from six to 10 ½, and my neck expanded from 11 to 14 ½. I weighed 145 pounds—thirty more than my father did. For the first time girls began to notice me—I'm not surprised considering what I was wearing! My sister Rita enriched my statue with dancing lessons along with some inside knowledge about the opposite sex. I later discovered that it was prejudiced to their point of view, and usually made me more a favorite of mothers rather than their daughters—regardless I was getting some much needed exposure.

My initial "dates" were family arranged—primarily the younger sisters of my sibling's friends. A rather ignominious beginning, I might add. "Ill at ease," would be a perfect description of my persona, but I soldiered on. I don't recall too much about these early encounters, except that my forced partners were just as nervous as I was, and that I never kissed any of them, even goodnight. I may have not been a budding Don Juan, but I possessed the protocol of a British Ambassador! I later learned that all the mothers called my sisters to compliment me on my manners. I'm sure the girls were thinking, "Where did they find that one?"

But in spite of these arranged meetings, there was something exciting just being in the company of a girl with whom you weren't related. They felt different and smelled different. Some of them had sweaty hands, obviously brought about by their nervousness. Sweaty or not, sometimes the touch of a hand was enough to get my internal electricity flowing—sometimes it was too much. The birds and bees were nesting!

As green as I was, I could sense their unease and my heart went out to them. I yearned to say; "Look I know exactly how you feel. I was forced into this as well. So just relax and we'll make it through this ordeal." Of course I never did. I didn't know how to begin to engage a girl in conversation. Once I got past, "Hi, my name is Jack. You come here often?" my conversation lagged. I progressed through trial and error—mostly error. In the end what saved me was my innate sense of humor. Once I got them laughing, we usually had a fun evening.

I knew inside that I had to broaden my exposure beyond the circle of my sister's friends. It wasn't easy, but I jumped in.

CHAPTER THIRTY-SIX

NAVY DAY 1945 –
MY BRUSH WITH HISTORY

N ew York City had been physically untouched by the war, but just a few weeks before the conflict ended everyone was jolted by an event that had always seemed impossible: a plane crashing into the tallest building in the world: the Empire State Building. At 10 A.M, on a Saturday morning in August, a B-25 bomber became lost in the fog and crashed into the 79th floor killing thirteen persons and injuring twenty-six. It was fortuitous that the accident occurred on a Saturday when most of the offices were empty. A year later, a single-engine private plane crashed into the Bank of the Manhattan Company a block from Wall Street. Again, luck was with the city as the plane hit the building at night. Both the bank and the street below were deserted. Only the pilot was killed.

As the sun rose over New York City on the 27th of October 1945, its first rays struck the masts and radar screens of a group of unfamiliar warships anchored in the Hudson River. The growing light revealed each vessel dressed in a bright array of signal flags, rippling in the morning breeze.

Even at this early hour, those who were awake and observant would notice that the decks of these ships were alive with sailors making the final preparations for one of the city's greatest outpouring of affection and gratitude.

My close friend Harold Czubaruk and I had dutifully celebrated New York's frenzied recognition of the Japanese surrender in the middle of August in Times Square. Being part of a million celebrants, it was truly a "night to remember." We arrived early enough to witness all the shops closing and boarding up their windows. Nedick's a frankfurter chain, gave everything away to clear the shelves. Harold and I remained until 6 A.M. This singular event was followed by a muted but thankful observance of the formal signing on the battleship MISSOURI in Tokyo Bay on September 2nd. These two historic events effectively rang down the curtain on World War II. But the Big Apple wasn't content to let things rest, and seven weeks after the ceremony in Tokyo Bay, New York City still yearned for one last opportunity to show its deep appreciation for the men in blue. She got that chance on October 27th.

Home to the nation's largest port and the Brooklyn Navy Yard, the city always had a special place in its heart for the U.S. Navy. For as long as most bluejackets could recall, New York had been the best liberty port in the world.

On that day many remembered the strong ties New York had to the fleet. Through its long past, the Navy Yard had produced such historic vessels as MONITOR, MAINE, ARIZONA and MISSOURI: ships that were as closely linked to the American saga as Bunker Hill or the Alamo.

The city's history was replete with a long line of triumphant parades. Many could recall Fifth Avenue thundering to the glorious return of the Rainbow Division after the "war to end all wars."

But this would be different. Now for the first time, a victorious task force fresh from battle would anchor in the Hudson and be reviewed by their Commander-in-Chief. If this event didn't contain drama enough, the celebration would take place on the birthday of Theodore Roosevelt, the Modern Father of the fleet. Since his time the date had been remembered as Navy Day.

Today, when its nearly impossible to muster more than a few hundred people to view a Memorial or Veterans Day parade, a younger generation may find it incredulous that hundreds of thousands of New Yorkers would stand for hours applauding major holiday marchers and military service anniversaries. One of the lesser casualties of the Armed Forces Unification Act in 1947 was the elimination of Army Day, April 6th, and Navy Day, October 27th. As a member of a marching band in the 30s and 40s, I well recall participating in every one of these patriotic events.

The forty-seven gray ships of the Task Force had arrived ten days earlier and moored at piers extending out like outstretched fingers into the Hudson. Their crews had sailed thousands of miles on this final journey and now they were almost home. Feelings ran high as the sleek men-of-war moved slowly up the Lower Bay, greeted by huge signs and banners proclaiming, "Well Done" and "Welcome Home." Scores of tugs, ferries, lighters and pleasure boats hailed their passage, every ship in the harbor sounding its whistle in a salute to the fleet.

When the first liberty parties reached shore they happily discovered that nearly every thing was "carte blanche." Never had the Navy been treated more royally. If you were wearing dress blues, buying a drink in Manhattan was practically impossible. A common response was, "Put away your wallet, sailor, it's our turn now." It was "open house" on Broadway, along with the Polo Grounds and Yankee Stadium. Many bluejackets were invited into private homes for dinner, but always closer to a sailor's heart than a home-cooked meal, it was the young girls who carried the day. With most of the men still overseas, there was simply no competition.

From the depths of the subways to the heights of the Empire State Building, sailors dominated the landscape. In turn, curious New Yorkers descended by the thousands to the piers, waiting patiently for hours to visit the battleships, carriers, and smaller vessels. For three consecutive evenings the night sky over Manhattan was illuminated by the ship's giant searchlights, turning the harbor into a fantastic kaleidoscope.

Finally the big day arrived, and none too soon: All this hospitality was taking its toll on the fleet: some of the sailors never wanted to leave.

President Truman began the day at the Brooklyn Navy Yard where his daughter, Margaret, christened the battle-carrier F.D. ROOSEVELT. Then he moved on to Central Park, where before a crowd of over a million people, the President made a major policy address. Finally, after lunch on the battleship MISSOURI, he boarded the destroyer RENSHAW with the presidential party and proceeded to review the assembled units of the Pacific Fleet.

As the RENSHAW made her way upstream, zigzagging her way past each ship, first of the New York side, then on the New Jersey flank of the armada, the sounds of saluting cannon resonated across the water, echoing and re-echoing among the skyscrapers. Each ship fired a 21-gun salute, and for awhile it almost appeared as if New York was under siege.

The famous battleship MISSOURI, upon whose quarterdeck the Japanese had surrendered scarcely sixty days before was there along the old battleship NEW YORK, which had seen service in two wars. The cruisers BOISE, AUGUSTA and COLUMBUS, the light carriers BATAAN and MONTEREY, and a flotilla of other veterans all rendered honors until the northernmost ship, USS ENTERPRISE, CV-6, in her rightful place of honor, ended the ceremony. ENTERPRISE was the most decorated ship in the U.S. Navy, earning twenty out of a possible twenty-two battle stars in the Pacific War. I'd last seen her picture in a newspaper a few months before, with her forward elevator being blown hundreds of feet into the air as a result of a kamikaze attack.

ENTERPRISE wasn't the only battle-scarred carrier in the harbor. A few miles away, at another pier rested the USS FRANKLIN, the most badly damaged ship of the war. Much too ravaged to be repaired, she's sit out her days awaiting the cutting torch. She stood in mute evidence of the price the men of the Navy had paid for victory. Nearly eight hundred men had died during her ordeal off the coast of Japan the previous March.

When the smoke cleared and the crowds began to disperse, it took the better part of the evening for everyone to get home. But in spite of the heavy traffic, I don't recall much horn blowing. I think everyone was still reeling from his or her brush with history.

Earlier that day, my friend Larry McBride, who like me, was a couple of years shy of draft age, had accompanied me into the city wearing the sea-scout uniforms of our marching band. Except for our tender age and a conspicuous patch that identified us as members of the American Bluejackets, we were indistinguishable from the real thing. Someone from the local American Legion had given us tickets for the Central Park mall where the President would speak. That morning we found ourselves milling around among thousands of people. As we were searching for our place, suddenly, an official-looking gentleman wearing a broad ribbon reading "Committee," collared us. Quickly glancing at our tickets, he snatched them from Larry's hand and in a menacing voice, demanded, "What are you doing with these?" We thought we'd somehow come into the possession of unauthorized passes and began to make explanations. But he brushed aside our entreaties, and right before our eyes, tore our precious tickets in two. "These are worthless," he said, smiling. "Take these." With that he handed us two engraved cards that bore the Presidential Seal and directed us down a long aisle. His parting words were, "Just keep walking."

Walk we did—and every time we came to a barrier we were motioned on toward the front. Finally we found ourselves in the third row, directly in line with Truman's podium. The only people in front of us were wounded servicemen, in wheelchairs or on stretches. Every time some official or naval officer came close we thought we'd be ejected, but on that day, no one paid us the slightest attention. Two WAVES studied our patches and left convinced that that we part of some special group similar to the OSS!

After Truman's address, we joined the mass of humanity heading west toward the Hudson to watch him take the salute of the task force anchored in the river. By the time Larry and I reached the shoreline, the crowd was ten deep. We were about to give up when we noticed hundreds of onlookers on every apartment roof along Riverside Drive. Encouraged we followed this group, but they were all turned away at the elevator by the doorman. All except us, that is. "Come right this way sailors. There's always room for the Navy." We were royally ushered into an elevator and whisked up to the roof. There we were greeted like long-lost brothers, given front row seats, and plied with sandwiches and drinks. Fortunately, no one asked us to relate any of our "war" adventures.

Gradually, the warships left their piers and headed to back to various ports for eventual deactivation. The city returned to an unfamiliar peacetime routine and we went back to high school. After sixty years, hardly anyone recalls that event: too much was happening at home and abroad. The troops from Europe were at last starting to return, and family reunions were the order of the day.

After the most deliriously wonderful week the fleet had ever experienced, there was no doubt that the America they'd dreamed of all those countless nights not only existed, but had been waiting just as longingly for them. A few lines from a popular hymn summed up the feelings of a grateful nation:

Now the laborer's task is o'er;
Now the battle day is past;
Now upon the father shore,
Lands the voyager at last...

With war's end I could finally concentrate fully on the two most important things in my life: high school and girls.

CHAPTER THIRTY-SEVEN

COUPLES

O ddly enough, it was the Church that greased our path to the opposite sex. Aware that our raging hormones couldn't be stifled, but had to be channeled, nearly every parish offered dances over the weekend. With an entrance fee of fifty-cents, we found ourselves in a spacious area monitored by a few Holy Name men and sometimes a parish priest. No liquor was served, but the music was good, with plenty of soft drinks and soft girls to go around. We were offered a multitude of partners that could have been matched by a computer. Same age, same economic background, and primarily Irish. For awhile I reasoned that 90 % of the young Bronx females had to be Colleens! It developed that there were plenty of Italian girls as well, but they were more closely watched. And everyone was Catholic with a capital "C."

Most of the dances for teens were held on Fridays and Sundays— Saturdays being reserved for older couples. For us the most popular locales were St. Philip Neri on Grand Concourse, St. Benedict's, and St. Helena's. The latter was barely two blocks away from my apartment, but along with my friends, I soon became enmeshed with a group of girls from Throggs Neck. This placed St. Benedict's in the forefront. Like most parishes, their dance was held in the school gym—a space encompassing a series of small alcoves, each one an unofficial den. Arena seating encouraged socialization. As both sexes tended to travel in tight groups, once you met one girl, you were automatically introduced to all her girlfriends. This eliminated a great deal of stress. The pattern never varied.

Standing around much like a row of mannequins in a dress shop, each girl prayed that she'd be asked for a dance. Chicks in a farmyard never appeared more insecure. Like ships in a convoy, they hovered in a pack. I guess our erstwhile partners regarded us as a mixed blessing. They wanted us and they didn't want us. Those moments preceding the initial encounter were pure hell. I don't know who had it worse: the guy who was rejected or the girl who was never asked. That's why it was so important to build a bridgehead with a like clique of girls. Finding a friendly face among that array of females lowered a lot of heart rates. One Sunday we met such a group.

With our usual false bravado, Larry and I were trying to appear confident and nonchalant, acting as though all those ever-interesting creatures in plaid skirts, white blouses and saddle shoes didn't exist. But inside we were hoping for some opening to bring us together. One girl, Marianne Hockemeyer, walked over to Larry and said, "I know you, you're Larry McBride," and then pointing at me said, "and I know you too, Jack Sauter. You're both in the Bluejacket Band." We were stymied. A few months before her brothers had joined the band as drummers at P.S. 12, the school where we practiced. It was here that she and her parents had met my mother who collected the weekly dues. She was also that same 11-year old girl who had tried out for the Bluejacket band. I don't think she recalled the meeting.

Those Sunday evenings at St. Benedicts would spawn a multitude of encounters. And it was inevitable that all these new friends would live in Throggs Neck.

In spite of the fact that I never dated any of them seriously, these girls were very important to my relationship with women. I spent hours socializing, attending parties, dances, movies and sporting events. One of the major hurdles was learning that girls never said exactly what they meant. After an uncountable number of hours one began to bridge this gender gap and became gradually introduced into their special world. Eventually, I became comfortable in their presence—no small accomplishment. One or two of my close friends never crossed this barrier, and lived a life without the intimacy of the opposite sex. I don't know if this trait was inborn, or if somewhere along the way some girl turned them off. Sometimes one can be painfully rejected just one time too often. I had an uncle on my father's side who never married. He finally began to keep company when he was in his fifties. At the time we never gave any of this much thought. We were just happy to be accepted.

Our girlfriend's parents welcomed me and my friends into their midst with no reservations. If their daughters had to choose companions from a pool of available boys, we were everything they could ask for. They

only had to be with us for a few moments to see that we'd be no threat.
None of us had cars, or even much of an interest in them. (Friends from
other parts of the country are astonished when they learn that I didn't
drive until I was twenty-four, and inherited my first car from my wife.)
Everyone in our respective groups took their Catholicism very seriously,
and in fact lived their faith. Many of these girls stood next to us at mass,
and at times even joined us at confession. At the time we knew so little
about the opposite sex we couldn't fathom what they would have to
confess. With innocence surrounding them like a halo, we never imagined that they harbored similar thoughts or entertained sexual fantasies
just as wild as ours.

I'm sure that there were some "bad" girls in our neighborhood, but
for good or ill, we never met them. Very few of my friends ever ran his
hand up a girl's skirt or inside her blouse. That only came after some
serious time together—years perhaps. We lived inside our dream worlds.
When it finally came, it was all the more exciting and satisfying. At least,
that's what we kept telling ourselves. In the end, for me at least, it turned
out to be true.

All those names swim back through the decades, but one, Virginia
O'Malley, is most remembered for her wonderful house parties.

Mrs. O'Malley was a widow trying to raise three kids. She'd prepare
soda, chips and cookies, lower the living-room lights, and repair to the
kitchen where she'd listen to the radio and knit. She became the most
popular parent in the East Bronx. I guess her theory was it was better to
know where your daughter was and whom she was with than worry all
night. We couldn't have been happier.

For my friends and me, discovering girls was akin to Columbus discovering America. We had a lot in common. Most of us didn't know where
we were going, or had a clue how to get there. These creatures could have
landed in a space ship from another planet. That was about the limit of
our knowledge. But it was that very enigma that lent so much allure to
their presence. It was always the DIFFERENCE. They looked different,
smelled different, felt different, thought different, and moved different
than we did. And awaiting us were all those mysterious pleasures that
only they could dispense.

Looking back, it was all so innocent. We'd start with parlor games;
Spin-the-bottle and Post Office were old stand-bys. Anything to start
things rolling. Everyone would have an opportunity to kiss. There was
no picking and choosing, so no one felt rejected. Slow music was the

catalyst. It was an unwritten rule that no girl was left sitting alone. Those sororities were always "equal opportunity." Gradually we were learning that the most glamorous girls were not always the best partners. They were far more interested in themselves than meeting anyone new.

We were also far too inexperienced to realize that looks and figures change rapidly at this stage in life. Like many fifteen and sixteen year-old girls, Marianne wore braces, but in a few years she'd leave each and every one of the "glamour girls" in the dust. I was too stupid to appreciate this at the time, but the Gods gave me a second chance before someone with more nerve and charm carried her off. With my stuttering I was no prize either. I wore my insecurity like an ill-fitting suit. At any rate, all that lay in the future. I was concentrating on Virginia's living room.

Marianne

A stack of Blue Deccas featuring Bing Crosby, Frank Sinatra and Dinah Shaw were soon chosen and we settled in. The McKenna living room reverberated to the familiar melodies of the day: "Time After Time, Stardust, Falling in Love Is Wonderful, Mam'selle, Deep Purple and Tangerine." Without all those eyes staring at you in the auditorium, we could let ourselves go and mould our bodies into our partners. Slipping my hand around a soft, slender waist was always a satisfying prelude to a dance. Never had any complaints. There was very little talking ——just to hold them and deeply inhale their fragrant scent was reward enough. Cheek on cheek, then ear to ear, we would soon open the path to their lips. That first kiss was always a revelation—no two girls were ever quite the same. After the magic of the newness wore off, I found myself existing on a plane I scarcely knew existed. It seemed I'd waited forever for these precious moments, and I vowed to remember all of them. With racing pulse and labored breathing, I longed for this to go on and on and on. None of the girls would have won any contests (neither did we), but that never entered our minds. Remember it was very dark! Totally at ease with them, we knew that their limited experience precluded any judgments on their part as well. We were like research scientists; never knowing what new revelation lay ahead. In our total naiveté there were no "next steps." Our instincts took over, but within very proscribed limits. Had Mrs. O'Malley somehow disappeared, I doubt that there was one of us who could have brought this evening to what today would be considered its logical conclusion. In spite of more than a few cases of "lover's nuts," each of us floated home to sweet and intense dreams. We all looked forward to Emily's next party.

While not being overly concerned with women's fashions, I loved the standard female attire of that time. Every girl I knew wore a skirt and blouse. Skirts were always far more provocative than slacks. Nylons did wonders for every set of legs, and there was something about garters, or even the thought of them that set our pulses racing. The crossing and uncrossing of legs was far more sensuous in a skirt or dress than it was with trousers. Blouses of course were perfectly designed for showing off "coming attractions." Some of sheerer ones were little more than lingerie.

All these evenings led to some very ambivalent feeling towards the opposite sex. Our bodies were pulling us in one direction, the church in another. Waiting to go into confession, my mind is filled with vivid images of are naked girls. It's driving me crazy. How can I confess that I'm sorry for "entertaining" (the church's word) impure thoughts when that's exactly what I wanted to do: "entertain" them. I'd never entertained any girl, naked or clothed, but it didn't make any difference. Why did God create naked girls if you weren't supposed to think of them? That was a mystery the brothers never discussed.

In time we arranged to meet these Throggs Neck girls every morning on the 8:05 IRT subway at the Castle Hill Ave. Station. In a sort of a "musical chairs" in reverse, the first girls would entrain at Middletown Road, an earlier station, and others would join at Westchester Square. Finnegan and I would wait until we saw them in the last car and then complete the circle. Just about all them went to Cathedral High School at 51st Street in Manhattan, the female counterpart to Cardinal Hayes. Our friendship grew with each train ride.

Unfortunately this jostling subway ride would often bring some embarrassing physical effects. It wasn't so noticeable in the winter when we wore heavy coats, but once the calendar moved to May we were often reduced to riding a few extra stops until this "battle of the bulge." returned to normal. A number of us took to buying a newspaper every morning for cover and concealment.

While many of our new partners were as sexually naïve as we were, there were a few more enlightened ones who took perverse pleasure in capitalizing on our plight. If we were dancing, they knew just how to trigger this nearly instantaneous reflex reaction. Others would purposely sit on our lap at parties, shifting and wiggling to bring us to indescribable agony, all the while feigning total innocence.

Those Sunday evening church dances eventually brought many couples into that topsy-turvy emotional state known as "going steady." At sixteen I wasn't ready to lock onto one partner, even if I could find one. But lightning struck a few friends and that first girl became his last. My long time friend, John Robben, had this experience. He spotted a pretty girl across a crowded room and instantly proclaimed to his dumbfounded buddy that this was the girl he was going to marry. And marry Margie he did. Two of my longest high school and Navy friends, Vin McCaffrey and Don Roller, both met their wives in the same way.

While it limited your circle of possible partners, going steady had some distinct advantages. For openers you always had a date. No more engaging in that Chinese water torture more commonly known as telephoning a girl and asking (begging?) for a date. How I detested that stupid game. For reasons I'll never fathom the girl you called almost never said yes the first time. Even if she liked you and was dying to go out to a movie or a dance, it was de rigueur to come up with some reason to say no. Playing "hard to get" seemed to be every girl's motto. Washing their hair was always Number One on their excuse list. I'm sure that they washed many a potential good husband down the drain along with the soap.

I engaged a few girls in that "going steady" routine. It usually lasted but a month or two. Every time we broke up, there was always that sinking feeling that I'd never find another partner. I always did. When I mourned my recent loss, my mother would say in her best philosophical manner, "Jack, remember this. There's nothing as dead as a dead love." In the end, most of my relationships with the opposite sex had all the permanence of a permanent wave.

My father's art books included several detailed anatomical drawings of the female body. A cursory glance at their internal organs would reveal how much more infinitely complex women were than men. If we were "long division," they were "calculus." Like music, this subject would entail a lifetime of study, always knowing that no matter how long you lived, you'd barely scratch the surface. At this stage of my life I was more than ready to begin scratching any surface!

That summer at work I briefly dated a girl who lived on Staten Island. It was quite a haul from the Bronx, but the ferry was but a few blocks from the insurance company. She decided to broaden my "education," and while I moved up a few "grades," I never took the "final." After she left the company, a friend of mine in Personnel revealed that Eileen was nearly twenty-three! I always thought her "lessons" routine was unique, but years later mentioning my experience to a much older woman, she said, "Jack, there are girls out there who are looking for a page not yet written on. You were lucky to find one.

CHAPTER THIRTY-EIGHT

WAR'S END

The European War ended on May 8th, 1945, but on the other side of the world another and perhaps more bloody campaign awaited us—the defeat of Japan. With the estimated casualties running as high as one million, many troops in Germany, France and Italy would have to be shuttled to the Pacific.

My brother-in-law, Johnny McDonald was onboard one of these transports when the Japanese suddenly surrendered in August. Being close to New York, the captain decided on his own to head for the nearest port. As a result, Johnny was home only a few weeks after the war's end. With no new homes and apartments built for over a decade, living space was incredibly tight. My mother offered Dot and Johnny the second bedroom of our apartment, and thus began a sort of "musical chairs" inside the Sauter family. Rita took over my couch in the living room, and I was shuffled into a small alcove just off the kitchen. We would live like that for nearly two years—three male and three female adults in four rooms, all sharing one bathroom. To compound the situation further, it wasn't long before my sister had a baby girl. I received a free lesson on what marriage was all about, beyond the kissing and caressing.

With living arrangements almost as tight as the army, my brother-law coped quite well. My mother tried mightily to smooth the transition and for the most part it worked. There were a few uncertain, but usually humorous moments when the ingrained habits of a soldier reared its head at the dinner table. "Pass the fuckin'salt, please!" would result in a deadly silence, but we'd soon all laugh and life would go on. More of a problem was created by the arrival of my niece who required two o'clock feedings. This meant a trip to the kitchen with the light shinning right in my eyes. I'd never had a baby underfoot before, so the whole experience was a revelation. On the up side, Johnny was an ardent New York Giants fan, fanning my interest in baseball. He bought me a copy of the baseball record book, and in my usual fashion I soon had nearly all the accomplishments set to memory. I was on the cusp of seventeen, but in a "better late than never" fashion, I embraced the sport. Soon photos of Mel Ott and Bill Voiselle replaced Halsey's carriers and battleships. This was the first time I ever lived with a male who wasn't my father. Johnny and I never developed as deep a friendship as I had with my other sibling's husband, Buddy, but he moved me in the direction of more conventional pastimes.

In time, apartments opened up, and Dot and Johnny moved a few blocks away to the same building where he grew up. In the meantime Rita got married, and facing the same tight market, replaced Dot and Johnny in the second bedroom. At least I was away from the kitchen. My chance for a room of my own was put on hold for another year and a half, however. Having known no other existence, it was no problem. In time, besides my father's air-compressor, we had to make our way around a baby carriage, a stroller and all the flotsam and jetsam that accompanies infants.

Buddy, Rita's husband, was crazy about jazz and the music of the twenties. He'd sit for hours listening to Fats Waller, Bing Crosby and Buddy Clark. Moving beyond the record book, Buddy took me to my first ballgame: Giants versus Cincinnati. Typically, the Giants lost, but I loved being inside the Polo Grounds. To me, it resembled an open-air Carnegie Hall.

Soon I was exposed to finer points of the game: bunting, base-stealing, and the apex of the sport: the battle between the pitcher and the batter. Television had yet to grace our apartments, but Buddy and Johnny played softball nearly every night after dinner. The game continued until it was too dark to see the ball. Afterwards, we'd discuss how they'd won or lost. It was the best way to learn that baseball was mostly a cerebral sport.

For Christmas that year my father once again leaned towards an "educational toy" for me. Ever since I was thirteen I'd been the recipient of books and study materials designed to make me use my brain rather than something tangible such as camera or a pair of binoculars. My gift that December was the Beethoven's Fifth Symphony—the Toscanini recording. He later recounted a humorous story. He was in a store during the Christmas holiday and was looking for some help in choosing my present. My father asked a salesman what he thought would be an appropriate educational gift for a sixteen-year-old boy. Without hesitation the salesman replied, "A sixteen year-old girl!"

A family friend bought a local bookstore on Castle Hill Avenue, only a block from our apartment. He and his wife kept the former name: Elna's Book Shop. They asked my mother to help out part time, but once they saw how perfectly suited she was to the job, she became a permanent employee. Blessed with a winning personality, and a naturally helpful attitude, she could literally sell snowballs to the Eskimos. She always took time with customers and helped them find just the right sentiment for a birthday or anniversary. Close to the store was a home for the aged, and many of these customers had difficulty writing. My mother would compose a suitable message in her John Hancock script and soon the entire home became devoted customers. She remained in this position until she was in her mid-sixties—a perfect job for a family of readers.

CHAPTER THIRTY-NINE

CATCHING UP

In September 1946, I entered my senior year. Academically, I blossomed. With the ending of World War II, I could concentrate wholly on my studies. I was also rewarded with excellent teachers. Some were new —some were old friends. Surprisingly, for the first time, I loved math. I'd just about squeezed through my first three years with 65-67 grades. In a change that I would have welcomed earlier, the two final math courses were split right down the middle. I studied Solid Geometry from September until January and Trigonometry for the balance of the school year.

Unlike algebra or plane geometry, I could see a practical reason for each of these courses.

Solid Geometry related to such problems as measuring the volume of liquid in a barrel or drum or the cubic area of a house. That I could understand. I also had a terrific memory for memorizing theorems; the rules created by Euclid and others. The second half of the Regents always gave one an opportunity to utilize that memory if you possessed it. The same applied to Trigonometry, only more so. Trig' was the basis of navigation, a science I was acutely interested in. My ultimate dream was to join the Navy and become a navigator. I couldn't imagine a more exciting life or responsible profession than being able to mathematically determine exactly where you were in the middle of the ocean. That smacked of black magic!

For English I had Father Grace. Grace ran the senior Debating Society and I spent a number of hours after school drilling in rebuttal arguments and summaries. As a fascinating sidelight in his formal English course, we dissected magazine articles in LIFE, TIME and COLLIERS to study how writers can slant material to establish a point of view. We did the same with the DAILY NEWS and the N.Y. HERALD TRIBUNE. Very enlightening.

By now my writing skills had reached a level where I could compose an essay or a debating speech in one sitting.

Everyone paid attention in the English class, as it was a required Regents credit. For many students, this was critical, as college hovered on the horizon. Unfortunately for Grace, he also had to spend an hour as our Home Room moderator, and he lived to regret it. Home Room was sort of a study period, a time-filler just before lunch. Announcements were read and the material was for the most part left up to the priest or brother. Communism was Grace's burning passion. He loved to read long passages from Das Capital, the Red Manifesto. With his monotone and a restless group of hungry 17 and 18 year-olds, it was a recipe for mayhem. There were forty students in 4I, our class. For this period we were assigned to a physics lab room with theater seating. The rows rose just like a movie house. Underneath this wooden flooring was a hollow space.

At some point during every class a Student Council member came by to collect the attendance report. Most of the time the teacher would leave the slip with the student nearest to the door and never even lift his eyes from his book. It was our last April in high school and everyone itched to raise some hell. When the attendance card was picked up, unknown to Father Grace one of his students would slip out. About a minute later there would be another quiet knock on the door and another student would leave. It became a disappearing act! When the lunch bell rang Grace would look up and discover to his horror that only five or six students remained instead of forty. Before he could recover, everyone would be gone in that mad rush to the underground lunchroom.

Other times, someone would crawl through an access trap door at the back of the room and position himself in the open space under the rows of seats. Then, right in the middle Grace's soliloquy, he'd begin to sing softly, "You are my sunshine, my only sunshine..." Poor Grace thought he was losing his mind.

Father Brady returned as my History teacher. Now we were studying U.S. History from 1900 to F.D.R.—right up my alley. Brady said my grasp of the issues gratified him. Having read everything I could get my hands on about this period for five solid years, I was well grounded. In my History Regents I scored 100%.

In 1946 something happened in lower Manhattan that affected nearly every working man and woman in New York. The clerks in the New York Stock Exchange went on strike to improve their working conditions. They formed a picket line that nearly everyone ignored. Soon mounted police appeared and began to push these pickets—mostly young girls, into the street. Their attempts at a strike became a laughing matter. But labor had come a long way since the thirties and soon members of a sister union: the longshoremen joined their picket line. The first time a mounted policeman tried to force them onto the street he found himself on his back in the gutter surrounded by two or three burly men. Since this confrontation had all the makings of a pitched battle in front of national media, Mayor O'Dwyer stepped in and forced the Exchange to negotiate with the union.

Father Brady

While this struggle was going on, union organizers were passing out literature to all the bank and insurance company employees in the area, including my own. Seeing the handwriting on the wall, major concessions were granted which effectively ended the threat. In the fallout from the settlement, every bank and insurance company followed suit. No more Saturday work, paid two-week vacations, hospitalization and group life insurance. A major upturn for working class New Yorkers. The Stock Exchange wasn't organized, but the union had won a tactical victory and in the process changed New York City. Father Brady was in his glory, but not many of the other clergy shared his viewpoint.

In many ways Brady reminded me of my father. He insisted on documentation for all your positions and arguments. Never accept the current popular notion—dig deeper, he cautioned. At the time many newspapers, especially those owned by Hearst, were strongly against unions and any government interference with the economy. Reciting major passages from Pope Leo XIII's famous encyclical, RERUM NOVARUM— On the Condition of Workers, Brady explained how the Pontiff espoused a philosophy that brought government into the forefront in the struggle between labor and management. Leo said, "It was not only the right of government to protect the rights of workers, but an obligation. Since wage earners are numbered among the great mass of the needy, the State must include them under its special care and foresight. It is shameful and inhuman to use men as things for gain and to put no more value on them than what they are worth in muscle and energy. Oppressed workers, above all, should be liberated from the savagery of greedy men. Equity commands that public authority show proper concern for the worker so that what he contributes to the common good he may receive what will enable him, housed, clothed, and secure, to live his life without hardship. When injury has been done or threatens the common good or the interests of individual groups, it is necessary for public authority to interfere. The right to organize and form protective organizations to guarantee the right to negotiate for better working conditions is a natural right that must be protected by the State."

At the time I wasn't aware of it, but Brady's comments were forging my lifetime political philosophy, one that I've never changed. Skillfully excerpting passages from the New Testament, he demonstrated that Christ was certainly on the side of the poor and the downtrodden. He asked the rich man to give away his possessions and follow Him. It was easier for a camel to enter the eye of a needle than for a rich man to enter heaven. "What politician echoed these sentiments?" Brady asked. Didn't FDR say, "I'm not worried about the man on the top of the ladder. It's the man on the bottom I want to give a helping hand." All the Democratic initiatives: Social Security, Child Labor Laws, the 8-hour day, the right to bargain collectively, Unemployment Relief, were all directly related to Christ's teachings. Brady continued, "Christian morality doesn't just mean policing the private behavior of individuals, but changing the unjust structures of society. You can pray to God to right the wrongs in the world, but real Christians engage in these tasks themselves."

Looking back, I can see than Dan Brady was a pivotal influence on my life. I was lucky to know him. Coming on the scene right after the Great Depression, his timing couldn't have been better. French Three brought a similar satisfaction. We read DeMaupassant and Moliere, and engaged in basic conversation. Again a repeat teacher—Brother Theodore. He looked severe, but possessed a quirky sense of humor. He loved plays on words. One of his favorite stories that remained with us involved a French restaurant. The patron orders eggs and out comes a plate with one egg. He complains to the waiter, but to no avail. "Don't you understand," the waiter explains. "In France, one egg is un oeuf." (enough!)—the word for egg.

I passed another milestone that final year. It required a great deal of "catch up ball," but 1947 saw me at last achieving a coveted place on the Honor Roll (90 or above in every subject) for the last two marking periods. Moving to an exalted plane, I could claim my reward—using the elevator while moving between classes!

School boat ride Ed Menninger, Don Roller, Arthur Leone

Another close friend, Eddie Menninger, also garnered a few prizes that year. Eddie and I went way back—to the Bluejacket Band where he was our drum major. Aside from being a brilliant student (he was offered a number of scholarships when he graduated the following year), he was an accomplished public speaker. In 1947 he won the Journal-American as well as the American Legion speaking awards—each one bringing a tidy sum of money. Much like my other close friend, Larry, Eddie was also blessed with an engaging personality. He didn't share Larry's musical talent, but he mastered a number of comedy routines that made him one of the most popular boys in our group.

With my studies in hand for the first time, I thoroughly enjoyed every minute of my last high school year. It was a time to get involved with football games, big dances in the gym, field trips to the United

Nations in Flushing Meadows and even Broadway plays. As a member of the Debating Society and the French Club I was taken to see "The Best Man," "High Button Shoes," and "Harvey." The band, the orchestra and the Choral Group spent a day at Steeplechase Park at Coney Island. Late that afternoon we couldn't locate one of the brothers who accompanied us. He was later found with a beer in his hand joyfully watching the passing parade.

In retrospect, I have a few criticisms. Had it only been for a single semester, typing should have been mandatory. And a four-year well-rounded education should have included a basic instruction in the use of hand tools. Living in an apartment I never saw anything more exotic than a hammer or a screwdriver. I also possessed only the vaguest knowledge of what went on under the hood of an automobile or under a dress. (Cars I didn't worry about!) Considering the world that we were moving into, these were not minor shortcomings.

Lastly, it always seemed odd that for a school steeped in the teachings of Christ, we were rarely taught tolerance. There were certainly enough glaring examples right under our nose. Racism was practically a way of life in America.

We never thought it would happen, but as the date for graduation approached, nearly everyone was sorry to see high school come to an end. It took awhile to appreciate that this was a critical and immensely rewarding time in our lives, and that every moment should be cherished and remembered. Four years had passed as if in a dream. When we first stepped through those bronze doors, time had stretched interminably— a straight highway disappearing in the distance. But faster than we'd imagined, the years had become seasons, the seasons months, until now we faced the final hours trickling through our fingers.

Four years had gone, and what a four years! Nations had been vanquished, millions killed, and now the world was slowly and agonizingly trying to pick up the pieces. Our brief spell on the Concourse had spanned the invasion of Italy to the first murmurs of the Cold War. No wonder I was distracted.

We didn't know it then, but we were living in a golden age: for the city and the Bronx. Every positive factor that would influence our lives had come together to forge a destiny that would shape our future. We could look forward to a world at peace after a long and terrible struggle. The economy was booming. Even at full production, it would be years before American industry could come close to meeting the pent-up demand for consumer goods. Not only the war, but the Great Depression had left the country without most of the basic ingredients of the "good life." For awhile there was an abundance of disposable cash, but little to buy. When the first new automobiles in four years reached the dealers, it was a "sellers market." Most purchasers were forced to pay an extra fee under the table to get behind the wheel. In spite of this there was a heady feeling of optimism that permeated every facet of society. We had won the war and put the Great Depression behind us. America was the most powerful country in the world. Nobody was even close.

All the daily newspaper featured photos of the largest ocean liners moving up the bay packed to the gunnels with soldiers returning home. On one voyage, the QUEEN ELIZABETH carried in excess of 15,000 men. People lined the shoreline with welcoming signs and banners. Nearly all the ships were met with a flotilla of private boats. On more than one occasion the Sanitation Department Band was pressed into service on a ferryboat to serenade the happy soldiers.

Every serviceman's dream was a home of his own, but it at this time it was an impossible dream. As the soldiers and sailors were discharged in record numbers, the housing shortage became all too apparent. In desperation, to help fill the need, the city constructed scores of Quonset huts in open tracts around New York. These basic structures were light years from the home of their dreams, but to a young married couple, it gave them that priceless element—privacy.

In many respects the United States was replicating what it done to raise an army and prepare for war in 1940. Then it was thousands of barracks that were being raised to house new recruits. In a twist of fate, many of these same recruits, now veterans were experiencing the same phenomenon in reverse.

Our pastor, Monsignor Scanlan, established a parish housing office to list every available spare room, basement or attic space. In a throwback to the Great Depression, many families—our own included, doubled up to fill the need.

Some far sighted builders, Levitt prominent among them, knew that we were on the cusp of a population explosion. Converting hundreds of acres of potato fields on Long Island into land for tract housing, it would irrevocably change the face of New York City and its surrounding counties.

But before I could dwell on these momentous changes, the Senior Prom was upon us.

CHAPTER FORTY

DOUBLE THE PLEASURE,
DOUBLE THE FUN

Ballroom of Hotel Pennsylvania

One of the highlights of our last year of high school was the Senior Prom. This premier event had been advertised to death as "the" social apex of our four-year stint at Cardinal Hayes, and one not to be missed. Having two older sisters didn't help—I was awash in tales of their "big" night. The culminating evening would take place in mid-May 1947, about a month before graduation. It was, by all accounts something of a "coming of age" milestone in our young lives. Nearly everyone in my senior class was looking forward to it with keen anticipation. Me,

I was scared to death.

If I was going to this ball, I wanted to share this night of nights with someone very special. But for all my dating, I hadn't met anyone even remotely close to my goal. It was my fault. I was painfully insecure, and usually after mumbling my name to a girl on a dance floor, I was at a loss for words. I usually got little help from my partners; I didn't know that they were just as numb as I was. I'd had "girlfriends" but it was a revolving door. I never really got to know any of them.

I spent hours wondering what it took to crack the mystery of girls. Some of my close friends never appeared to have a problem. They would go to a party or a dance and within a few minutes they would be surrounded by two or three pretty co-eds. Was there some magical chemistry I needed to possess? I had spent the last two New Year's Eve's with my parents. No fun. What I really wanted was a soft girl to hold and relate to. Physically, I'd "come of age," but it was all wasted. For the first time I experienced an intense loneliness. I soon discovered that one can be terribly alone even in a crowd.

Things drifted along like this for the first two months of the fall of 1946, but then against all odds I met the right girl. My parish lowered the age for admittance to their Saturday night dances in the school auditorium. Now I could meet a whole new crop of girls rather than keep recycling my original group. Those Throggs Neck girls knew our "lines" better than we did.

A dozen Bronx parishes employed this weekend dance formula, and it worked beautifully. Engaging a small group of live musicians, or using the "canned" popular melodies of the day, the churches attracted scores of teenagers from all over the Bronx. And the odds were heavy that every girl you met would not only be Catholic, but also be within a year or two of your age. St.Helena's school was easily reached by subway or trolley car—still a nickel in that wondrous year. (I lived two blocks away) As a result there was a fresh mix of female faces every Sunday.

One entered a rather austere basement hall—a chamber of cinderblock walls encompassing a hardwood floor that was also pressed into service as a hall for Sunday mass, and on other evenings as a roller rink. But the music was good and it was crowded. Like the proverbial birds of a feather, each sex tended to stick together, seemingly afraid to mingle individually. For all our bravado, it took more than a little courage to break away from your protective male cover and sally out alone to test the waters. What would you do if the girl you asked to dance said no? Everyone you knew would witness your denial. This little game of advance and retreat, acceptance and rejection could turn the toughest guy's guts to jelly. But finally a few brave souls ventured forth. Lo and behold, every girl they asked said yes.

Looking back, it must have been much more difficult to be a girl in that situation. We were concerned about being turned down, but we had innumerable bodies to choose from. The odds were in our favor. Even the homeliest guy could eventually find a soul mate. On the other hand, in the custom of the day, the female couldn't initiate the encounter; she had to wait to be asked. Her great fear was that no one would, and she would stand there like a sentinel all night, dying inside. We were too dense to grasp this truism, but these girls had come here, some traveling long distances, for one purpose—to dance and meet boys. They weren't looking to get married (yet!)—they only wanted a few minutes of our time. My friends all grabbed partners and joined the pack on the floor. One didn't have to be Fred Astaire—the dance floor was so crowded it resembled the I.R.T. at rush hour—with music! You just held on to each other and the mob bore you along. I waited and watched, trying to get up my nerve.

After about a half-hour, I decided to get a Coke and walked over to where some church volunteers were handling the sodas. These affairs were well chaperoned—no liquor or rowdiness permitted. There was a crowd at the soda table, but suddenly it melted away and there in front of me stood this gorgeous girl—all alone. I was astonished that nobody had asked her to dance, so without further thought I blurted out, "Hi, would you like to dance?" She rewarded me with an engaging smile and slid into my arms. "My name is Terry Corrigan, what's yours?" It was as easy as that. Rather than place her right hand on my shoulder, she encircled my neck, drawing me closer. An appropriate song was on the turntable. Connie Boswell crooned, "I need no soft lights to excite me, to thrill and delight me, Oh no, it's just the nearness of you." I couldn't have ordered a better lyric to express my feelings. When that number was over, she didn't break away immediately as most of the other girls did, but remained loosely in my arms. A rising warmth consumed me and I must have looked it. The music resumed and we continued. In the next half-hour I discovered that she had five older sisters—no brothers— and lived about a mile away. Terry was a year older, and had just graduated from Aquinas High school the previous June.

I thought she'd want to meet some new boys after an hour passed, but she made no move to break away. Gliding along to the popular songs of the day: "Linda, Mam'selle, and Racing with the Moon," I was enveloped in a fragrant cloud of Tabu. We talked about getting jobs and going to college, but neither of us had made any definite plans. Terry was working for the Telephone Company while she sorted her life out. Very few girls thought about careers in 1946; it was assumed that they'd work for a few years and then get married.

Much too soon I heard the strains of "Goodnight Sweetheart," the band's swan song. I offered to take Terry home and she readily accepted. She liked the idea of an ice cream soda and we headed for an all-night diner nearby. Sitting across from me, she looked terrific. Light brown hair fell to her shoulders, and her open jacket revealed a fine figure. I liked everything about her, especially that winning smile. We sat and talked for more than an hour until she looked at her watch and said, "I'm really enjoying this, Jack, but tomorrow is 'Labor Day,' and it's getting close to midnight." I had never before been so relaxed in a girl's company.

Approaching her home, with my heart pounding, I took the plunge, "Terry, how would like to go to my prom with me?" Without hesitation she replied, "Oh Jack, I'd love to." I think I can borrow one of my sister's dresses and alter it in time. I guess it's going to be in January, right?" It took me a minute, and then I realized that she thought I was graduating in January—about six weeks away. I said no; it won't be until May. A bewildered expression came across her face and then she began to laugh. "I guess you really wanted to make sure of me, didn't you? Well, you needn't have worried. I think you're a pretty nice guy and I'd love to go with you. What's more, I like the way you dance. You didn't know this, but I never made it to my own prom. I had a date, but he broke his leg playing football a couple of weeks before the affair and that was that." Before I had a chance to agonize about making the first move, she did it for me, leaning forward and giving me a delicious kiss, whispering, "I had a lovely time. Thanks." I don't think my feet touched the ground the whole way home.

We met at the same church dance for a few weeks and then we began to go other places; mostly movies. My mother told my sister that she was concerned about me going out with an "older woman" while I was still in high school, but my sister Rita just laughed. "I don't think you have anything to worry about Mom. I saw her. She's only a few months older than Jackie, and he told me that they start their Saturday night date by going to confession in her parish."

Terry was the first girl I'd gone even remotely "steady" with and it was paradise. How I hated to call girls for dates. Most of them didn't want to appear too eager, so they'd make up a series of excuses I could probably recite better than they could. With this girl I never had to be concerned with rejection. We always arranged the coming weeks' date at the end of the current one. If she couldn't make it on Saturday, she'd always suggest another night. Best of all, she was naturally affectionate, usually ending a date with long necking session in the park near her home or on the sofa in her parlor. She invited me to a party at her house and I enjoyed meeting her family. Each one of her five sisters could have been a starlet.

The prom was a relatively expensive affair with the hotel dinner tickets, a rented tuxedo, a corsage and a nightclub afterward. At seventeen I wanted to be my own man, so I went hunting for a job. By October, one of my close friends, Jim Skinner, who worked in an A&P supermarket managed to get me in. The store was very much like the Navy, in that the work was physical and there was a tremendous camaraderie. Except for Jim and me, the rest of the workers needed this job as a livelihood. These were real men doing real work. No one cared that you were only seventeen. You were treated as an equal as long as you held up your end. The pay was outstanding for that period, and I soon had more money than I needed for my big night; May 18th, 1947.

Jim and I were going to be accompanied by my best friend Larry McBride. Larry worked after school for Collier's magazine in midtown Manhattan, and this became the subject of a peerless prom night experience.

Our prom was on a Friday, and everything was well in place long before that. The three of us ticked off our plans—nothing was left to chance. Jim, being the oldest, and the sole possessor of a driver's license, borrowed a car for the evening and picked me up after fetching Maureen, his date. We drove over to Terry's house and her whole family greeted us, escorting her out the door. Ravishing in her white gown, Terry took my breath away. Jim was still ogling Terry's gorgeous sisters as we drove off, just narrowly missing another car.

Arriving at Larry's house we expected to find him standing outside, but there was no sign of him. Jim and I walked in and to our surprise found him sitting forlornly in a pair of dungarees. "Larry! What the hell are you doing? Dorothy is waiting for you and we don't have a lot of time. Hurry up and get dressed." He looked even more despondent. "I'm not going. I blew all my money." Then he proceeded to relate his sad tale.

Larry McBride

Larry had the kind of genes that made him look as if he needed a shave ten minutes after he put his razor away. While working that afternoon, his boss, knowing that he was going out that night said, "Larry, why don't you take the rest of the afternoon off. Go downstairs to the barber and get spruced up. That way, you won't have to rush yourself." What Larry didn't realize was the barbers in these midtown office buildings were far different than the local Mario in our neighborhood. In the Bronx, thirty-five cents was the going rate for a haircut and hot towel. A shave was twenty. Sliding into that comfortable leather seat Larry felt totally relaxed. The barber placed a warm towel over his face and asked what he'd like. "Give me the works," Larry responded and dozed off. In this case, the "works" included a haircut and shampoo, a shave, a manicure and a singe. Looking at the finished product, Larry beamed. Then he got the bill—$11.50, without the tip! After the tickets and flowers, Larry had saved all of $20.00 for the evening. He was devastated.

The trouble was the more he looked for sympathy, the more Jim and I laughed. His unique tonsorial adventure reminded us of O'Henry's classic story: THE GIFT OF THE MAGI." Jim and I quickly held a little council of war and figured we could easily bankroll Larry for the night with our extra money.

In most cases in life, when one earnestly longs for something, in the end it's usually a disappointment. But our prom night was everything we'd wished for and more. The dinner dance at the Pennsylvania Hotel was outstanding, and the Latin Quarter show afterward was just raunchy enough to make us feel all grown up. Sophie Tucker came down and sat on Larry's lap during one of her numbers, and we topped off the evening (morning) with a round-trip on the Staten Island ferry. Our dates looked like candidates for Miss America and were totally exhilarated by everything. Crossing the harbor in the cold breeze, Terry cuddled so close that my studs left a weeklong imprint on my chest. She looked and smelled so enticing I could have remained on that ferry all night.

Back in her living room, with the first rays of dawn brightening the room, she asked me to give her a hand unhooking her long gown. With two sisters and a mother I was a past master at that chore, but my hands were shaking. Even without the gown she had more on than any girl on Orchard Beach, but that brief glimpse of her was intoxicating. Somehow the sight of a girl in her underwear, no matter how conservative, is always arousing. I was tempted to take advantage of this opportunity and break new ground, but it was a little late in the day. The living room was also much too close to her sisters and parents bedrooms. She slipped into a robe and we shared a pot of tea. I had another big night in the wings, so after a few goodnight (or in this case, Good Morning) kisses I headed home.

In the end I was just happy to have been given this "coming attraction." If I can carry this movie analogy a little further, there would be a seven-year intermission before the "main feature," and that would star an entirely new leading lady—Marianne. She was already playing "bit parts" in my scenario, but at this time neither of us could have imagined what lay ahead.

That would have been enough of a prom night for any red-blooded boy, but fate had more in store for me.

Four years before in my 8th-grade class at St. Helena's grammar school, I met a studious classmate, Jenny McCoy. At thirteen and fourteen, the rest of the girls in the class liberally applied as much makeup as Sister

Ann Veronica would allow. But not Jenny. Blessed with an alabaster skin, the kind I'd only seen on actresses like Maureen O'Hara and Vivian Leigh, her deep brown eyes only accentuated the contrast. On the down side, she was short and still a bit pudgy, needing a little more time to rid herself of the baby fat that plagues so many teenagers. I'd had the same problem, but I didn't wear a skirt. It wasn't her looks that I recalled most, however, but her studious manner, always fully prepared in class and acting far more mature than her age. We were friendly, and more than once she helped me through an algebra assignment. Aside from that we parted ways after class ended, never socializing.

As the years passed I saw her regularly at the 11 o'clock mass with her parents. Occasionally, I'd be pressed into service as an altar boy to help distribute communion and I would have to hold the plate just beneath her extended tongue. Just for fun, I'd sometimes press the plate into her chin so she'd know it was me.

One Sunday in mid-April she was waiting for me after mass. She looked worried. "Jack," she murmured, "Can I ask you a big favor." "Sure," I replied. "What can I do for you?" "I'm embarrassed to ask you, as we've hardly spoken since we left school, but I hope you'll help me." By now, my curiosity was aroused, and I stood there waiting. "Well, it's like this. My senior prom is coming up next month and I'm dying to go. My problem is I don't have a date. I really don't know any boys, but I do know you from school and the neighborhood. I was wondering if you'd take me." Before I could open my mouth, she quickly blurted, "It won't cost you a nickel. I have the tickets and enough money to cover any expense you would have. I know you have to rent a tux." I was at a loss for words, but she looked so vulnerable and pleading that I had to say yes. It seems that every girl has that secret weapon and they learn how to use it from about the age of two.

The next day I made the mistake of mentioning my encounter to a couple of my neighborhood friends who knew Jenny and they kind of sneered when I told them I was taking her to her prom. "That dog? You must be hard up for a girl. I thought you were a lady killer." I was sorry I'd opened my mouth.

In a stroke of good fortune, Jenny's prom was the night after mine. I could get two nights out of my rented tuxedo for the same price. But that was only the beginning of my good luck. When her prom date came around, I was still a bit the worse for wear after my big night, but by Saturday evening I was ready for another whirl at the Big Apple. The recuperative power of youth. The Square Florist remembered me and gave me a discount on another orchid. I wrote a short note on the card and slipped it in with the flower. (I had a favorite corny line lifted from a movie: "You're the only girl I know who can wear an orchid. Usually the orchid wears the girl.") They ate it up. My mother had meantime sponged and pressed my tux and washed my dress shirt. I looked spanking new.

Jenny lived in Parkchester, a pretty fancy address at that time, and I looked forward to a pleasant, if not exciting evening. Her father greeted me at the door and said that Jenny was still getting dressed with her mother's help. Inviting me into the living room, he lowered his voice. "Jack, Jenny is our only child and this a very important night for her. She's been looking forward to this affair for a long time and I want her to have everything possible to make this evening perfect." He made a furtive glance toward to bedroom door and then leaned in close to me, lowering his voice. "Jack, I know you're a good boy. I've seen you going to communion on Sunday and I'm not worried that you won't be a gentleman. This is Jenny's first dance with a date, so treat her gently. I understand that you went to your affair last night, so you know the routine. Please show Jenny as good a time as you gave your other girl." With that he reached into his pocket and handed me fifty dollars!

It took me more than two weeks to earn that at the A&P. I tried to refuse the money, but he insisted. "Jenny's mother and I think it's a wonderful thing that you're doing. Not many boys would take the time and effort with just an acquaintance."

Jenny looked completely different when she walked out of her bedroom. She'd been to the hairdresser (probably the first time in her life) and her mother had helped her with some lipstick. That marvelous complexion remained unsullied however, and the plain duckling had become a serene swan. Her dress was from Arnold Constable, her mother said. That didn't mean much to me, but my mother and sisters nearly swooned when I told them. Mr. McCoy was a Wall Street attorney, and Jenny was "daddy's little girl."

Insisting that we take a taxi to the hotel for her prom, he paid the driver in advance. Two of her girlfriends and their escorts joined us at the dinner table. It appeared that this was a "first night" for both the other couples. I may have been their "man about town," but I was still drinking Coke.

Prom group at Village Barn

After the dance, I suggested the Village Barn, a nightclub down on McDougall Street in Greenwich Village. My brother-in-law recommended it. They featured a variety show, very clean, and very vaudevillian. I didn't think Jenny or her girlfriends were the Sophie Tucker type. By the time the show ended it was close to midnight. The other two dates decided to call it quits and one of them suggested sharing a cab back to the Bronx. Laughing I said, "Do you think Jenny is some kind of Cinderella who has to leave by midnight? We're not ready to say goodnight." She beamed at that remark. I called a taxi, but instead of going uptown, I told the driver to take us to South Ferry. The Staten Island ferry was packed with many prom couples, some from her private school. She got some very curious looks from her girlfriends, surprise mostly, and I secretly hoped, envy. I'm sure she was going to be a topic of conversation in her school for some time. I took her up on the open deck where it was crowded, and placed my jacket and arms around her. It was a warm, moonlit evening, but there's always a breeze underway. She held onto me like a drowning swimmer. For Jenny this was a totally new experience. I didn't want to come on too strong, so we didn't kiss on the way out. I had to remind myself that in spite of all the trappings, this was our first date. Alone for the first time, she started to tell me a great deal about herself. She was very shy and insecure, and completely unsure of herself with boys. Then she lifted her head toward mine and whispered something. "Jack, I'm so ashamed to tell you this, I hardly know where to start, but I think it's only fair that you hear this from me. I hope I won't hurt your feelings, but you were the third boy I asked to my prom. The others turned me down. You have no idea what this means to me."

I couldn't even begin to imagine how difficult it was for a girl to admit this. I related my similar feelings and how much I feared rejection. She confessed that she never thought boys had any problems. They always looked so confident. I told her a few jokes, and once she began to laugh, she totally relaxed. I could feel all the tension drain from her body. Returning to Manhattan, we found a sheltered spot on deck enveloped in darkness. I told her that she looked absolutely radiant and that I was so glad she'd asked me to share this special night with her. I leaned close and our lips just touched. From her reaction I knew it was her first real kiss. For Jenny, it was like the first sip of wine and she came back for more. By the time we reached South Ferry I was wearing more lipstick than she was.

Just before we reached Parkchester on the ride home, I saw a White Castle hamburger diner and told the driver to let us out. Since he was the only car on the road, he asked us if we'd like to have him wait while we ate. I agreed and we brought the curtain down trying to satisfy that ravenous hunger that always seems to follow evenings like the one we just had. Jenny suggested that we bring a hamburger and coffee to the driver. He was all smiles. (Amazingly, that diner still stands on the same spot.)

Her mother was still waiting up when we got home. She invited me in, but I said I'd burned my candle too long at both ends. That was no lie. Mrs. McCoy gave me a kiss and a hug and thanked me for showing her daughter such a good time. I said I was the one who should be saying thanks. Jenny will never have to ask another boy to go out. They'll be lined up at her door. That was a bit of a reach, but I'd been well versed by my sisters to tell a few white lies.

I didn't see Jenny again for seven years. I'd just been married and was in Parkchester to visit my parents. Coming out of Macy's our eyes met in instant recognition. She'd lost all that baby fat, and was now a slender, attractive woman. However, she still carried that serious demeanor, a real asset in her case. Jenny would never be mistaken for a glamour girl. But there was something far more important than glamour in that angelic face. This was the kind of a girl some lucky guy would marry. I could see that Jenny was a completely different person than the girl I'd kissed goodnight in May 1947. We exchanged pleasantries. "Jack, you didn't know this but I know your wife, Marianne, from the Parkchester library, "Jenny said. Marianne had worked there while she went to high school. "I even made it to your wedding. My mother and I heard the bands at St.Helena's. You've probably forgotten, but we live only two blocks away from the church. Marianne's a lovely girl. Best of luck."

Just before we parted, she took hold of my hand and said, "I don't think you ever knew how much that night meant to me. I still have the faded leaves of your orchid inside my prom night program." She kissed me on the cheek, turned and walked away. I left her feeling very good about the world and myself.

Fifty-nine years have passed since those two memorable nights in May. I don't have any faded flowers or even a program, but I don't think I'll ever forget my fabulous weekend with two lovely girls.

CHAPTER FORTY-ONE

BREAKTHROUGH

1947 was a year to remember. All my life it seemed as if I was waiting for something— waiting to grow taller, waiting to pass a test, waiting to meet girls, waiting to get promoted, and waiting to enter high school. Now I'd accomplished all these things. But leaving Hayes was akin to moving to another plateau—the cusp of maturity. I had a strong feeling of inner satisfaction, but one tinged with ambivalence. I was climbing a hill and there was no turning back. My clock was running and there was no stopping it. There would be other plateaus.

Father Sheehan, my old English teacher and close friend had volunteered to say mass at my parish during the war. So many priests had gone to become military chaplains, the local churches were shorthanded. As a result, the archbishop asked those priests in teaching and hospital work to say a mass or two in the parish of their choice. Father Sheehan chose St. Helena's and decided to remain after the war. Every Sunday I'd attend his mass and then join him afterward for coffee in the rectory. By this time my family and I were familiar to the Monsignor and the other clergy as part of a family who helped the parish in many ways.

After Mass, I would often wait for the church to empty before moving up to the sacristan. I wasn't aware of it, but my conduct triggered speculation that I might be seriously considering the priesthood. Even my mother was curious. That particular morning I found that question particularly amusing considering what had transpired the night before.

My good friend, Harold had arranged a blind date for me to accompany him and his girlfriend to a dance at the Merchant Marine Academy in Throggs Neck. My partner, Audrey, was rather quiet, with average looks and a good figure. She liked to dance, but said little. After the dance Harold suggested a drive to City Island for a pizza and a walk along the shore. It was a gorgeous night. Once in the car however, Harold's girl put a hammerlock on him and soon they were all over each other. Harold's girl began to emit these deep moans while the car windows completely steamed up.

Audrey and I began what appeared to be a standard necking session, when all at once she opened her blouse. She placed my hand on her bra. She was warm as toast. I felt as if I was on the edge of a tremendous revelation—an experience that I'd only dreamed about. She whispered just two words—the best words I could have heard: "Unhook it." My heart pounding, I reached back across the warm, smooth flesh of her back and found the clasp. The bra flew apart. Reaching up, she pulled it away with one motion. At first, I couldn't see much, but then the headlights of passing cars in the parking nearly floodlit the backseat. Under different circumstances things might have gone much further, but it's difficult to erase the inhibitions of a lifetime in one stroke. People were moving around the lot looking for their cars, so we weren't exactly alone. If I'd had a long relationship with Audrey things might have been different, but everything happened so suddenly that night, I was more than satisfied to have reached this momentous stage.

The only downside to this evening was that Audrey had splayed herself across my lap, making it impossible for me to move my legs. Of course the inevitable happened and I was in excruciating pain. I kept thinking about that science lesson about an irresistible force meeting an immovable object. Unfortunately, that night my body contained both of them.

In spite of all the distractions, it was a landmark experience. I never saw Audrey again. I thought about calling her, but our relationship might have moved into uncharted waters— seas I wasn't ready to navigate. So I settled for a fond memory and quit while I was ahead.

With the images of those recent hours still burning inside, I found the thought of entering the seminary the furthest thing in my mind. For the first time I didn't feel any guilt. I figured that anything that beautiful just couldn't be sinful. I was just celebrating one of God's most enchanting creations.

The next time I saw Harold he said, "I have a little gift for you—something to help you remember last Saturday night." I opened the bag and inside was a box of Mounds!

For someone below the age of fifty, my conduct may seem more than a little strange. But the reader must understand how different life was prior to 1960. Religion played a major role in most people's behavior. Nearly everyone I knew spent his or her first 12 years in a parochial school. There were no Playboy or Penthouse magazines, and the movies enforced a strict moral code completely controlled by the Hays Office. Television was if anything else, more restrictive. Words like "pregnant, hell, damn, and breast" were deleted or bleeped. Clark Gable's final line in GONE WITH THE WIND—"Frankly, Scarlet, I don't give a damn," was much debated before being finally approved. We never experienced the temptations that arrived with the sixties, so it was easier to remain on the straight and narrow. As one's friend's father put it, we were all fasting before a feast.

Women's fashions from 1945 to 1960 were among the most modest of the century—the "new look" which featured hems nearly touching the ground. The sight of an uncovered breast was limited pretty much to art museums or the National Geographic! If someone depended on the media to learn about sex and reproduction, he or she would probably think that the stork delivered all babies!

In my circle, regardless of gender, the chances were very good that you'd enter your marriage bed a virgin. In retrospect, this wasn't all bad. As in most things in life that are postponed, it only heightened the experience. We discovered that the only thing better than sex is the anticipation of it.

I had one more unusual evening concerning females that year, but this time they were seen from a far greater distance than Audrey. Under the stern morality of Mayor La Guardia, New York City was about as raunchy as a seminary. But just across the river in Newark stood the Hudson Theater, where burlesque was featured. One night we were supposed to go to a concert, but instead decided to broaden our non-musical knowledge. Big surprise! When we arrived outside, we saw entire families going in. The comedians were easily the stars of the show, but the women, who we'd come all this way to see, were nothing to brag about. When they started doing their "bumps and grinds," the lights became dimmer and dimmer. All the men in the first row of the balcony leaned so far forward I worried than some of them were going to fall out. In the end it was all shadows and imagination—mostly the latter. In spite of our disappointment, it was a fun evening. We all felt very grown up. Burlesque had shed its mystery.

CHAPTER FORTY-TWO

BONDING

*The whole family: 1949: My father, Rita, Buddy, her husband, Jack,
John McDonald, Dot's husband, Dot, and Mom)*

While all of these events were certainly notable, what remains paramount in my memory that year was my rapprochement with my father.

From the time I was seventeen my father and I began to enjoy long and spirited conversations about politics, and music and art. I yearned to discover the details of his early life, but that revelation wouldn't be aired until I joined the Navy three years later. That fall, we spent a Sunday afternoon exploring the Bronx Botanical Gardens. I was never aware just how pristine this stretch of landscape was, right in the heart of a bustling commercial district. His knowledge of trees and flora astonished me. He pointed out that much of the East Bronx looked exactly like this park when he was growing up in the early years of the century. Finding Indian arrowheads and other 18th century artifacts was not that uncommon in some of the more rustic areas of Morris Park and Throggs Neck.

More rewarding, I became privy to nearly every facet of his artistic creation. I learned, for example, how much more difficult water color technique was than working with oils. If an artist made a mistake in an oil rendering, it could be painted over. There was almost no limit to how many times that could be done. Often, when my dad was short of canvas and short of money, he'd create a new work right on top of the original. Watercolor painting required an entirely different method. Instead of canvas, the artist employed an absorbent paper-based material. Should he exceed the allowable amount of moisture to any given point, a stain would run down the work, rendering the work useless. This made water-color painting an infinitely more painstaking and stressful a medium to master.

Half-finished canvases stood against every wall. Sometimes in the middle of a rendering, he'd lose inspiration or become more interested in another subject. To me, what made these "works-in- progress" far more intriguing than those framed landscapes or portraits, was the opportunity to see the building blocks as they were being assembled. In the Louvre Museum in Paris, there are a series of partially completed sculptures by Michelangelo. Each one reveals a half finished human torso trying to "escape" from the stone. I don't know if the artist intended it that way or he just ceased work part way through, but it demonstrated the same insight.

One day during a walk he paid me a rare compliment. "Your mother and I are happy with the way you and your sisters have matured. You've kept your nose clean and you've been the recipient of a first class education. Over the past few years working with the Great American, you've gotten a pretty good background in the business world. You could easily have a good job waiting for you when you leave college. Remember one thing. Learning isn't over at twenty-one. It should be just the beginning. That's why they call a graduation a "commencement." Continued learning will give your life purpose and direction."

During one of these conversations, I took advantage of his unusual openness and tried to break new ground. How did he cope with being unemployed for so long? Would he have done anything differently? There was a long silence, and at first I thought I might be treading too heavily on a sensitive subject. But he smiled and said, "That's all behind me now. Sometimes it seems as if it never happened, but I know all too well that it did. I'm glad that I had a second chance to prove that I still had it. Someday I'm going to write a book about Wall Street in the Twenties. It was the most exciting period in my life. The high rollers, the phonies, the memorable people I met—what a decade! I just hope that you never have to go through what I did. I had a lot of company, but that didn't make it any easier. There were times when most of us thought the country would never come out of this."

"You're coming of age at a wonderful time. We're on the cusp of a tremendous expansion. When you get out of college and start earning some money, you can invest in any large company and just watch it grow. So put some money away. General Motors, US Steel, US Rubber— you can't go wrong. Right now, we're experiencing an economic phenomenon that may never be repeated. The long Depression, followed by World War II, has created an incredible demand for practically every kind of consumer goods that will take years to satisfy. Remember this. Right now and for some time to come America will have almost no competition. The British are bankrupt. The continent is devastated, and it will take years to recover. If we don't blow ourselves up with the atomic bomb we could be seeing the start of an economic "golden age." I didn't know how prescient he was.

My knowledge of economics was practically nil. I should have trusted my dad's savvy about the stock market, but my personality shied away from "risk taking," a key element of investing. With no money in hand, all this was purely academic, but it was good advice nevertheless. Down the road I'd benefit from his expertise, but for now I was happy to have him share these confidences.

My birthday and Christmas fall within ten days of each other. That year, 1947, my father gave me a reference book for each occasion. For my birthday it was a standard Webster's Dictionary. Christmas brought a similar, but quite remarkable companion volume. It was titled: THE WORD FINDER. Essentially what it accomplished was cataloging every adjective and adverb that could modify a noun or verb. It was invaluable. I still have and use both books. Dog-eared and braced with heavy tape, I handle them with the utmost care. I carried them through four years in the Navy, onboard three aircraft carriers and across countless oceans and seas. What I find most rewarding isn't the books themselves, but rather the inscription found inside the front leaf. Sadly, it's the sole surviving record of my father's writing. In THE WORD FINDER he wrote: Christmas 1947

> Dear Jack:
> It is my sincere Christmas wish that you learn to use this book in conjunction with your dictionary, as an artist uses his palette. Your dictionary can be likened to the three basic primary colors. This volume should widen the range of your palette so that each word picture you create, will have a style, and color that can only be reached through a true sense of "values."
> —Dad.

CHAPTER FORTY-THREE

A LOVE AFFAIR WITH LINERS

Liners at piers on the Hudson

Along with the returning troops, ocean liners of many flags began to return to New York. By 1947, Europe once again became a destination for tourists rather than soldiers. And among these ships were fortunately some of the crown jewels that had set the standard for ocean travel back in the thirties: ILE de FRANCE, QUEEN MARY, LIBERTE' (nee EUROPA).and AMERICA. At the time all one needed was a few spare hours on Saturday and a copy of the New York Times that listed the schedule of the departing ships and their respective piers. In those halcyon days, the great vessels lingered three to four days, but access was limited to sailing day.

During that first year, I joined my friend Bob Lipeles who had spurred my interest in liners, and took the subway nearly every Saturday to visit the ships. Initially, Bob and I just walked aboard with the passengers and their guests. Later, a quarter was collected, ostensibly to fund seamen's relief program. For ocean liner buffs this was the best money ever spent—a unique opportunity to see in the "flesh" what previously been restricted to travel brochures.

Stepping on that tilting gangway, one was transported into a completely new world. Perhaps the best part of that brief journey was a quick glance down into the narrow, but awesome canyon separating the steel hull from the pier. I can't imagine a more dramatic way to grasp the enormous height of these towering vessels. Once inside, the scene is best described as controlled chaos. Scores of passengers crowded the Purser's desk, while stewards and stevedores moved with purpose through a sea of bodies, bags and bouquets.

Searching for elbow room, we struck out on our own. Even armed with deck plans (which on occasion we were smart enough to carry), we often found ourselves hopelessly lost in a labyrinth of corridors and stairwells. We quickly learned that liner decks aren't flat, but curve gently, following the contours of the hull. And we never fully grasped the immensity of these huge ships until the first time we looked down the Promenade Deck on one of the QUEENS and watched it disappear in the distance. It seemed a miracle that something this enormous could float, let alone move.

In 1946 and 1947 we were a distinct minority—individuals wandering about the ship who were neither sailing or seeing someone off. One phenomenon struck us immediately: everyone appeared to be deliriously happy. And why not? Most of them were departing on a great adventure to strange lands that only a few short years before had seemed forever out of reach. For a week or longer, they would be ensconced in an unbelievable floating cocoon where everything that was promised in those brochures of old would come true, and in spades. On top of that, there would be an entirely new cast of characters to share this with. What could be more delightful?

Often in the course of admiring the breath-taking beauty of a grand salon, we'd be caught up in one of those elaborate bon voyage parties where all the well-wishers were plied with Champagne and canapés. After the first hour of uncounted refilled glasses, no one seems to care who you were, and assumed that you were part of the farewell ensemble. As a result, on many an occasion, our Saturday lunch became caviar or smoked salmon rather than a hot dog and Coke wolfed down on the street. Dressed in a jacket and tie (de rigueur for Manhattan in those days –and still for me today), we just became part of the scenery. Even more agreeable, there appeared to be an over-abundance of pretty girls eager to make our acquaintance, thinking perhaps that we might make suitable dancing partners on the upcoming voyage.

Away from the tumultuous public rooms, more intimate parties spilled into the narrow passageways from open stateroom doors. Occasionally, passengers in adjoining accommodations would join forces until there was barely enough room to squeeze by all the merry-makers holding drinks and shouting to be heard over the din. In the midst of this gaiety, sweating stevedores struggled to deliver suitcases, while stewards deftly maneuvered flowers and baskets of fruit. Locked in this crush, I half expected to hear Groucho's inimitable voice exclaiming, "Make that two more hard-boiled eggs!" (One of the memorable lines from the stateroom scene of A NIGHT AT THE OPERA)

In spite of all this warm hospitality, Bob and I had to break away. It was, after all, the ocean liner we'd come to see. Making our way to the upper deck, we'd find anxious knots of serious travelers huddled with deck stewards carefully choosing their deck chairs for the coming week. Walking beneath the towering funnels (predominantly three in those days) we'd gaze down on the neat rows of lifeboats, invariably thinking of the TITANIC. None of these behemoths boasted an outdoor pool— the sole open air activity being shuffleboard. Later, poking around in what were actually the bowels of the ship, we located the pools, intricately tiled affairs, often adorned with faux mermaids and fish.

With the exception of the QUEEN ELIZABETH, which moved directly into wartime service after completion, every ship we explored had seen many years of passenger service prior to performing their patriotic duty carrying thousands of troops. Regardless of how many coats of paint and miles of new carpeting the owners had added, there was no denying a welcome "lived in" quality that invited your company. To me, these traits were reminiscent of an old pair of shoes: resold perhaps, but eminently comfortable. And from the quiet efficiency and confident maturity of everyone onboard, it was evident that many of the stewards and ship's company had invested a fair chunk of their lives in these hulls. Since the host countries subsidized nearly all these magnificent ships, a strong sense of national pride ran throughout the crew. At the government's urging the lines tended to hire crewmen from economically depressed areas of their countries. Unlike today's cruise ships, this wasn't just a short term job it was their life's work.

Resuming our tour, we entered the dining room; always the most lavishly decorated public space on every ship. I particularly recall the architectural grandeur of the Salle de Manger onboard ILE de FRANCE: three decks high and looking for all the world as if it had just been lifted intact from the stage of Radio City Music Hall. If our liner was sailing at noon, this most popular area would be bubbling with activity with scurrying waiters and maitres'd assigning tables.

Not all the departures were during daylight hours however, and I recall one memorable evening onboard CARONIA as she was preparing for a 92-day world cruise. For a change, the bars were open and serving drinks gratis. The crowd was smaller, much more subdued, and elegantly attired. Jewels sparkled from the overhead lights and full length minks were sprawled carelessly across couches.

The beguiling melodies of Cole Porter blended with the sounds of tinkling glasses and soft laughter.

Bob and I wouldn't have been aware of that sailing were it not for story in the New York Times about two wealthy women, traveling alone, who had each booked an extra cabin just for their evening dresses! They brought a different dress for each evening.

The SATURNIA had a chapel, complete with stained-glass windows and pews. For those who needed more physical uplifting, every vessel boasted a multitude of bars. And there was always a grand lounge for dancing in the evening and sometimes movies. Whether the departure was afternoon or evening, one thing that didn't change was the sound of chimes signaling that all visitors were to leave the ship. This was always the most painful part of the visit. I entertained this wild fantasy that someone would step forward and offer to take me to Europe—perhaps as a companion to his lovely daughter. (I did say fantasy, didn't I?) Soon we joined a crush of passengers and friends in varying degrees of sobriety, heading for the gangways. Reality set in quickly when we found ourselves on the cold concrete of a dreary pier looking up at all those happy faces crowding the rails. For those die-hards who harbored doubts about the seriousness of those chimes, three deep-throated blasts on the whistle rang down the curtain in no uncertain terms. Feeling that no ocean liner visit is complete without the departure, Bob and I always lingered at the pier. A transatlantic sailing encompassed all the drama of a grand opera.

While the passengers and relatives shouted themselves hoarse (secretly wishing that all this forced gaiety would come to a hasty conclusion), two or three tugs quietly positioned themselves to help ease our levia-than on her first step to the high seas. Longshoremen manhandled thick hawsers over the bollards, and they were hauled in by the ship's capstan. Then slowly, ever so slowly, a gap of water appeared between the pier and the massive steel hull. After a few more high-pitched whistles, boiling white water suddenly erupted beneath the tug's sterns.

Now the moment everyone had been waiting for arrived, and the huge mass began to move ponderously out into the Hudson. This triggered another round of cheers and wails, until, with ever-increasing speed, the bow passed from view. Some onlookers rushed to the front of the open pier to take a last lingering look at the disappearing liner as her bow turned southward. Others slowly made their way back to the street, the traffic, and the real world. Our venture into this dream world had been satisfying, but all too brief.

Later, my friend Harold joined us on our Saturday outings, and we continued our visits until 1950. Among other ships, we managed to explore QUEEN MARY, QUEEN ELIZABETH, MAURITANIA, AMERICA, ILE de FRANCE and SATURNIA.

Of all the leisure activities I enjoyed growing up, ocean liner viewing was one of my favorites. This mode of transportation was unique, elegant, sophisticated, and adventurous. For the only time in our lives we thought we were on a movie set. All those Saturday Hudson River visits were carefully deposited in our memory banks, where they've drawn rich dividends.

CHAPTER FORTY-FOUR

THE SEVENTH REGIMENT

The Armory

"A fort on Park Avenue." This was the description given me to find the armory on 66th St. In spite of my exhaustive explorations of nearly every city byway, Park Avenue remained terra incognita. Housing no museums, historical buildings or even well known shops or restaurants, its rows of elegant apartments held no interest for me. Soon it would.

With the Senior Prom, a permanent job, and the impending decision on college, the year, 1947 would have been momentous enough. But that fall, just after being accepted by Fordham University, Larry McBride asked me if I'd be interested in joining the Seventh Regiment of the New York National Guard. John Carroll, his boss at Crowell-Collier, had been in the regiment prior to the war and had gone on active duty in

1941. During the Second World War the New York State Guard took over the duties of the regulars when the 7th went to Fort Stewart, Georgia. The State Guard was comprised of men who were ineligible for the draft because of age or disability. Now they had all moved back to full-time civilian life and the regular National Guard was set to return to its rightful homes.

Larry's boss was a Captain who desperately needed a crew. Following the path of least resistance, he leaned on his eligible employees to flesh out "B" Company. To have his unit "federalized" and be paid, he needed a minimum of twenty-five men. Drills were held once a week at the Seventh Regiment Armory, at 66th Street and Park Avenue, in Manhattan. I jumped at the chance.

Like most of my companions, I had expected the war against Japan to continue until at least 1947 or 1948. Japan had a fanatical population of more than 90 million, ready and eager to die for their Emperor. If the Okinawa campaign was any indication, landing on the home islands would be a long and bloody struggle. I'd be 18 in December of 1947 and planned to enlist in the Navy before being drafted. The atomic bombs dropped on Hiroshima and Nagasaki suddenly threw a wrench into all our plans.

Having worn a military uniform since we were ten, Larry and I didn't take much convincing. Besides, we were getting a bit old wearing leggings with our marching band. Another incentive was the pay (assuming our captain could corral twenty-five recruits) —$2.50 per weekly drill, plus the same daily rate for the two weeks at camp during the summer. This time we'd wear real army uniforms and fire live ammunition.

With World War II now history, I think all of us desperately wanted to prove to ourselves that we were real men. A last chance, perhaps. This would carry us, if not to the "real" thing, then to the threshold. It was time for a change.

By the time Larry and I came on the scene, the halls were filled with Gatling Guns and decades old cannons, as well as bronzes and other objects of art. Huge paintings graced the corridor walls. Imbued with tradition, it reeked of history. Permeating the interior were a mélange of odors— the lingering scent of cigar smoke, rifle oil, and the just plain mustiness of Victorian New York. In Manhattan, its nearest counterparts were the Dakota apartments, the Custom House, and the Museum of Natural History.

The regiment was drenched in tradition. Founded in 1806, it saw service in the Civil War where it endeared itself to the residents of Manhattan by being instrumental in putting down the infamous draft riots of 1863. But its most memorable duty was in World War I where it suffered heavy casualties breaking the Hindenburg Line in 1918. Two members of the regiment were awarded the Medal of Honor. In a brief ceremony in September 1947, we were sworn in for a three-year enlistment and quickly outfitted with a set of uniforms.

Joining this regiment was a sea change in my life as well as Larry's. For the first time we were in the company of real soldiers, many of whom had seen action in Europe or the Pacific. We were treated like soldiers, even though we were a long way from the real article. I reveled in the close-order drill, an exercise I'd been engaged in since I was ten. It was like another life—one we had all lived in our fantasies. That this world was real and could still exist in 1947 was astonishing. Above all, it was a maturing process par excellence.

This was no kid's game. Mackey, Cotter and Bonning were different from anyone I'd ever met in the insurance company. They'd all seen combat—some in Europe, others in the Pacific. It left a mark on a man. It was as if they had somehow seen the other side of death and returned. That was my theory anyway. It was difficult to remember that they were part-time soldiers, this duty occupying just a small compartment in their lives. The regiment loomed larger than most in my makeup since I was essentially a college student, locked in a job shuffling papers. After a few months I began to look forward to those Thursday drill nights. Watching all those war films, one never fully grasped the incredible number of skills one needed to master just to survive in combat. In a series of lectures and films, we were indoctrinated in the arts of cover and concealment, how to dig a foxhole or slit trench in a few minutes, and the importance of not bunching up under fire. Having the high ground was paramount. In the infantry, topography was fate. Stripping and reassembling the M1 and carbine until we could accomplish it blindfolded took a lot of hours of practice, and I guess most of us were astonished to discover that we'd completed our task without leaving out any parts.

With a company of scarcely twenty officers and men, esprit de corps was a given. After two hours of drill, we'd repair to the company room for cokes and sandwiches before changing back into civilian clothes. Some nights we'd play softball with another company in the drill shed. Finishing around midnight, we'd take a quick shower and board the subway for the journey back to the Bronx. The fact that we had to get up for work and night college the next day at 7 A.M. never seemed to deter us.

Enlisting in the military is like asking a girl to marry you. If things don't turn out right, you only have yourself to blame. On the other hand, if you were drafted, it was a shotgun wedding. We were serving in "B" Company simply because we wanted too. All this changed in 1948 when President Truman reinstituted the draft. Within one week our company strength went from twenty to one-hundred twenty-five men. While this change made us federalized and brought a welcome pay check, we lost some of the dedicated and generous spirit that made our tour so much fun. Some of new arrivals spoke disparagingly of 'playing soldier." In time most of this attitude changed. The alternative of serving two years active duty was far too strong for anyone to leave the regiment.

As much as I enjoyed these weekly drill nights, this routine put a crimp in my social life. Fordham School of Education claimed four evenings every week. As a split English/History major I was saddled with endless book reports and term papers nearly every weekend. Fortunately my new job as the receptionist/aide to the executive floor at the Great American afforded me a couple of hours of study time every day. No one particularly cared what I did at my desk as long as I was readily available when the Chairman of the Board, the President or the VPs buzzed me. That's how I got the job. A series of young girls had preceded me. They always seemed to be in the Ladies Room or on a coffee break when they were needed. Since I wasn't interested in a career in insurance, this arrangement worked well for all parties. The Chairman, Jesse S. Phillips, was more than a little impressed that I was working my way through college. Sometimes, to the consternation of my boss he'd invite me in to his richly furnished office for long conversations. Apparently he had some grandsons who were squandering their lives away driving convertibles and chasing young girls. How I envied them. Phillips was a lonely man, yearning for company. I became a good listener.

In July 1948, the 7th Regiment went to Camp Smith for their two-week summer maneuvers.

To accustom us to the "real thing," our showers consisted of a series of open wooden enclosures dispensing only ice-cold water. This awakened us in a hurry. I accepted this without too much discomfort, but what I couldn't abide was the horrible smelling open latrine we were supposed to use. One had to squat over this reeking mess to relieve

Jack Sauter

yourself. Instead, I took my entrenching shovel and walked a few yards into the woods. That was the first thing I disliked about the infantry.

As I dug innumerable foxholes, my entrenching tool soon took on all the properties of another appendage. One day the importance of digging these holes deep enough was brought home by having us observe the effects of a mortar attack on a prepared unmanned position. The real thing is much more impressive than any movie. Camp Smith was too small for any artillery demonstration; that would have to wait until next year when we traveled to Pine Camp (later Fort Drum), close to the Canadian border for our exercises.

The weather was hot and humid, perfect for mosquitoes. We soon discovered that camping out wasn't as it looked in the movies. Communing with nature might sound romantic, but after you were eaten alive by a swarm of insects, it certainly took the edge off. Stretched out under the stars, we spent the early evenings telling stories. This was the first time I'd been away from home on my own. It took a bit of getting used to, but there was just too much going on for me to feel homesick. That summer, I discovered that the long bull sessions were one of best things about the military life. Cloaking any embarrassment, the darkness allowed even the most reticent among us to open up. Most of the conversation revolved around girls, but except for an occasional veteran, it was all just talk. Everyone in our tent had been subjected to the rigors of a religious education, and it would take a few more years to rid us of all of these hang-ups.

Don related an incident that happened just before he'd left for camp. He was sitting on the darkened porch of his girlfriend's home engaged in some heavy petting. Her parents arrived home unexpectedly and his girl grabbed her clothes and beat a quick retreat. When the light was turned on, there sat Don with a brassiere in his lap. Luckily her mother didn't notice, but her father said, "I see you're in the lingerie business now, Don! It must be interesting work."

Early that first week we had to line up for what is colloquially known as a "short arm" inspection. The medics were checking to see if anyone harbored a venereal disease. It was bit of a shock to one's sensibility to be asked to expose himself to a perfect stranger and, to further demonstrate that his genitals were unsullied. This was just one more step to removing some of the vestiges of your civilian life. Communal showers were another revelation, but with ice-cold water, everyone's penis was reduced to the size of a cigar butt and we laughed it off. No embarrassing comparisons here.

Our first day on the rifle range was an exciting experience. Range safety was taken very seriously. This was our initial experience handling live ammunition. There were no restrictions on firing. We were to become as familiar with the various weapons as possible. Each of us was paired off with a veteran. I had sergeant Boning, a Marine Corps non-com who had seen combat on Iwo Jima. We made some "dry-runs," pulling the trigger without a shell in the chamber. On my first try I yanked the trigger. Boning was all over me. "Jack, don't jerk it. Take a deep breath, let it half out, and then squeeze the trigger—very slowly. Don't jerk it. Squeeze it soft and gentle just like the nipple on a pretty girl's—Bang!" The army certainly had a fool-proof way of making you remember.

But there were some surprises. Not being forewarned, the first time I squeezed the trigger with live ammunition, I temporarily lost all my hearing for a few hours. One was also taught to be extra cautious inserting the .30 Caliber clip into the chamber of the M1 rifle. The feeder mechanism was controlled by a powerful spring. The idea was to quickly push down the eight-shell clip deep into the aperture with your thumb, and then quickly release your hand before the bolt snapped shut. Those who didn't move fast enough received a painful lesson—M1 finger! I did fairly well on the range garnering a Marksman badge on my first afternoon. I did even better with the BAR.

Every afternoon at 4 P.M. we knocked off drills and returned to our tents in the company area. But we weren't free. We had to shower and change into Class "A uniforms (summer suntans) for evening parade or Retreat. The entire regiment was formed and the flag was lowered to the strains of Retreat. A cannon was fired, and with our band playing a Sousa march, we passed in review. Before this ceremony we resembled the image of a recruiting poster soldier—combat boots polished to a high gloss, creased trousers, rifle stocks oiled and gleaming. But whatever grass once graced the parade ground at Camp Smith, had long since disappeared under the weight of a thousand boots and the heat of a mid-July sun. As a result, huge clouds of dust enveloped every company as the dry earth was churned into a veritable sandstorm. Once the dust was so thick an entire company turned the wrong way on the parade ground.

The second week brought the field maneuvers.

At Camp Smith-summer 1948

Now we marched out into the "field" as they called it, although with the rather compact size of Camp Smith, the distance was probably no more than five miles away. Foxholes dug, we mounted our pup tents over them. We felt as if we would be snug as a bug in a rug until it began to rain hard during the night. It didn't take long before our foxholes were filled with six inches of water. Soon, I gave up bailing with my hands and helmet, and wrapped myself in my damp poncho. With battalions of hungry mosquitoes, I feel into a fitful sleep if one could call it that. There was no reveille, but a whistle awakened us at 0530. It was barely light and still raining. Our cooks had followed us into bivouac, so we stood in line with our mess kits waiting to receive pancakes and sausages.

In the downpour, we soon gave up trying to keep our folding aluminum plates dry, so the cold hotcake (a misnomer if I ever saw one) half floated with the soggy links. At least the coffee was hot. Everyone tried to find some relief from the rain, but we were under pine trees; not the most practical cover. Standing in the heavy rain, with wet feet and wet fatigues, I began to have second thoughts about all this. Captain Carroll's recruiting talk made no mention of nights and mornings soaked to the skin. No matter how much I tried to avoid it, the cold rain always seemed to find an opening in my poncho and trickled uncomfortably down my back. But better to be exposed to this real world of the infantryman now than be surprised later. If nothing else it gave me a deep respect for our relatives and friends who had gone through this experience in the recent war. No war movie, no matter how realistic could match the physical discomfort of this occupation. One of our noncoms said that it once rained steadily for twenty-six days in Italy during the winter of 1943-44. There was no campaign ribbon for rain. It went with the territory.

That night B Company took part in an assault against another company, defending a ridge on a small hill. We were issued blank cartridges, so when we squeezed off a round it sounded like the real thing. Instead of a steel bullet, however, the cap was composed of compressed paper. You knew if you were hit, but it rarely broke the skin unless you were very close. Sometimes the ammunition was dyed so the results could be evaluated.

Fortunately, the rain stopped before evening, so other than crawling through wet underbrush and mud, it was a lot of fun. As boys, we had played "war" in the empty lots of the Bronx, so this was merely an extension of those games. It's always a game when no one is using live ammunition.

Our evening meal was a big step up from our earlier fare. "C" Rations were heated in empty oil drums and everyone received a can of pork and beans, biscuits, a chocolate bar, fruit juice and cigarettes. I never understood the rationale for including cigarettes, until years later. Many youths became "hooked" after that first pack. Our mess kits included all the basic utensils. The spoons perfectly fit the "C" ration can. I traded my cigarettes for another fruit juice.

Our platoon commander, Sergeant Nichol, explained our plan of attack, which would be in nearly total darkness. There would be a few flares now and then, but we'd have to follow our squad leader who had a compass. Stay close, he said. If you lost your way you could easily fall into a shallow ravine. It wasn't deep enough to kill you, but you could break an arm or leg. Don replied, "Hey Jack, Look at the positive side. We're getting $2.50 a day for this!"

Off we went.

I was the third man in a single file, allowing me the advantage of having another pair of combat boots to follow. I always stayed within inches of those boots. Crawling on my elbows, sweat poured into my eyes, sharp branches tore at my arms and legs, and every mosquito in the camp seemed to have zeroed in on my face and neck. Their incessant buzzing was the most disturbing part of the exercise. Maintaining absolute silence, we couldn't even smack the little devils.

After about twenty minutes we arrived just below the ridge and my squad was deployed in a wide circle to flank the defense. Moving solely by instinct, I strained to hear any sound. We pulled up the night's darkness like a blanket. As we moved closer and closer, my nerves were screaming. Once up the rise a flare briefly illuminated the scene in stark detail. Looking down on the other company's foxholes, we saw that we'd achieved complete surprise. We all ran down the hill, screaming and shooting and tossing mock hand grenades. The rest of the platoon soon attacked, and overran their foxholes from the front. In a few minutes it was all over. Captain Carroll was ecstatic. .

As a reward for our evening's work, Carroll arranged trucks to take us back the five miles to camp the next morning where hot showers awaited us. This exercise would have been the highpoint of our summer camp except for one drawback, which revealed itself all too soon—poison ivy! Unknown to us, we'd been crawling through massive patches of this horrible greenery –both poison ivy and poison sumac. About half the men had it in varying degrees of discomfort. The worst part was the terrible itching. Because of the darkness none of were aware of the effects of the ivy, and we'd inadvertently spread it by scratching ourselves everywhere. Within 48 hours the blisters erupted. It was agony. Our medics had nothing to help with the itching. We all suffered.

In wiping the sweat from my forehead, I'd infected my eyes to the point where I could barely see. Obviously I couldn't function like this, so they decided to send me home by train two days early with two other guardsmen. All my gear was sent back to the armory by truck. As bad as I felt, my buddy, Dick, was in worse shape. During the night he'd relieved himself right in the middle of a patch and he couldn't sit down.

Dressed in suntans and combat boots, with my face and hands swathed in bandages, I was given a railroad voucher on the NY Central, along with ten dollars for lunch and carfare. When I arrived at the Tremont Avenue railroad station, I jumped in a cab for the four-mile trip home to my apartment. The driver told me how his heart went out to veterans like me. I just nodded. When we reached Gleason Avenue, the meter read $1.45, but the driver waved away my money, saying, "I don't take fares from "wounded soldiers!" Seeing the bandages, my mother almost fainted. Once I explained, she was all right, but she insisted that I strip down and take a scalding hot bath to open all the sores.

Then she liberally painted the infected areas with a heavy coat of calamine lotion. It eased the itching, but did little to dry up the oozing sores. Only time would do that.

I couldn't face another summer like that, so I contacted our family physician, Doctor Rosenthal. There were some shots I could try, but he cautioned that they were only about 60% effective. I took them right away and continued to take boosters before the next summer camp in 1949. Luckily, I fell within the right 60%.

During the winter and spring the Cold War heated up and our training schedule was intensified. I made PFC and was assigned to a heavy mortar platoon. Instead of the Garand M1 rifles, we carried sidearms, but before I could congratulate myself on my good luck, I discovered that the 81-millimeter mortar weighed more than forty pounds. Everyone in the squad rotated carrying the various pieces in the field, but the base plate was a real back-breaker. It was like hauling the hood of a car!

The summer of 1949 the 7th regiment moved up to Pine Camp, (now Fort Drum), next to the Canadian border. It was 500 miles from Park Ave. and a real honest-to-goodness Army base. With a couple of hundred square miles of rugged countryside, we had ample area to interact with armor and artillery. Living in two-story barracks was a great leap from tents. There was a movie theater, a large mess-hall and numerous ranges for every conceivable weapon. Our war games were more realistic, joining forces with two other regiments, but essentially the two weeks were a carbon copy of 1948. By now, I was used to life in the field. The novelty had worn off.

One incident on maneuvers brought home more vividly the seriousness of what we were doing far more than any lecture or film. During an artillery demonstration, a 105 mm round fell short, killing three guardsmen. Their bodies were so badly mangled that one soldier was identified solely by his high school ring. No more remarks about "playing soldier."

Having four weeks away from work during the summer was one of the best parts of being in the National Guard. No matter how bad the mosquitoes were at night, it was far better than riding the Lexington Avenue subway every morning. I was also becoming toughened to the military regimen and never got tired of marching to a good band. Strong friendships were forged, and in a way it was very much like living on another plane.

Much as I enjoyed the close comradeship in B Company, I had strong doubts about my ability to go to war with this group. Sergeant Bonner said that everyone felt like that, because no matter how much you train, there's no substitute for the real thing. Aside from my misgivings, at this very time I was completely engrossed in the early volumes of Samuel Eliot Morison's US NAVAL OPERATIONS IN WORLD WAR TWO. The Navy had always been my first love and this stirring account only rekindled my loyalty. I gave serious thought about transferring to the local Naval Reserve Chapter at Fort Schuyler when my National Guard enlistment expired the following summer. They met one weekend a month. That would play havoc with my social schedule, but it would open up an extra evening every week. With the draft now filling the ranks, I no longer felt any obligation to Captain Carroll. I had plenty of time to mull it over. My enlistment didn't expire until September 1950 and I still had more than a couple of years of night classes remaining at Fordham.

In spite of the poison ivy, the mud, the heat, the long marches and the backbreaking effort of hauling a mortar, it was clear that my stint in the Guard was just what I needed to cross that threshold from adolescence into manhood, albeit on the installment plan. I found I could measure up with my contemporaries, especially on the rifle range, and living away from home—even for two weeks—was an effective preparation for the real thing. I fired live ammunition, ate C-rations out of a can and slept outside in the rain. More important, I never let anyone down. But always in the background was the certain knowledge that in two weeks I'd be back at my desk in the insurance company. One old sergeant described the difference between the Guard and the Army perfectly: It was just like using a condom, he said. You were there, but you weren't there!

CHAPTER FORTY-FIVE

COLLEGE NIGHTS

In the spring of 1947, with high school graduation fast approaching, I formulated my plans for higher education. I had pretty much decided on a career in teaching, which is another way of saying that I had no firm idea of what I wanted to do with my life. I later discovered that this wasn't unusual for those in my age group. I was more than a little envious of students who had settled on a firm course, but it remained a lifelong mystery how one determines that he'll be a dentist or an accountant at age seventeen, never having been employed as either.

Since there was no money for private college in my family, I took advantage of the city universities that were essentially tuition free: one of the many perks of growing up in New York. I applied to Queens College and was accepted on my high school average alone.

It may seem strange that I'd chosen a school across the Long Island Sound, but Queens had a fine ciricculum and was convenient to a bus that ran only a few blocks from my apartment and crossed the Whitestone Bridge. My plans were to attend days and work in my off hours to pay my modest tuition and help the family.

I was well into what I imagined would be my last summer at the Great American Insurance Company, when suddenly all my plans were upset. A letter from the college Admissions Department explained that while I was eligible to be enrolled, their charter required that they give first preference to residents of Queens County. Ordinarily this would pose no problem, but a surge of returning veterans were availing themselves of the GI Bill, and all the slots were filled. To help soften the blow Queens College had taken the liberty of sending my academic transcript to City College and Brooklyn College, both free universities. Each in turn accepted me.

Unfortunately, the distance involved to either school would involve a commute in excess of three hours a day, as opposed to thirty minutes for Queens. I had to reply to each admission office within ten days to be accepted, too quick I thought, for such a major decision. I decided to work for a year, and sort things out later.

It was July when Frank Whelan, an attorney in the Legal Department of the Great American, came to my aid and made me privy to another alternative. He asked me if I was aware that Fordham University had a downtown branch right next to City Hall, practically within walking distance from my job at Liberty Street. I inquired and discovered that there were three schools available: Law, Business and Education. I was a bit apprehensive at first because I knew the Liberal Arts College in the Bronx required either Latin or Greek to qualify, and I had neither. But the School of Education offered a straight Batchelor of Science that required neither language. Essentially it was a liberal education with only a few basic science courses like Anatomy and Physiology, and General Science. The rest of the ciricculum comprised the usual Jesuit regimen: Philosophy, Religion, Foreign Language, History and English. Best of all, the tuition—$9.00 a credit was something that I could handle on my modest salary. I applied and was accepted.

Because I'd experienced such difficulty early on at Hayes, I still felt some apprehension about my ability to survive at the college level. In retrospect, my insecurity extended well beyond dealing with the opposite sex. At the time the rest of my close friends were following a similar path, so I took the plunge.

Arranging my schedule around the National Guard gave me four nights to play with and I used every one of them. I carried fourteen credits the first semester—only two less than a full day schedule. Speech, Religion, two History courses (my major), English literature, Logic and Epistemology. From my initial few minutes in Philosophy, I could see that this was a huge change from high school. Still unsure if I was "college material," I hit the books with a vengeance. My job on the executive floor not only gave me a few hours of study time a day, but also access to some very sympathetic secretaries who wanted me to excel. Whenever I had a term paper or book report to write, they would take my long-hand and transcribe it on to an IBM electric typewriter and bond paper. This placed my efforts in the gilt-edged category. My reports were truly "works of art," and I'm sure that some of the "A"s I received were helped immeasurably by their appearance.

A course in Ancient History required a term paper with mandatory footnotes. Finding the saga of the ruler Justinian and his remarkable wife, Theodora, fascinating, I used them as my subject. Our 1905 Britannica contained forty pages on this Byzantine emperor and empress, complete with detailed references. Fleshing out my research, I found two other books about their reign. With four footnotes to every page, I hoped it looked professional. I was buried in "ob cits" and "ibids." My bond paper thirty-six page report garnered me an A+ and was held up as an example of the perfect term paper! It was my turn to be stunned. Miss Corcoran, the Chairman's secretary, was thrilled when I showed her my grade and told her that she was largely responsible for my good fortune. She in turn loved basking in my reflected glory. She said I'd given her a priceless gift—the son that she never had! I may not have had a great deal of luck with the younger set, but the older women were sure making my life easier.

The first semester passed like a breeze. I became enamored of English poetry, especially Keats, Byron, Shelly and Wordsworth; General Science revealed the mysteries of our universe, and Logic more than held my interest. Deductive reasoning would hold me in good stead in nearly every subject down the road. Remarkably, that first year I made the Dean's List, eliminating any doubts about my ability to survive. .

My History professor, Doctor Manning, was a carbon copy of Father Brady. Much older than Brady, he was a feisty Yankee, relocated from the coast of Maine. Favoring English tweeds, and bearing a remarkable resemblance to the Former Secretary of War, Henry Stimpson, he was a college "prof "straight out of Central Casting. He always came to class burdened with magazine articles, newspaper clippings, and copies of the Congressional Record. His course was tracing the Progressive era from La Follette to FDR. He was so well versed he could have written a book on the subject. We spent a solid month on the causes of the Great Depressions and the solutions offered by the New Deal. Growing up in the middle of Roosevelt's revolution, my knowledge of the politics and economic policies of the twenties were limited to say the least, but light years ahead of my fellow freshmen. I had no idea that the situation facing the farmers and the average wage earners was so precarious. As my parents had lost all their savings in a bank failure in 1932, I didn't need much convincing.

Downtown Fordham University was located just above City Hall in an old office building on Broadway, just off Duane Street. Stifling in the winter, it was warm and stuffy as well in the spring and fall. As a result, during the 8 to 10 P.M. periods, half the class would be fighting to stay awake. The school's only concession to social activity was a basement space, which included the bookstore and a coffeepot that ran constantly. Furnished with a few battered leather couches dating from the thirties,' this is where we gathered before class on cold evenings, and held our dances at Halloween and Christmas. A rubber plant sat forlornly by the elevator bank. Some wag placed a large sign next to it, proclaiming: PLEASE DON'T LEAVE YOUR BUTTS ON OUR CAMPUS!

In spite of its drawbacks, it was eminently convenient. Leaving work at 5 P.M., I had plenty of time for dinner at an Automat on Nassau Street (40 cents for a hot meal) and a leisurely walk up Broadway. Most evenings, a panhandler would accost me. In my dire financial straits I had little money to spare, but I'd always give them a smile and wished them luck. One night the same man hit me twice, about ten blocks apart. I told him he must have been an Olympic runner! The City Hall Station was two blocks away for my ride home. I literally rode the Pelham Bay line from one end to the other, exiting only a few stops from the end.

Marianne 1950.

In 1950, an old friend often joined me on the ride home—Marianne Hockemeyer. She was following my path, also studying to be a teacher. Her brothers were still in the Bluejacket marching band. Marianne had matured beautifully. Tall, with radiant brown hair that glowed in the reflected light, she wore clothes as if they were made for her and her alone. In many respects she bore a remarkable resemblance to Loretta Young—my favorite actress. She told me that she was studying ballet. In my eyes she didn't need any exercises to improve those marvelous legs. From what I could see in the dim light of the subway, the rest of her didn't require any enhancement either. She could have stopped traffic! I was astonished that this was the same girl I recalled from the Bluejacket band when she was eleven, and more recently at church dances. Many a night Larry and I would stop by on any excuse to sample some of her mother's succulent pies and cakes. At least that's what we told each other. Subconsciously, I think we were hoping to run into the daughter.

Then one night in late May I saw her in the lounge at school. She was wearing a skirt and blouse. I had known Marianne for nearly ten years, but I never really looked at her closely before. Right under my eyes she'd become a stunning beauty. Tall and slender, she had an engaging smile that locked you in. Seeing her in this new light, she made me forget everything. She was transmitting teasing images and I was tuned right in. Revealing legs that were both long and beautiful made her every step liquid motion. She radiated an aura of sensuality I'd never seen before. Watching her walk across the room was enough to leave me breathless.

Marianne had changed and so had I. I made sure we rode home together on the subway after class. This girl who I'd always taken for granted was now fully confident and reveling in her femininity. Later, when we got to know each other better, she said she had no confidence in herself—nothing but a bundle of insecurity. She sure fooled me.

I didn't tell her, but I began to formulate plans to see her one on one. Unfortunately, events took that option away from me and she nearly slipped out of my life. I didn't have much to offer an attractive girl. But fate was kind and I got another chance.

Although I was approaching twenty and had been working full time for nearly three years, I was basically poor. No car, a limited wardrobe, and still living at home. Those days everyone lived at home until they got married. Aside from the expense, people were always suspicions about why someone would need their own apartment. For a girl it was considered downright indecent. While many of my friends were driving—I didn't even have a license. There seemed little reason to bother. My father didn't drive, and I'd long become accustomed to public transportation. A car was well beyond my limited finances. Often I became envious when I heard my buddies' tales of romantic interludes in some secluded spot. Mine were limited to the girl's living room couch, usually in close proximity to her family. However, my work, my classes and my time with the 7th Regiment neatly locked in my weekly schedule almost to the minute. Weekend nights were my one break.

While I didn't have my own car (wouldn't until I got married at 24!), some of my friends bought ancient models that were now plentiful since war's end. New cars were coming on the market in ever increasing numbers. Joe Cavelli purchased a 1935 Chrysler and took us all for a ride. Six of us squeezed in this vehicle that had initially seen a showroom during Roosevelt's First Term. Joe hadn't been driving long and only had the barest knowledge of automobiles. On this cold night, Joe learned a timely lesson about mechanical brakes. We were coming down a hill when the car in front of us stopped for a red light. Joe hit the brake pedal, but the Chrysler only slowed. It was immediately evident that we weren't going to stop in time. Joe turned around and said, "Men, brace yourselves, we're going to hit that car!" Since all the old vehicles were equipped with sturdy bumpers, the damage was minimal, but there was a mighty jolt. We just sat there. The other driver came out of his car ready for a fight, but when he looked at the inside of our sedan and saw what he took to be six big men, he made a quick exit.

John bought a 37'Ford that came with a starter crank under the front bumper. He picked up his date for a formal dance and halfway there he stalled out. The Ford's cranky starter was such that only John could manipulate it. So, clad in white gown, his date had to get on her knees to manually crank the starter. End of romance!

Larry came up with a 1939 Nash—the big one that converted the back seat into a full-length bed. I guess it was designed for traveling salesmen to sleep on the road. At least that what their ads proclaimed. All these cars came with shades and possessed a distinctive odor. Once experienced, it was never forgotten. Someone said it closely resembled the smell from an open hamper.

I tried not to admit it, but by the third year, I was beginning to question my career choice. It would take at least five years to finish my B.S., and then it would be another two years to obtain my Masters in Education. And after all that effort, teaching remained one of the lowest paying professions. Other than insurance, in which I had little interest, I'd never been exposed to any other job possibilities. I seemed to be locked in a dead end. But most of my close buddies were in the same situation.

Larry followed in my footsteps, enrolling in Pace Business College. He had no definite chosen path either.

Among my high school friends, Don Roller had taken the biggest step. Wanting to study electronics, but without the means to go to college, he took a Navy test that guaranteed him a year's electronics technical school. Don had enlisted in 1948. By now he was stationed in a squadron at Quonset Point, Rhode Island. From time to time he'd drive down to the Bronx on weekend liberty. He was still going with his high school sweetheart, Dot Johnson, and there was little doubt that they would get married. In many ways I envied him, but in my family there was no way I could join the service. My mother would have considered that a step down in peacetime. I may have been 19, but in her eyes I was still 9!

1948 held two surprises: the Berlin Airlift and Truman's reelection. The former had the closest effect. The 7th Regiment was put on an alert to be prepared to go on active duty. We were not permitted to travel more than a hundred miles from New York during the emergency. I had a chuckle over that one. I'd never been more than the distance to the Jersey shore! After a few months the Russians understood that we were in Berlin to stay and the crisis passed.

While the privilege to vote wouldn't be granted until my 21st birthday—three years away, I was a solid Democrat. After living through the Great Depression, I couldn't be anything else. All during the summer of 48' I suffered along with Truman who seemed to be the only one in the country who thought he could win. Thomas Dewey, the Governor of New York, was well financed and seemed unstoppable. To compound Truman's problems, a large block of Southern States bolted the convention over a Civil Rights plank and formed the Dixiecrat Party headed by Strom Thurmond. On the other side, a number of other Democrats didn't think Harry was liberal enough, and they left to form the Progressive Party. They were headed by Henry Wallace, Roosevelt's former Vice-President. Watching Truman in the newsreels became almost painful. He put up a good front, but everyone thought he was going to go down in a landslide.

On the executive floor, plans were being formulated for the arrival of a new Republican administration in January. Obviously, it would mean a big plus for their business—lower corporate taxes for openers. I sat up listening to the radio on election night. At midnight, the results were still inconclusive. At this point I'd finally achieved my lifelong ambition: my own room! I turned the volume down and decided to await the outcome. By 2 A.M. even I was too sleepy to continue, so I turned out the light. With some western states still up for grabs, it was still anybody's election. The next morning, we followed the news on the radio at breakfast, a first for our family. By now everyone was very excited by a race that had gone down to the wire. It would be 10 A.M. before the election was decided. California went for Truman and Dewey conceded. I had a portable radio in my desk, so it fell to me to break the news to the board of directors who were all huddled in Phillip's office.

I screwed up all my acting skill to appear downcast, but inwardly it was one of the happiest moments of my life. I tapped on the open door. "Excuse me, gentlemen. I thought you'd like to know that a few minutes ago Governor Dewey conceded to President Truman. I just heard the radio flash." The long shot had come through. The previous week, Life magazine ran an article about Dewey and referred to him as our "next president!"

As I progressed at Fordham, the world situation, commonly known as the "Cold War," began to look more ominous. In 1948 Czechoslovakia was taken over by the Russians, and Yugoslavia was under the control of a Communist leader, Marshall Tito. The following year in China, Mao's forces defeated Chiang's government, which fled to Formosa. Positions on both sides hardened. The grand alliance that had defeated the Axis was now in tatters.

Worse news followed. In 1949 Russia exploded an atomic bomb, ending our monopoly. Most military analysts felt that with the advent of the nuclear bomb, the next confrontation would be a "push-button" war. People seriously questioned the need for a Navy, a Marine Corps or for that matter, any ground troops. The Air Force was the only branch necessary for our defense. Congress and the President apparently bought this argument and massive cuts were made to all elements of the armed forces, except for the proponents of the big bomber. Russia was the only enemy in what appeared to be the beginning of a nuclear standoff. With both sides facing each other in Germany, it seemed only a matter of time before some incident triggered another war. There would be another conflict involving the United States in 1950, but it was far from Europe in a completely unexpected place.

And it would change my life.

CHAPTER FORTY-SIX

A NEW WAR, A NEW BEGINNING

In the spring of 1950 I'd just completed my third year at Fordham. I was still at my desk on the 9th floor of the Great American Insurance Company at 1 Liberty Street. If I hadn't looked at the calendar, for all the difference, it might have been 1947. I seemed to be on a treadmill. All my life I had felt and tasted adventure only between the covers of a book. From childhood on, my every move had been planned by others; parents or teachers. No surprises. Would there ever be a chance to let fate take control—to jump into the swift current of life and let it carry me along? Unknown to me, events unfolding half way around the world would soon give me the answer.

Just before the summer began, I joined a few of my buddies on a short vacation together in the Catskills. Larry and I needed a break from our night college regimen. An old friend, Vinnie Mc Murray, who had just left the seminary after three years, joined us. In our eyes his move took a great deal of courage. Vinny's parents, like many of the Irish, had their heart set on a son in the priesthood. But after some terrible soul-searching, he decided that the religious life was not for him. Obviously, this decision had caused great pain at home and he needed some time to get away.

It was Sunday, June 25th. We were just getting ready to leave the hotel when he heard word on the radio that North Korea had invaded the South. In a matter of hours events went on a fast track. President Truman flew back to Washington from Independence, Missouri and the armed forces were placed on immediate alert. It was a situation fraught with peril. On the drive back to the city, this act of naked aggression dominated our conversation, and unconsciously, we were beginning to formulate our plans for entering the active duty military. There was never any doubt that we wouldn't wait for either the draft in Vinny's case, or the National Guard in ours. This looked like a major war and we wanted in. All those movies, books, and war stories had prepared us for this day— over-prepared us perhaps, and we weren't going to be denied. Aside from a deep and abiding love of our country, there were another reasons, not fully grasped at the time. In retrospect, each of us in his own way was running away from something, and this would be our ticket out. I wanted to break away from the stifling regimen of night-college tied to a dead-end job. This war would be the perfect antidote, taking the wind out any arguments against my decision.

During the next few days the situation in South Korea deteriorated rapidly. The Republic of Korea forces were overmatched in every cate-gory: tanks, artillery, trained men. The capital, Seoul, was so close to the border that the government evacuated its offices within 48 hours. Truman asked the UN for a resolution condemning the attack and ordering North Korea to withdraw. The Communist leaders felt that the west would dither away precious time trying to get a consensus, and they in turn would achieve total victory in a few weeks. It would be a fait accompli. Fortunately for us, the Russians, angry over some issue, had walked out of the Security Council a few weeks before, so they didn't have the opportunity to veto any resolution. The measure passed unani-mously and Truman ordered MacArthur to take command of the UN forces. At first the president only authorized the use of naval and air power, but after a quick trip to the front, MacArthur told Washington that we needed ground troops to stop the Reds. Truman ordered them in and that sealed our decision to join them.

My mother was not too happy over my enlisting, but I think she sensed, in the manner of all mothers, that in this decision, there was no appeal. My mind was made up. I was six months shy of twenty-one. There was no way that I was going to sit on the sidelines while my friends left. My father just wished me well. They both knew how I felt about the Navy. The morning after Truman's order, my friends and I gathered outside the Navy Recruiting office on Broadway. Oddly, the Navy office was barely two blocks from Fordham. The three of us had stayed up most of the night before, mulling over our plans, and as a result arrived at Broadway two hours before they opened. A Daily News reporter and photographer came on the scene shortly after we did and interviewed us. The next day our picture appeared in the paper under the heading: NEW YORKERS ANSWER THE CALL.

My father had always told me, "When the next war comes, you'll be just like me, too young for the first war and too old for the second." He was 19 on a train heading for the Yaphank training camp when the armistice was signed in November 1918. At age 42, when Pearl Harbor was attacked, he was a father of three and too old. So he missed World War II as well. The North Koreans had other plans for me.

Our intentions were to stay together, but immediately our plans went askew.

Larry was rejected out of hand because of his chronic asthma. (We wondered how he'd passed the National Guard physical!). Vinny Mc Murray had albumin in his urine, and that put him on hold for a few weeks. The National Guard was loath to lose any trained men, so I was back in limbo. The Navy told me that I'd have to obtain a release before they could take me. I put in my formal request. (The 7th Regiment remained in New York for the entire war.)

Meanwhile I'd let my intentions to enlist be known to my employer. The Board of Directors called a hurried conference and invited me into their office. Since I was the first one in the company to enter the military in this war, they were caught a bit unaware, but wanted to do right by me. They gave me three months pay and paid my government life insurance for a year. Very generous. Since I'd been an office boy in the company as early as 1943, and had worked full or part time all those years, every department gave me a going away sendoff. I was buried in Sterling silver ID bracelets, shaving kits, Parker pens, leather writing tablets, and more than fifty messages of good luck. Aside from being taken to some trendy restaurants for lunch; Fraunces Tavern, among them, nearly every floor took up a collection, and as a result I was enriched by close to $300—a tidy sum at that time. I was kissed and hugged by nearly every girl and woman in the company, including many whom had never given me the time of day. An impending stint in the Navy apparently stirred a lot of juices. A few made it known that if I was interested, there was a lot more than kisses waiting. All I had to do was ask. I guess I could have lost my virginity, then and there, but that wasn't high on my agenda.

At home I had a similar reception from the opposite sex. Girls that never gave me a tumble were suddenly all over me. From what I'd read, every new recruit at the start of a war shared this experience. A couple of weeks passed while my request for early discharge went through channels at the regiment. I chafed over the delay. One of the old sergeants told me not to hold my breath. In the regiment's eyes I was a trained mortarman and they didn't want to lose me.

One day in late July, the Chairman of the Board called me into his office. I thought he wanted me to get his lunch, a common request. Instead, Phillips asked me to sit down. "I thought you were going into the Navy, Jack? What happened?" When I told him my tale of frustrating red tape, he exploded. "I can't believe that with the country at war, a man can be prevented from going on active duty." I explained my problem with the 7th Regiment, and he thought he could help me. "Just sit down Jack and give me a few minutes. I think I have a friend who might be able to solve your problem." Incredulous, I sat there as he put through a call to General Hugh Drum, a former Chief of Staff of the Army, and now head of the NY National Guard. When Phillips began to call the general "Hughie," I knew that I was home free. They were old friends and often played golf together. Drum explained that I didn't need to wait for a release. Active duty eliminated the need for that. I did, however, have to complete one very important process. I should go up to my Supply Sergeant at the armory and request a detailed inventory of all my equipment, accompanied by a signed receipt. Then I should take this receipt to Navy Recruiting. That would eliminate the last hold the regiment had on me—government property under my control. I accomplished that task the same afternoon and the Navy Chief told me to report at the Recruiting Office on August 2nd for swearing in to active duty.

I may have been the only sailor who ever utilized a four-star general to get into the Navy!

During those last crowded days while I agonized over my future, I took things as they came. Then, as the days dragged on, I began to feel more and more depressed. I was completely unprepared for this logjam. But the night of August 1st, after finally clearing the last hurdle, I went to bed with a profound sense of relief I'd never felt before. It was if my entire past life had been but a preparation for this day. Although I was impatient for the morning, I slept well for the first time in weeks.

A whole new road stretched before me. I couldn't see very far, but for me, that was its greatest advantage. For all the unknown detours and adventures that might lie in store, it could have been paved with yellow bricks. I was ready and eager to take the first step and let the journey begin.

U. S. NAVY RECRUITING STATION
346 BROADWAY
NEW YORK 13, NEW YORK

Mr. John Sauter,
2108 Gleason Ave.,   AUG 1 - 1950
Bronx, N.Y.

Dear Sir:

You are requested to report to the Navy Recruiting Station,
346 Broadway, New York, N.Y., at 8:00 on the morning of ___AUG 7 - 1950___.
If found physically and in all other respects qualified for enlistment, you will be sworn into the United States Navy on that date
and transferred to the U.S. Navy Training Center, Great Lakes,
Illinois, for Recruit Training.

You are advised to bring with you only toilet articles and
cash not exceeding six dollars ($6.00). It is not necessary to
bring articles of clothing other than what you will wear when reporting, as after outfitting at the Training Center, you will send
your civilian clothing home.

If you are a member of the Naval Reserve (Active or Inactive),
U.S. Marine Corps Reserve or the National Guard bring with you
some paper showing date of enlistment. If a member of the Naval
Reserve you should also have some paper showing your service number.
If a member of any Organized Reserve Unit you should turn in all
clothing issued you PRIOR to reporting for enlistment in the U.S.
Navy.

If you are a High School Graduate and qualify for a Navy Trade
School you should bring your High School Diploma when reporting
for enlistment.

If you are between the ages of 18 and 26 you Must present your
DRAFT REGISTRATION CARD. Otherwise you cannot be enlisted (sworn
in).

Since our space is very limited in the Recruiting Station, you
are requested not to bring friends or relatives with you.

Very truly yours,

John Csizmar

JOHN CSIZMAR,
Lieutenant Commander, U.S.N.

My recruiting letter

CHAPTER FORTY-NINE

EPILOGUE

The author in 1953 in the US Navy

I spent four years in the Navy. They were among the happiest of my life. Much like my marriage, it was a dream come true. All my childhood fantasies were realized: from going to sea, flying from and landing on a moving deck in a combat zone, and visiting a vast array of foreign ports of call. As a bonus, I met a cast of characters that could have easily populated a few novels.

After more than 15 month of intensive training in aviation electronics, I qualified to fly in the backseat of a Douglas Skyraider as a radar-navigator—a Navy Enlisted Aircrewman. I served in three flattops: MIDWAY, F.D.ROOSEVELT, and LAKE CHAMPLAIN making more than sixty carrier-landings. Off Korea, I was catapulted a half dozen times. In the air, I helped direct fighter and attack aircraft hundreds of miles out to sea and brought them home safely to our flight deck. This was the heaviest responsibility ever placed on my shoulders, but like my shipmates, I rose to the task at hand. In the entire crew of over 3,000 men in LAKE CHAMPLAIN, I was but one of twenty enlisted men entrusted with this duty. In the closing days of the Korean War, my Early Warning Squadron put me on the cutting edge of Task Force 77, where I was designated a Combat Aircrewman. I truly believed in the rightness of that war—my prime reason for enlisting, and I still hold that belief today.

Beyond the flying and the travel, perhaps the most profound change was the hard-won self-confidence I gained. I found myself engaged in technical subjects and crafts that had been completely alien to me. What's more, I derived great satisfaction from this often demanding and challenging work. For the first time in my life, I felt that I was doing something important, and lives (including my own) depended on my skills. This attribute carried me in good stead when I later took on a selling career—something I never imagined I could accomplish in a million years. In short, the most enduring lesson I took from the Navy was that I had the surprising ability to learn—practically anything.

Besides the technical knowledge I'd mastered, my view of the planet and the people in it expanded exponentially. I know it's a cliché—"Join the Navy and See the World," but I accomplished that in spades. From the boulevards of Paris, to the ancient temples of Japan and Southeast Asia, I immersed myself in multi-faceted civilizations I'd only previously skimmed in geography texts. Unconsciously, these foreign and often bizarre experiences were laying the foundation for a lifelong love of travel. Far more satisfying were the warm and lasting friendships I forged while wearing the blue. More than fifty years later, I still remain close to many of my shipmates—John Robben being the best example.

When the USS LAKE CHAMPLAIN ASSOCIATION was created in 1989, I became a charter member. Later I took over the editorship of the group's magazine: THE CHAMP, and a few years later, the presidency.

Aside from enlisting in the Navy, my biggest and most profound decision during that time was asking Marianne to marry me. This gorgeous girl, whose beauty often left me breathless, was and is the ideal mate. She was everything I always wanted in a wife. Whenever my old nemesis "insecurity," reappeared, she was the perfect antidote. Recently, we were fortunate enough to reach that landmark: Fifty Years of Marriage. I was extremely lucky and blessed. My good luck continues.

To go back in one's memory and try to recreate the events of nearly three-quarters of a century ago is both exhilarating and enervating. In a cascade of recollections, I recalled how I felt in grammar school, or experiencing my initial fumbling with the opposite sex. It was an enlightening exercise. I sensed time passing in a rich, profound, and inevitable manner. I never quite knew what I would rediscover until I sat before the word-processor. In the magical phenomena called writing, this experience was very much like reliving much of my early life. That was the exhilarating part. Organizing and putting all those memories into readable prose was the chore.

I find it remarkable that in spite of the passage of three quarters of a century, I'm still very much the same person I was when I sat in that freshman class at Cardinal Hayes High School. Feeling one's age can be deceptively elusive. When I was twenty, I imagined that I'd be totally different when I reached fifty or sixty, but it hasn't happened. Physically I've been very fortunate. I function much as I did twenty-five years ago. Two heart attacks and bypass surgery gave me the impetus to change many things—diet and exercise primarily, and they've borne fruit. Nevertheless, I know I'm living on borrowed time.

Enrolled in the First Grade a year earlier than my classmates, this led me to play "catch up ball" until I was well into high school. This pattern persisted into maturity, as I didn't play baseball until seventeen, tennis until thirty and the piano until forty. And I began to write seriously at the ripe age of sixty! Intellectually, we change in some ways, but the core remains. I haven't lost any of my inquisitiveness—three books still adorn my night table. As I matured I thought my reading would provide most of the answers I was searching for. But instead, what I acquired was even more questions. Very few blacks and whites—mostly grays. The more profound the question, the greater the enigma.

The big difference is that now I write articles and books rather than just read them. The pleasure writing brings is immeasurable. My great regret is that I waited so long. But better late...

From the year 1935, when I first began to remember events, to 2005 is, by any measurement, a long time. Many things have changed, but I still live within twenty miles of every site of my childhood, except for the summers I spent in Water Witch, New Jersey—that remaining within a couple of hours drive. Astonishingly, while a significant chunk of the Big Apple's landscape has dramatically changed, much of my physical past remains intact.

My first apartment on Seddon Street, where my mother could watch me playing in the empty lots still stands to this day. Alas, the lots are no longer empty—they've been filled with homes and apartment houses One day I decided to revisit the place of my childhood. I approached this five-story walkup with different eyes, trying to recapture that most elusive of senses: memory. An intercom had been added to the catalog of names and buzzers. When Alice passed through the looking glass her experience could not have been more imaginary than mine passing into the lobby. I felt myself shrinking to my old size. My feet fell back into the familiar rhythm; skipping down the steps to the mailboxes under the stairs. How the names had changed! No more "Schneiders" or "Rooneys."

A different super was mopping the floors, but that enduring smell of dust and ammonia had not changed. The weak light, the worn stairs, the battered mailboxes seem to be remembering me, but from the names by the entrance I knew there was no tenant in this building who knew me or would care that I had once lived in apartment number 57. I climbed the five flights that I had taken two-at-a-time for so many years, and finally stood outside our old entrance. I was tempted to ring the bell, but what would I say if someone answered the door? After a long minute I walked slowly back downstairs; back to a different kind of reality. Who lived there now I'd never know. Perhaps it was some other insecure ten-year old that enjoyed radio and music and books? The other signposts of my youth I viewed from the outside.

A few blocks to the west, St. Raymond's school and church remain a going concern, having added a secondary learning level from my days. My own high school, Cardinal Hayes, thrives as well on Grand Concourse, a beacon in a neighborhood that has seen both good and bad days in the half century since I left. The graduates now number two to three hundred instead of close to a thousand, but jackets and ties are still mandatory. The Westchester Square Public Library, where I spent so many happy hours, and religiously carried four finished books back to the front desk and picked up four new ones still stands, but it's no long a book repository. When the neighborhood changed in the late seventies, it became a drug rehab clinic, but now, as conditions improve, it's evolved into a Senior Citizens center.

The office buildings that housed the Great American Insurance Company on One Liberty Street, where I held my first job, as well as downtown Fordham University on lower Broadway where I labored all those nights are both gone. The sites are now primarily empty spaces. My college moved uptown to Lincoln Center, next to the Metropolitan Opera. Arriving for a performance, I often look at the new building, but except for the name on the façade, it holds no meaning. Incredibly, some years ago, the Great American Insurance Company relocated to Lake Success, Long Island, barely a mile from where I now live. Then they merged and the name disappeared.

The five-story walkup where I spent my adolescence, a most rewarding interval —2108 Gleason Avenue, is now just a memory—another victim of the infamous Cross Bronx Expressway. It was torn down in 1952. With it, went the "Z" trolley, whose endearing sounds kept me company on so many nights. But St.Helena's, my second grammar school, where I locked horns and wills with Sister Ann Veronica, remains, pretty much as I left it, sixty years ago.

Some things disappear and then almost inexplicably, return. The Hudson and East River ferries had nearly all been replaced by bridges and tunnels, but they're now enjoying a renaissance. New Yorkers are finally learning to appreciate their harbor and waterfront, just as I did in the summer of 1943. The advent of containerships put a significant dent in New York's port activity, but other activities have helped preserve our maritime heritage. While most of the transatlantic traffic has disappeared, along with such stalwarts on the Hudson as Holland-American, United States, French, Italian and American Export Lines, a unique historical enterprise was created in the South Street Seaport Museum, at the foot of Fulton Street. Through the efforts of many preservationists, two 19th century sailing ships were resurrected and restored, along with lightships, tugs and ferries from another age. While those Saturday ocean-liner sailings have met morphed into cruise ships, a true liner—another QUEEN MARY still spans the Atlantic. The urban preservationists were doubly delighted when the bulldozers by-passed the ancient buildings on Front Street by, thereby saving the last slice of New York's 19th century seafaring history.

The Times Square I knew, with Nedicks and Toffenetti's and the old familiar Hollywood palaces: the Roxy, the Astor, the Strand, the Capital, and the Paramount have disappeared. But a few blocks to the east, the jewel of movie houses—Radio City, still inspires crowds of tourists as they gasp in wonderment at the theatre, and marvel at the Rockettes on stage. Sadly, McDonald's and Burger King have replaced the Automat and the orange-roofed Howard Johnson's and their heavenly twenty-eight ice cream flavors. Ice cream itself has become a casualty of an encroaching continental taste. Today, Latte and espresso are all the rage. But back in the Bronx, our writing group still lunches once a month at a landmark restaurant: Charlie's Inn in Throggs Neck. And the timeless Arthur Avenue's Italian trattorias, along with the unique seafood temples on City Island still require advanced reservations.

Large segments of the Bronx that were devastated in the dark decade of the seventies' are in the midst of a rebirth. It's a monumental project, and one of its prime movers is Father Gigante, a priest from my old high school, Cardinal Hayes. My borough has made great strides in the past two decades, regaining much of its former glory.

Rediscovering these haunts from my childhood was an unexpected revelation, a catalog of cherished memories to help warm the closing days of my life. Thomas Wolfe once said, "You can't go home again." Perhaps not in a literal sense, but in this case the magic of memory trumps everything.

Considering what time has done to this city, I'm grateful that so much from my past remains intact. That "past," from 1930 to 1950, was a remarkable and memorable period. Shaping that era were all the films I reveled in from the time I was five years old— from KING KONG to THE BEST YEARS OF OUR LIVES. Looking back, I could almost frame these two decades within the parameters of my own movie, albeit a long one.

And now, just like in those theaters of old, it's time for me to say, "Let's go. THIS IS WHERE I CAME IN."

ACKNOWLEDGEMENTS

The most frequently asked question about THIS IS WHERE I CAME IN is "How did you remember all of this from sixty odd years ago? What's the trick? Is it just memory, or are there other factors that came into play?

A good memory is important, but it's more than that. Memory, while often elusive, can be helped and jogged in a number of ways. Having written another memoir: SAILORS IN THE SKY, about my naval service, ten years earlier, I had an edge. The same methods were utilized. Essentially, I had to completely immerse myself into the time frame. Old movies, newspaper clippings, histories of the era, and conversations with contemporaries all helped. I recall reading that when Carl Sandburg was writing his monumental multi-volume biography of Lincoln over a number of years, he became, in a real sense the 16th president. Walter Cronkite once came upon Sandburg in deep thought. Without being seen, he quietly approached and in a conversational tone said, "Mr. President?" Sandburg immediately answered, "Yes."

Fascinated by World War II, I began to keep a detailed scrapbook when I was ten. That was in 1940. I continued, rarely missing a day, and filled the book with hundreds of clippings from newspapers and magazines. Only years later did I uncover the real hidden riches—examining the flip sides of the articles and photos. Here were the nuts and bolts of everyday life—the shirt and dress ads, the comic strips, letters to the editor, radio listings, baseball box scores, and even on occasion, advice to the lovelorn; A newspaper is nearly an exact chronicle of day to day existence. Family photo albums were equally indispensable. We had no movie camera, and video lay far in the future, so black and white photography was the norm.

Whenever I experienced "writer's block," (fortunately rare for me), all I had to do was concentrate on another "block"—one of my neighborhood streets, to dispel it. Except where I had permission, the names have been changed to protect the privacy of individuals.

About ten years ago John Robben, Jim Hewitt, Bill Twomey and John McNamara joined me in forming a social group linked by writing. We called it The Round Robben. We meet about once a month in a local Throggs Neck restaurant that all of us frequented in our youth. Much of what I recall about the 30s and 40s I can lay to the long conversations we shared over bottles of Pinot Grigio. Many of these luncheons jogged my memory and led to rich recollections long buried.

Did I leave anything out? You bet. There are some secrets that deserve to remain just that—secrets.

I'm indebted to a number of people who gave me indispensable help in completing the manuscript. Keith, my son, again stepped up to the plate to edit and organize my effort. My wife, Marianne, who's always been my toughest critic, corrected my spelling and helped distill much of my first draft into more readable form. John Robben, in spite of being heavily involved in his own manuscript—PARTICLES OF TIME, was never too busy to offer editorial advice and support. John, who more than anyone else encouraged my early writing, generously wrote an eloquent Foreword. Other friends who read much of TIWICI (as it became known) and offered their time and support were Bill Twomey, Dick Mohan and Mike McGrory. I'm in debt to all of them.

While I deeply appreciate all the support and criticism I received, any mistakes, omissions, or other gaffs are solely mine.

One last item: Just as this book was being completed, my sister Rita, the person who most shaped my character during those critical early teen years, died. Fortunately, she had an opportunity to read the manuscript. I'll miss her dearly.

—Jack Sauter